Garfield
gains weight

BY: JIM DAVIS

Ballantine Books · New York

A Ballantine Book
Published by The Ballantine Publishing Group
Copyright © 1981, 2001 by PAWS, Inc. All rights reserved.

All rights reserved under International and Pan-American Copyright Conventions. Published in the
United States by The Ballantine Publishing Group, a division of Random House, Inc., New York, and
simultaneously in Canada by Random House of Canada Limited, Toronto. Originally published in
slightly different form by The Ballantine Publishing Group, a division of Random House, Inc.

"GARFIELD" and the GARFIELD characters are registered and unregistered trademarks of PAWS, Inc.

Ballantine is a registered trademark and the Ballantine colophon is a trademark of Random House, Inc.

www.ballantinebooks.com

Library of Congress Catalog Card Number: 2001118231

ISBN 0-345-44975-4

Manufactured in the United States of America

First Colorized Edition: December 2001

10 9 8 7 6 5 4 3 2 1

A Talk with Jim Davis:

Most Asked Questions

How far in advance do you do the strip?

"Eight to ten weeks—no less, no more. I operate on what Al Capp termed 'the ragged edge of disaster.'"

When did GARFIELD first appear in newspapers?

"June 19, 1978."

Where do you get your ideas for the strip?

"I glean a lot of good ideas from fan mail. Cat owners are very proud of their cats and supply a generous amount of cat stories."

What GARFIELD products are on the market and in production?

"Books, calendars, T-shirts, coffee mugs, posters, tote bags, greeting cards, puzzles...in another few months GARFIELD will be on everything but pantyhose and TVs."

Why a cat?

"Aside from the obvious reasons, that I know and love cats, I noticed there were a lot of comic-strip dogs who were commanding their share of the comic pages but precious few cats. It seemed like a good idea."

Where did you get the name GARFIELD?

"My grandfather's name was James A. Garfield Davis. The name GARFIELD to me sounds like a fat cat...or a St. Bernard...or a neat line of thermal underwear."

What did you do for a living before GARFIELD?

"I was assistant on the comic strip TUMBLEWEEDS and a free-lance commercial artist."

What's your sign?

"Leo, of course, the sign of the cat."

Have you ever been convicted of a felony?

"Next question, please."

Are you subject to fainting spells, seizures, and palpitations?

"Only when I work."

Have you ever spent time in a mental institution?

"Yes, I visit my comics editor there."

Do you advocate the overthrow of our government by violent means?

"No, but I have given consideration to vandalizing my local license branch."

Are you hard of hearing?

"Huh?"

Do you wish to donate an organ?

"Heck no, but I have a piano I can let go cheap."

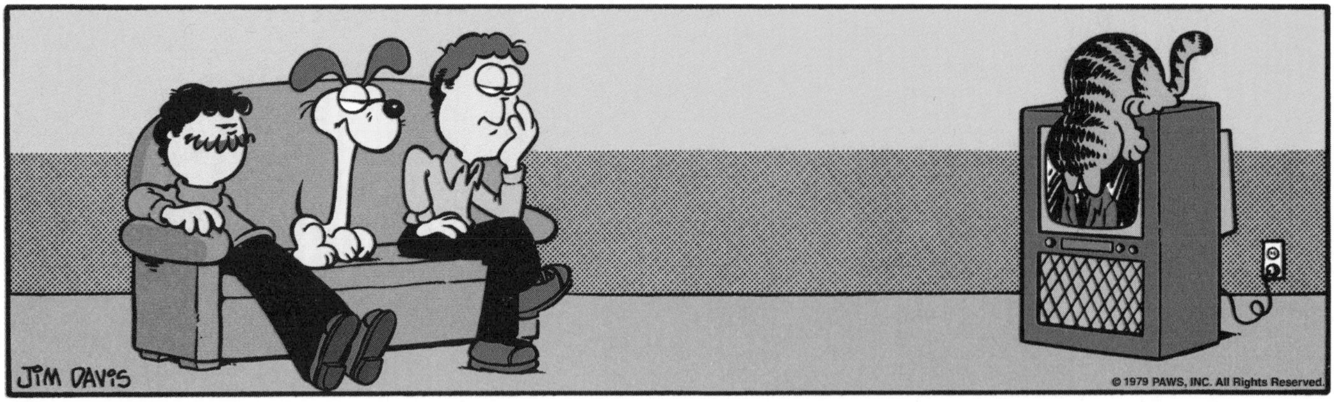
JIM DAVIS
© 1979 PAWS, INC. All Rights Reserved.

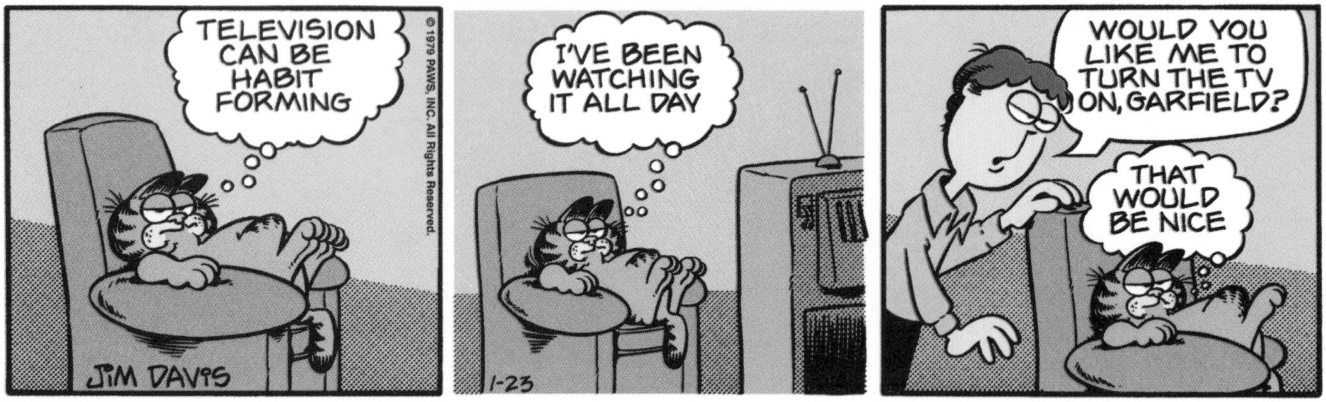
TELEVISION CAN BE HABIT FORMING
JIM DAVIS
© 1979 PAWS, INC. All Rights Reserved.
I'VE BEEN WATCHING IT ALL DAY
1-23
WOULD YOU LIKE ME TO TURN THE TV ON, GARFIELD?
THAT WOULD BE NICE

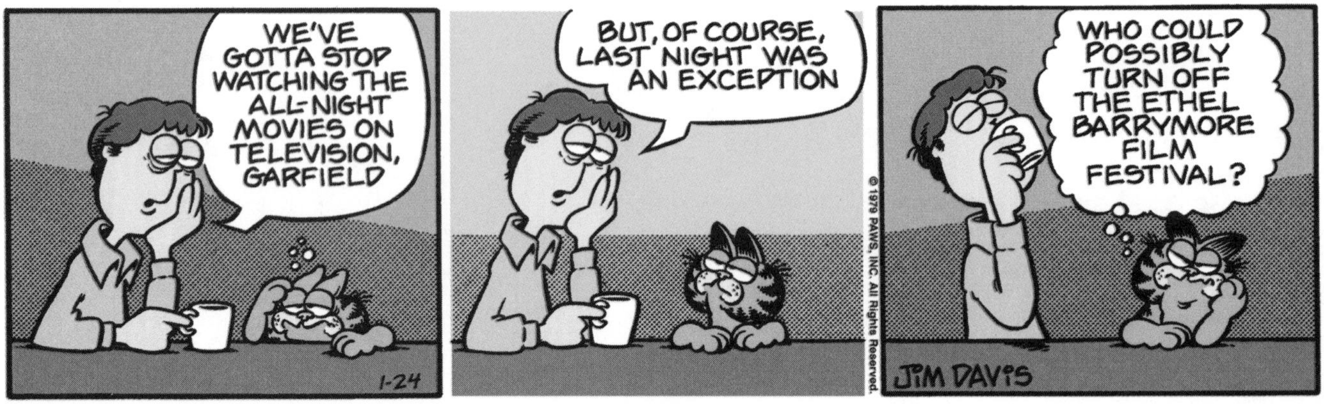
WE'VE GOTTA STOP WATCHING THE ALL-NIGHT MOVIES ON TELEVISION, GARFIELD
1-24
BUT, OF COURSE, LAST NIGHT WAS AN EXCEPTION
© 1979 PAWS, INC. All Rights Reserved.
WHO COULD POSSIBLY TURN OFF THE ETHEL BARRYMORE FILM FESTIVAL?
JIM DAVIS

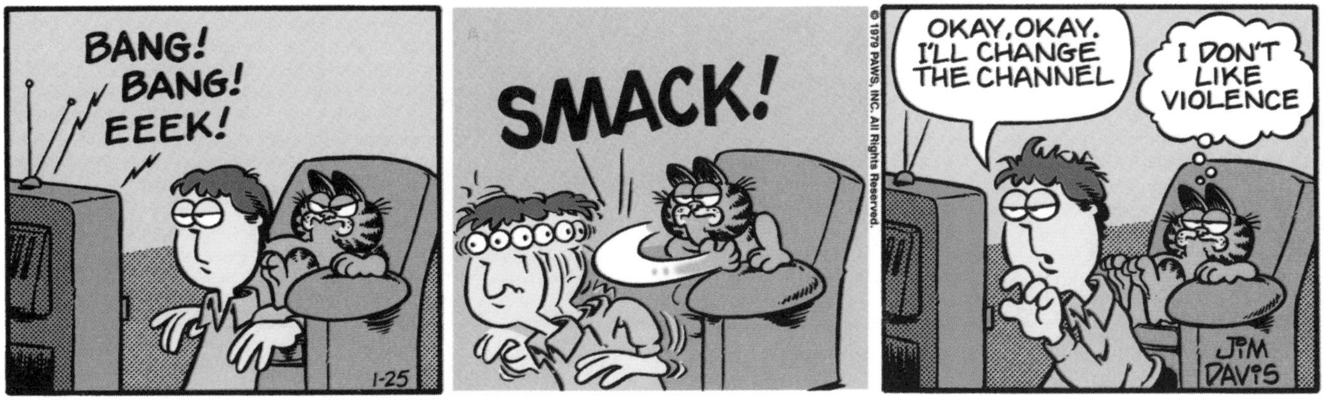
BANG! BANG! EEEK!
1-25
SMACK!
© 1979 PAWS, INC. All Rights Reserved.
OKAY, OKAY. I'LL CHANGE THE CHANNEL
I DON'T LIKE VIOLENCE
JIM DAVIS

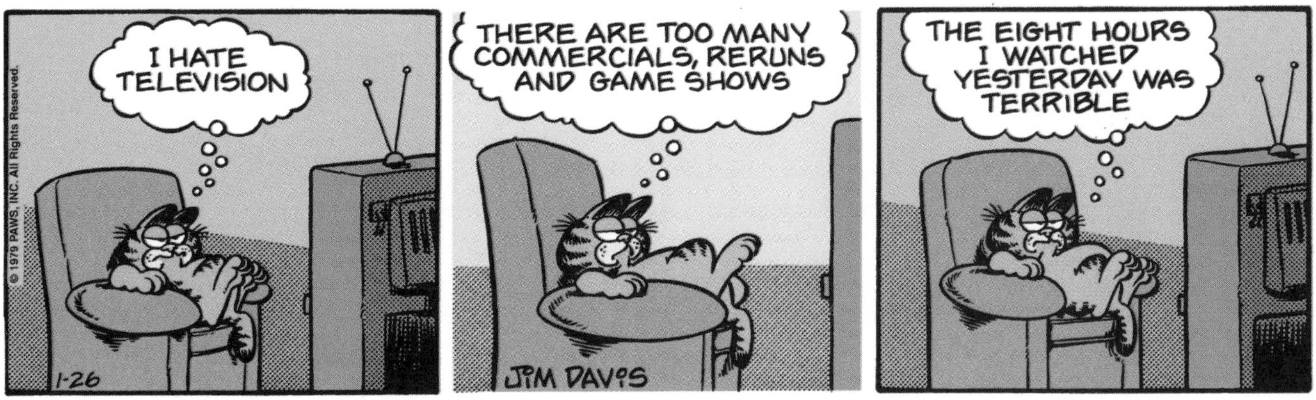
© 1979 PAWS, INC. All Rights Reserved.
I HATE TELEVISION
1-26
THERE ARE TOO MANY COMMERCIALS, RERUNS AND GAME SHOWS
JIM DAVIS
THE EIGHT HOURS I WATCHED YESTERDAY WAS TERRIBLE

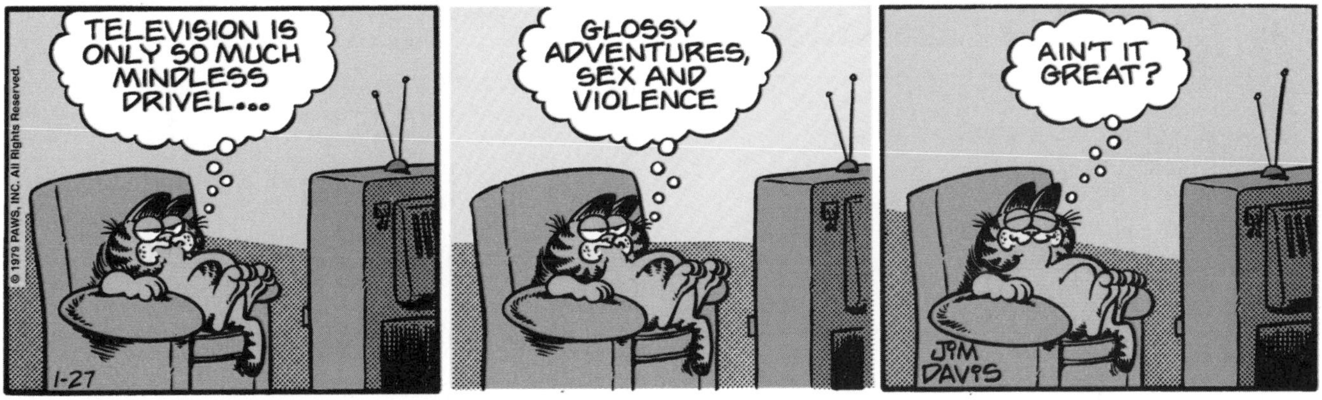
© 1979 PAWS, INC. All Rights Reserved.
TELEVISION IS ONLY SO MUCH MINDLESS DRIVEL...
1-27
GLOSSY ADVENTURES, SEX AND VIOLENCE
AIN'T IT GREAT?
JIM DAVIS

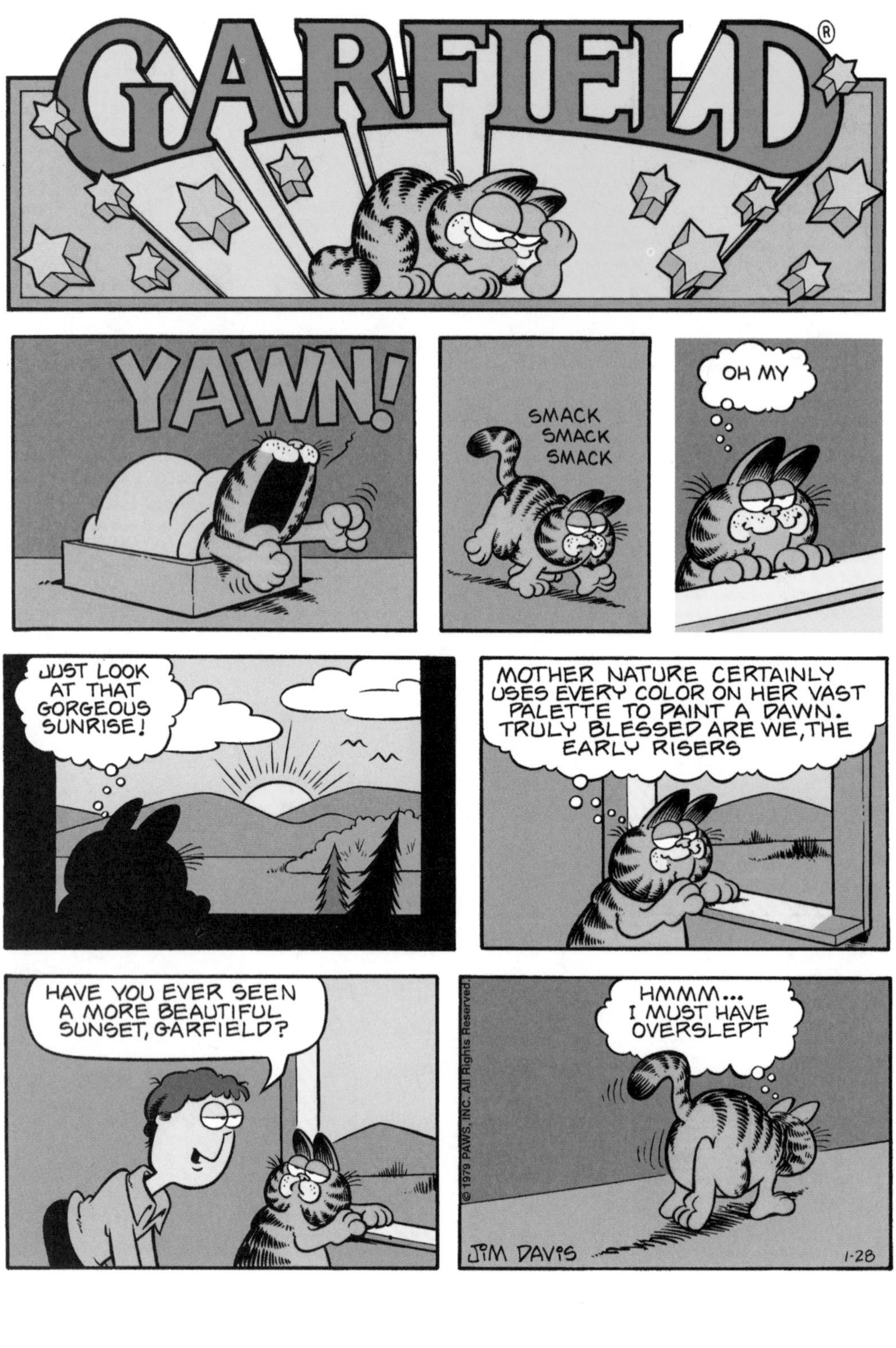
GARFIELD®
YAWN!
SMACK SMACK SMACK
OH MY
JUST LOOK AT THAT GORGEOUS SUNRISE!
MOTHER NATURE CERTAINLY USES EVERY COLOR ON HER VAST PALETTE TO PAINT A DAWN. TRULY BLESSED ARE WE, THE EARLY RISERS
HAVE YOU EVER SEEN A MORE BEAUTIFUL SUNSET, GARFIELD?
HMMM... I MUST HAVE OVERSLEPT
© 1979 PAWS, INC. All Rights Reserved.
JIM DAVIS
1-28

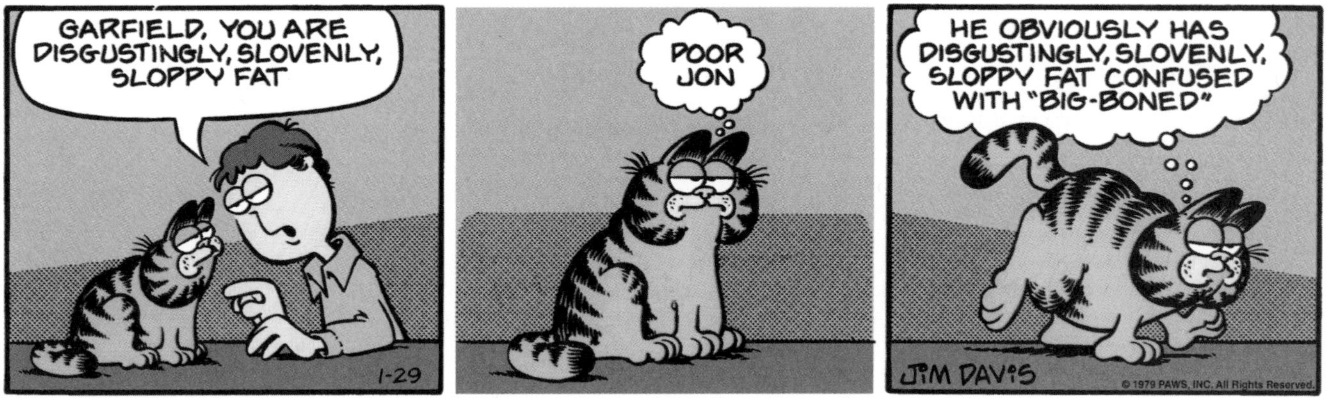
GARFIELD, YOU ARE DISGUSTINGLY, SLOVENLY, SLOPPY FAT
1-29
POOR JON
HE OBVIOUSLY HAS DISGUSTINGLY, SLOVENLY, SLOPPY FAT CONFUSED WITH "BIG-BONED"
JIM DAVIS
© 1979 PAWS, INC. All Rights Reserved.

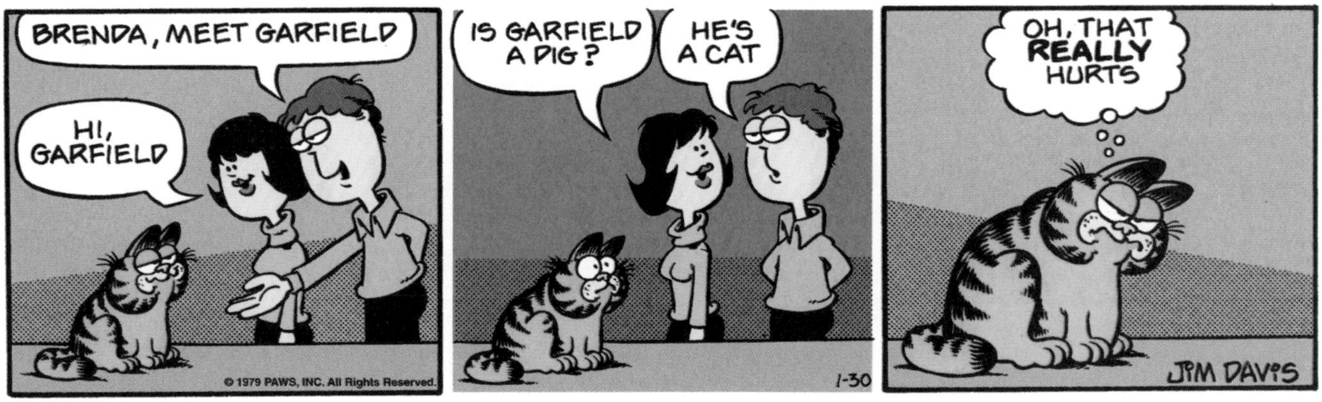
BRENDA, MEET GARFIELD
HI, GARFIELD
© 1979 PAWS, INC. All Rights Reserved.
IS GARFIELD A PIG?
HE'S A CAT
1-30
OH, THAT **REALLY** HURTS
JIM DAVIS

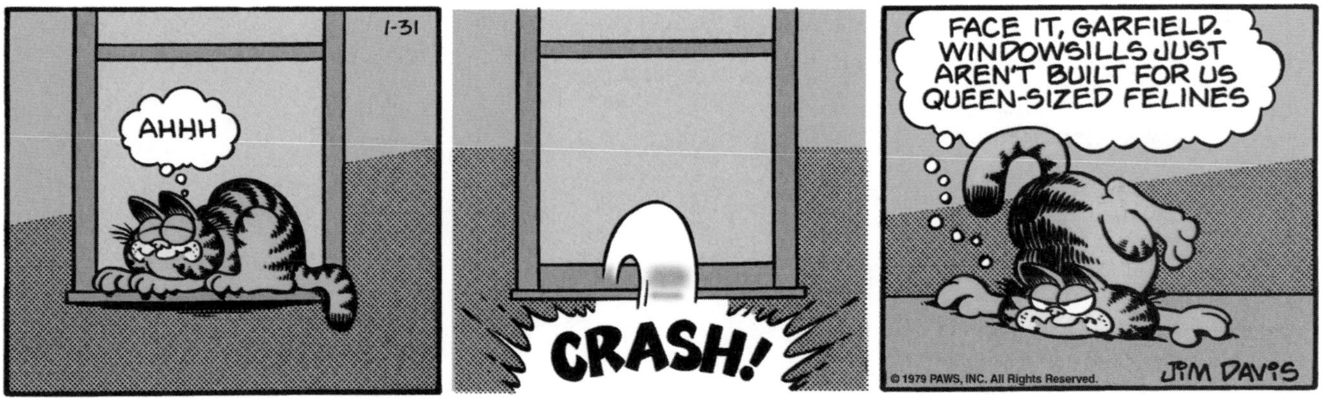
1-31
AHHH
CRASH!
FACE IT, GARFIELD. WINDOWSILLS JUST AREN'T BUILT FOR US QUEEN-SIZED FELINES
© 1979 PAWS, INC. All Rights Reserved.
JIM DAVIS

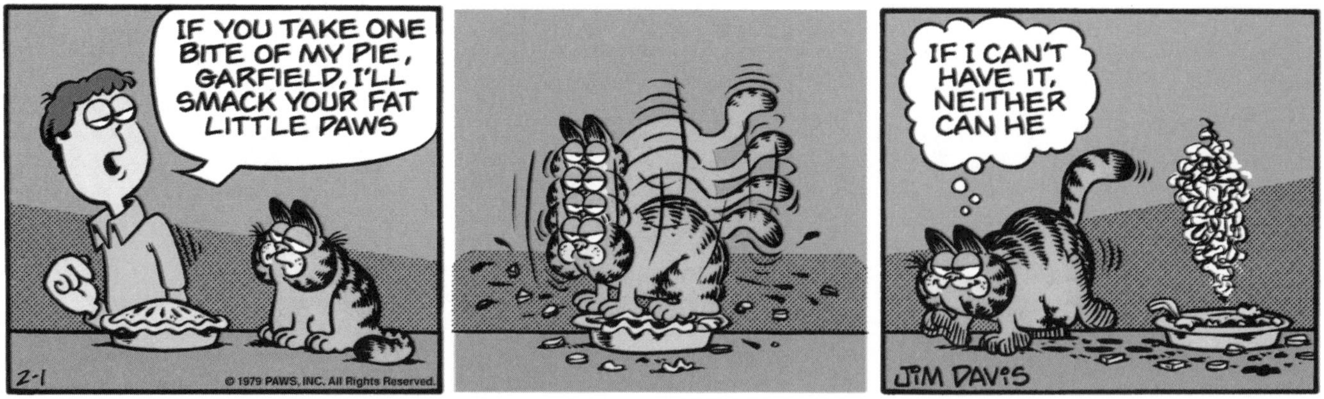
IF YOU TAKE ONE BITE OF MY PIE, GARFIELD, I'LL SMACK YOUR FAT LITTLE PAWS
2-1
© 1979 PAWS, INC. All Rights Reserved.
IF I CAN'T HAVE IT, NEITHER CAN HE
JIM DAVIS

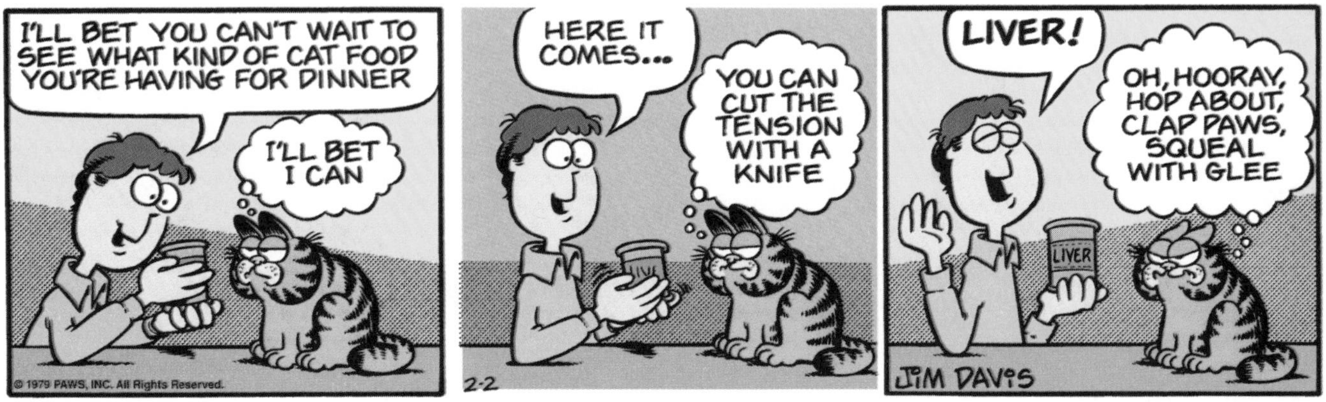
I'LL BET YOU CAN'T WAIT TO SEE WHAT KIND OF CAT FOOD YOU'RE HAVING FOR DINNER
I'LL BET I CAN
© 1979 PAWS, INC. All Rights Reserved.
HERE IT COMES...
YOU CAN CUT THE TENSION WITH A KNIFE
2-2
LIVER!
OH, HOORAY, HOP ABOUT, CLAP PAWS, SQUEAL WITH GLEE
LIVER
JIM DAVIS

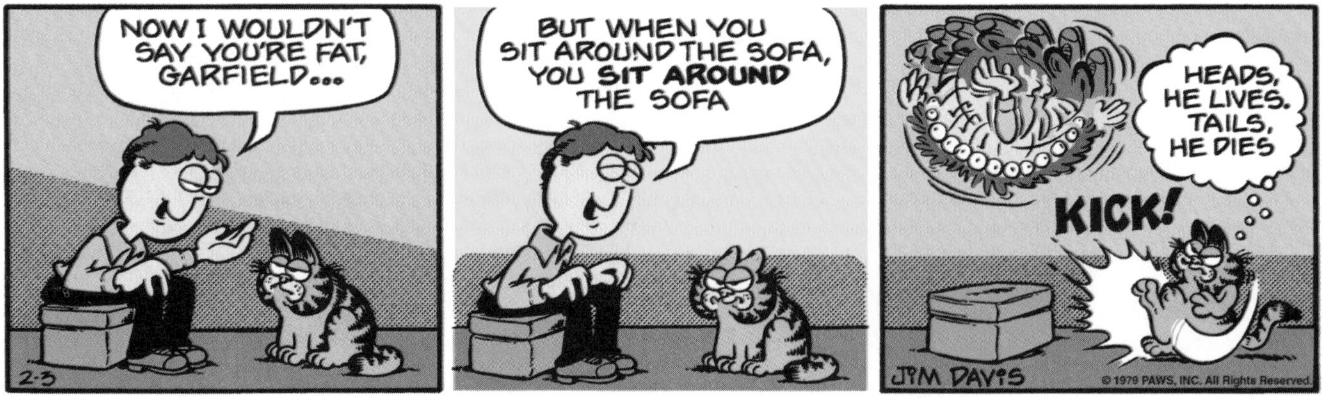
NOW I WOULDN'T SAY YOU'RE FAT, GARFIELD...
2-3
BUT WHEN YOU SIT AROUND THE SOFA, YOU **SIT AROUND** THE SOFA
HEADS, HE LIVES. TAILS, HE DIES
KICK!
JIM DAVIS
© 1979 PAWS, INC. All Rights Reserved.

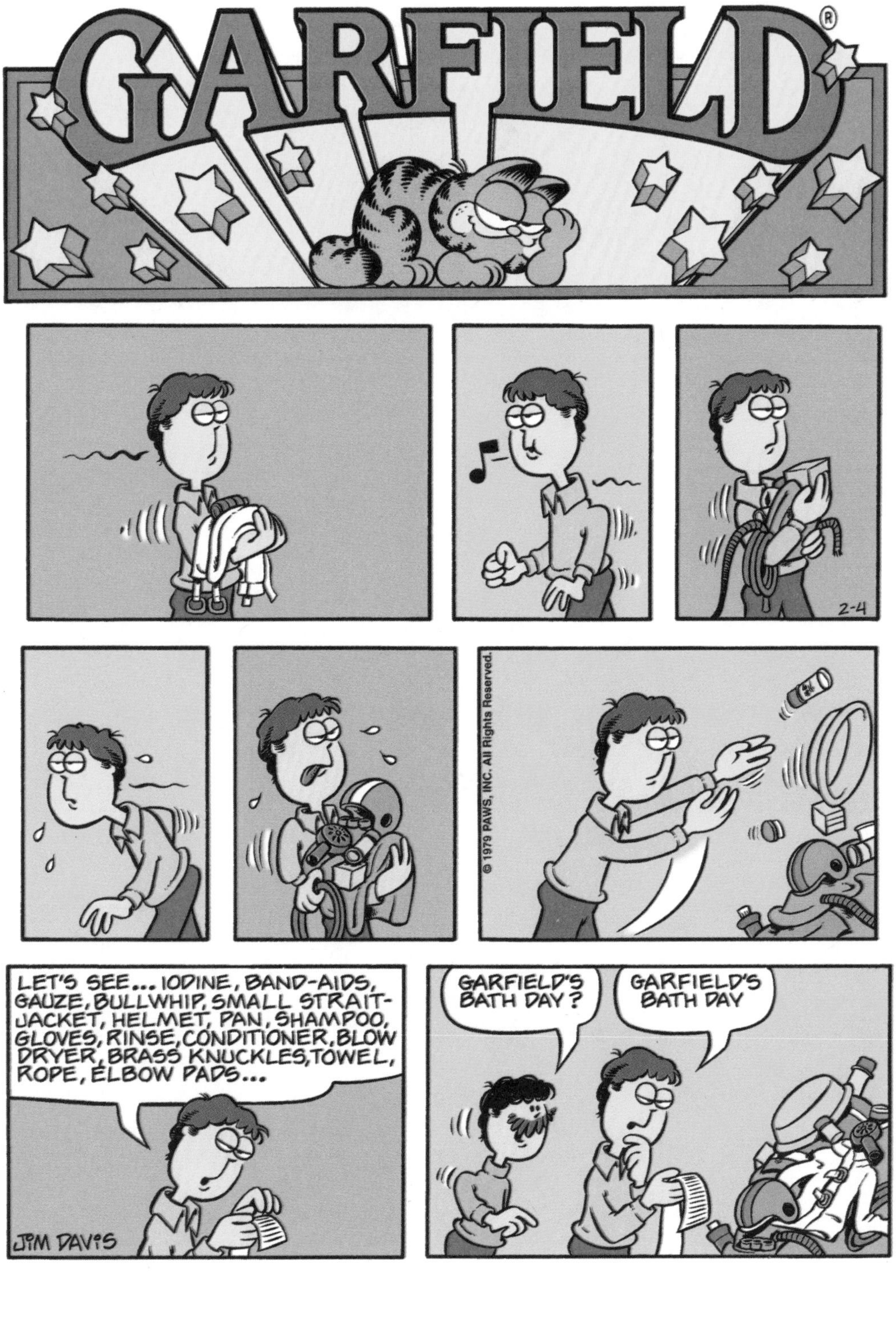
GARFIELD®
2-4
© 1979 PAWS, INC. All Rights Reserved.
LET'S SEE... IODINE, BAND-AIDS, GAUZE, BULLWHIP, SMALL STRAIT-JACKET, HELMET, PAN, SHAMPOO, GLOVES, RINSE, CONDITIONER, BLOW DRYER, BRASS KNUCKLES, TOWEL, ROPE, ELBOW PADS...
JIM DAVIS
GARFIELD'S BATH DAY?
GARFIELD'S BATH DAY

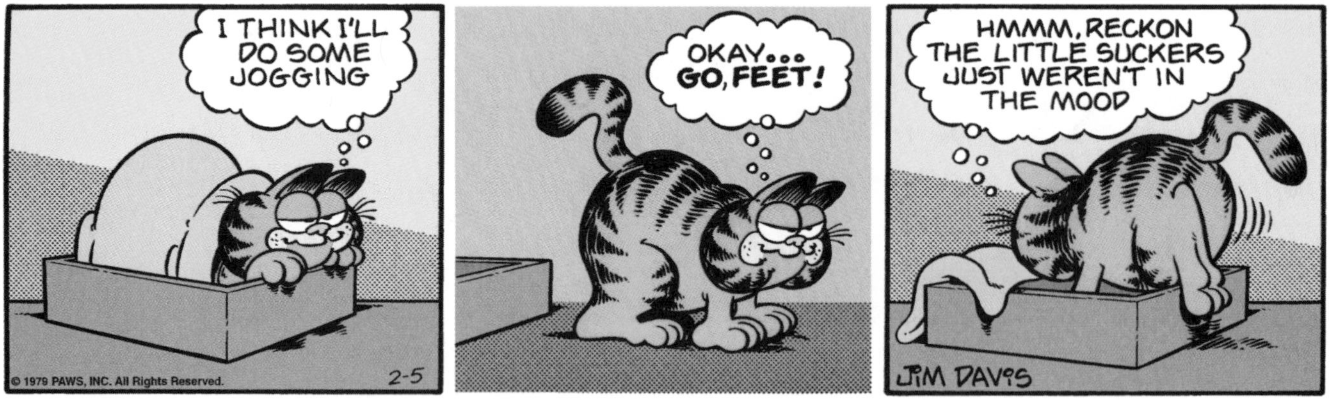
I THINK I'LL DO SOME JOGGING
© 1979 PAWS, INC. All Rights Reserved.
2-5
OKAY... GO, FEET!
HMMM, RECKON THE LITTLE SUCKERS JUST WEREN'T IN THE MOOD
JIM DAVIS

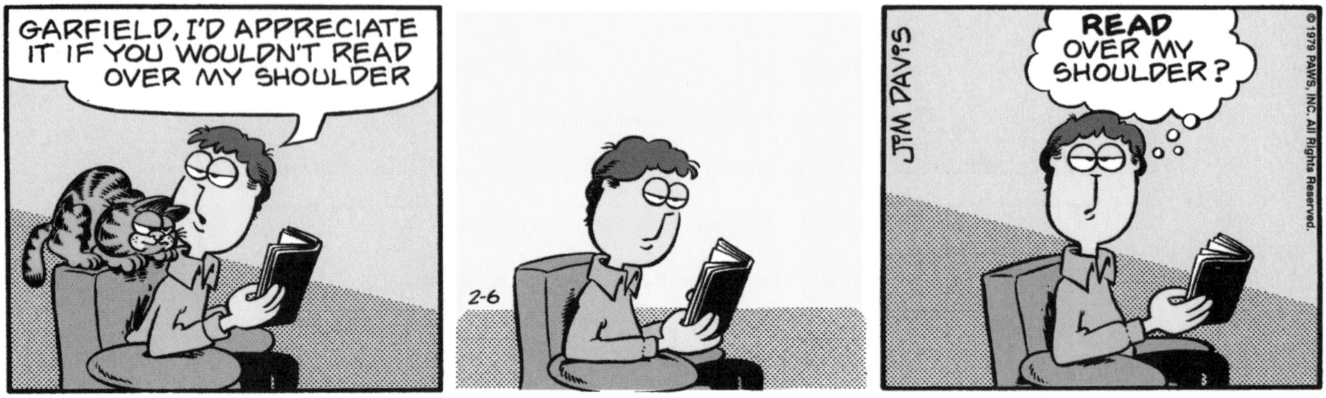
GARFIELD, I'D APPRECIATE IT IF YOU WOULDN'T READ OVER MY SHOULDER
2-6
JIM DAVIS
READ OVER MY SHOULDER?
© 1979 PAWS, INC. All Rights Reserved.

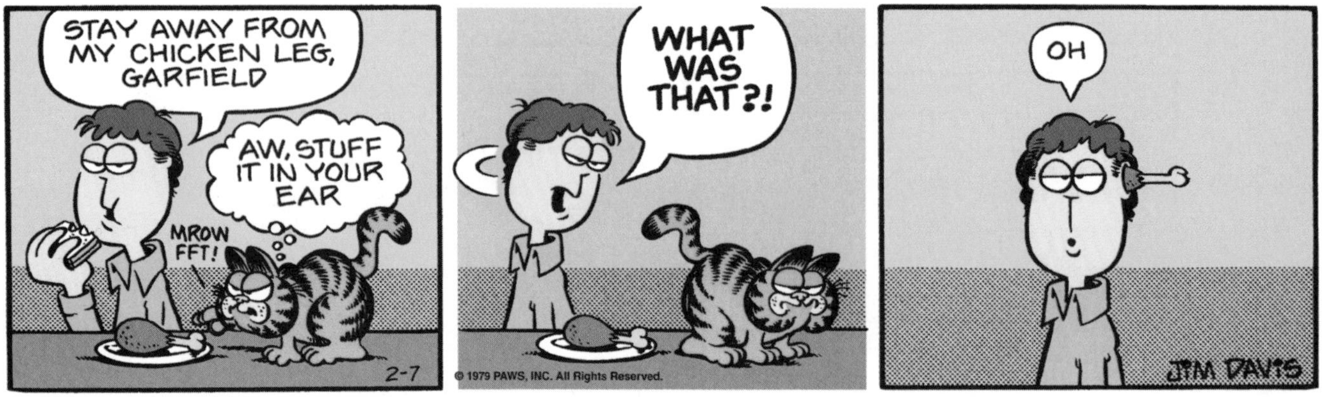
STAY AWAY FROM MY CHICKEN LEG, GARFIELD
AW, STUFF IT IN YOUR EAR
MROW FFT!
2-7
WHAT WAS THAT?!
© 1979 PAWS, INC. All Rights Reserved.
OH
JIM DAVIS

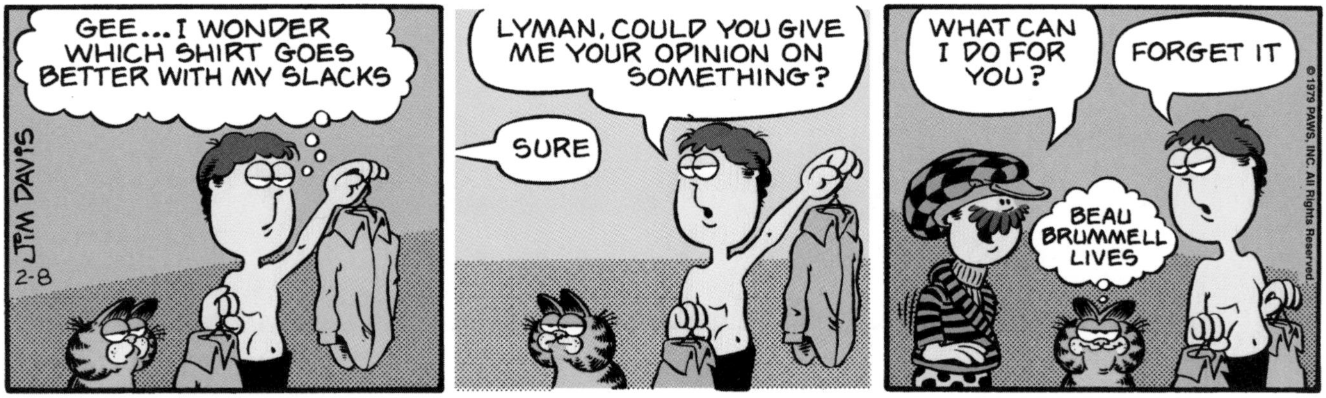
GEE... I WONDER WHICH SHIRT GOES BETTER WITH MY SLACKS
JIM DAVIS
2-8
LYMAN, COULD YOU GIVE ME YOUR OPINION ON SOMETHING?
SURE
WHAT CAN I DO FOR YOU?
FORGET IT
BEAU BRUMMELL LIVES
© 1979 PAWS, INC. All Rights Reserved.

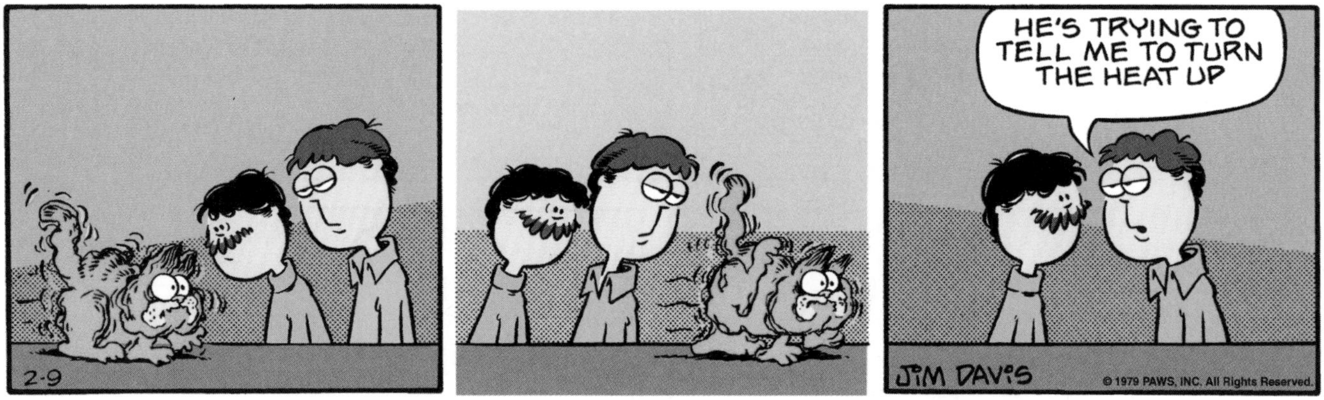
2-9
HE'S TRYING TO TELL ME TO TURN THE HEAT UP
JIM DAVIS
© 1979 PAWS, INC. All Rights Reserved.

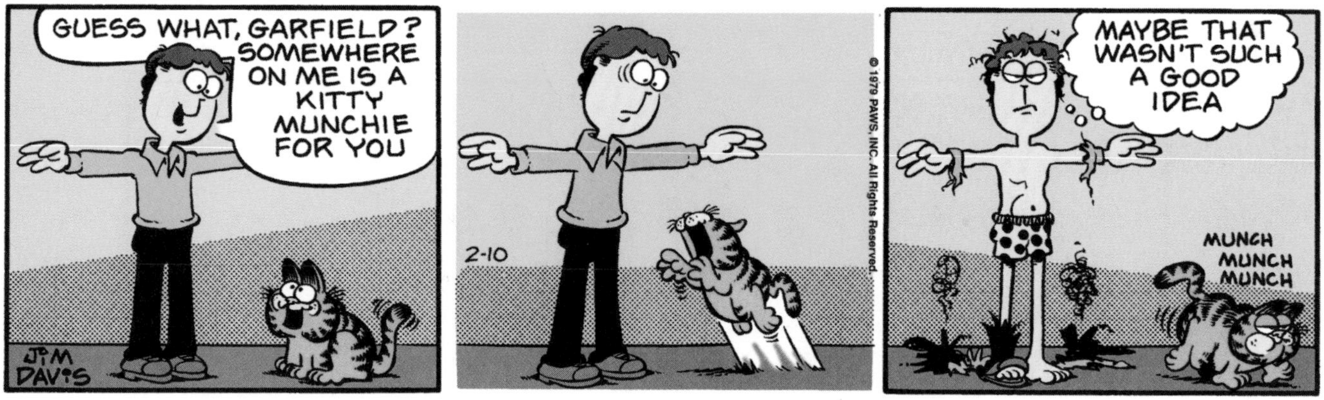
GUESS WHAT, GARFIELD? SOMEWHERE ON ME IS A KITTY MUNCHIE FOR YOU
JIM DAVIS
2-10
© 1979 PAWS, INC. All Rights Reserved.
MAYBE THAT WASN'T SUCH A GOOD IDEA
MUNCH MUNCH MUNCH

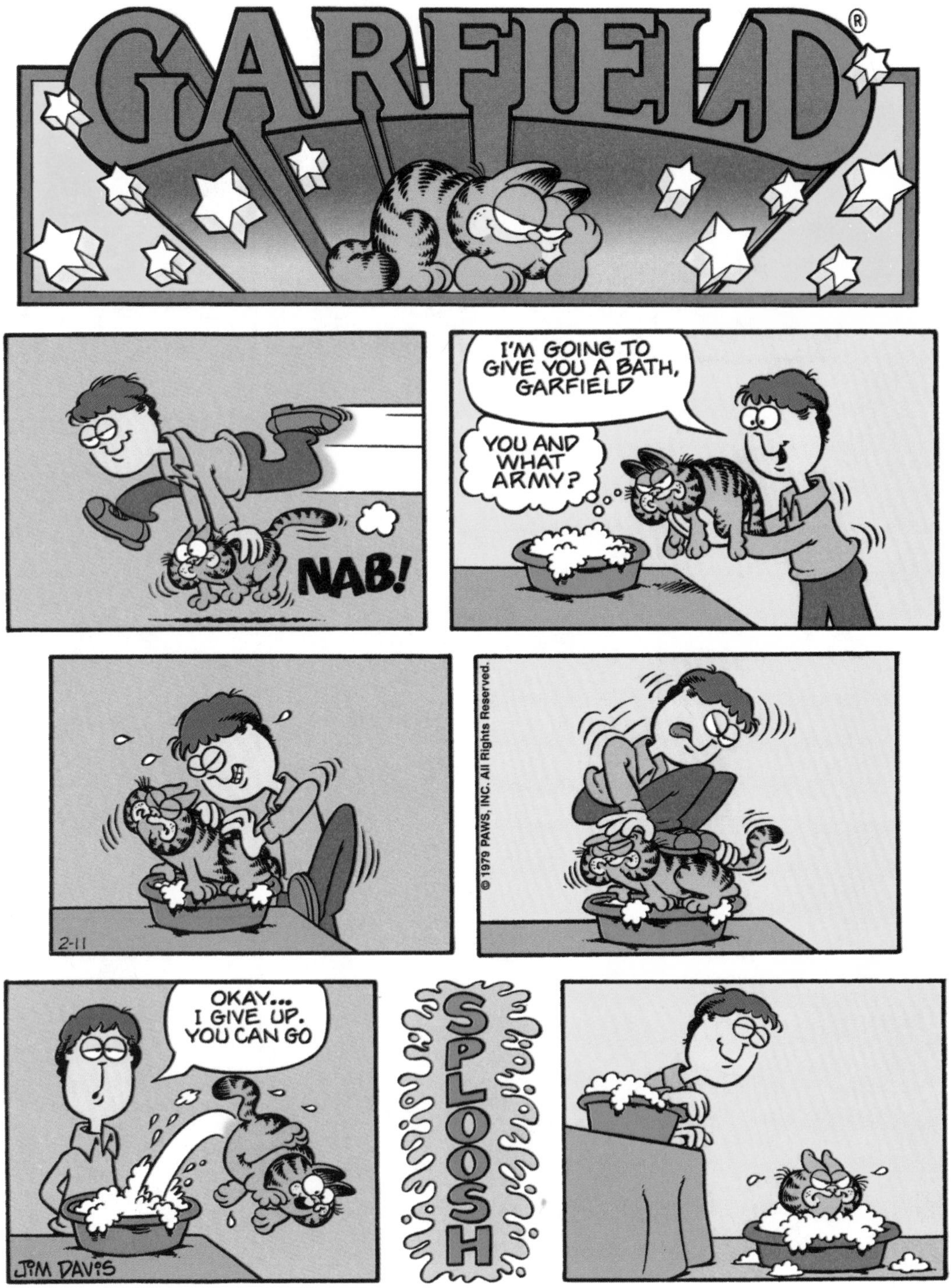
GARFIELD®
NAB!
I'M GOING TO GIVE YOU A BATH, GARFIELD
YOU AND WHAT ARMY?
2-11
© 1979 PAWS, INC. All Rights Reserved.
OKAY... I GIVE UP. YOU CAN GO
JIM DAVIS
SPLOOSH

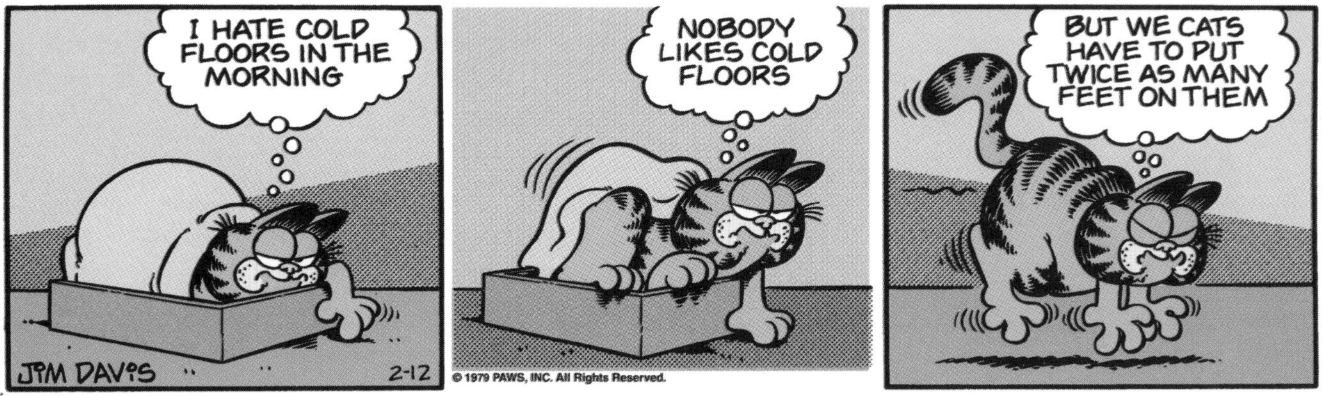
I HATE COLD FLOORS IN THE MORNING
JIM DAVIS
2-12
NOBODY LIKES COLD FLOORS
© 1979 PAWS, INC. All Rights Reserved.
BUT WE CATS HAVE TO PUT TWICE AS MANY FEET ON THEM

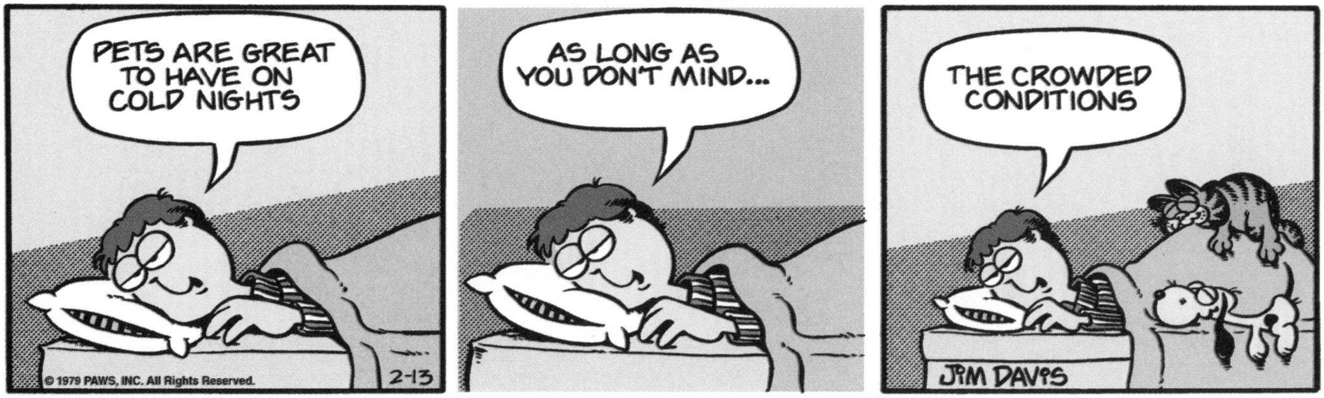
PETS ARE GREAT TO HAVE ON COLD NIGHTS
© 1979 PAWS, INC. All Rights Reserved.
2-13
AS LONG AS YOU DON'T MIND...
THE CROWDED CONDITIONS
JIM DAVIS

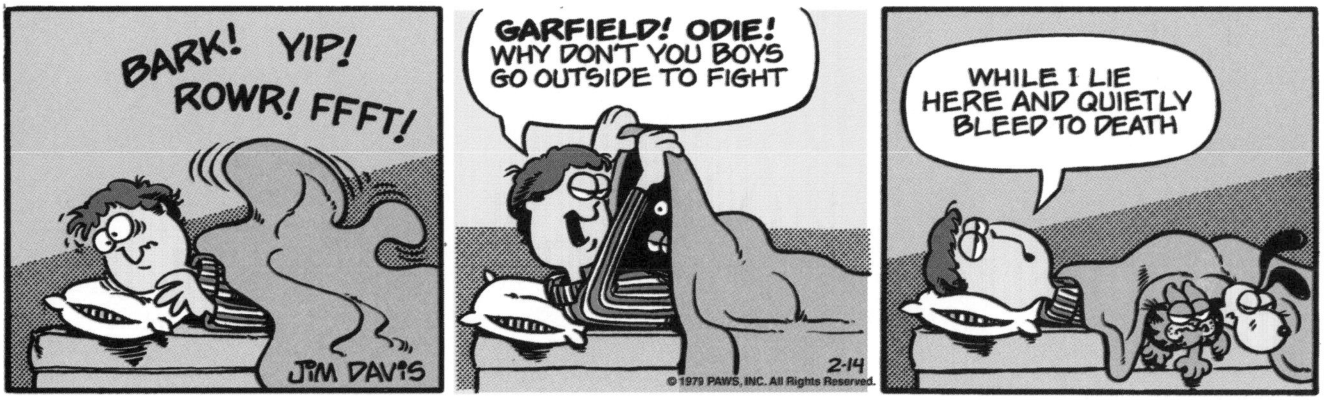
BARK! YIP!
ROWR! FFFT!
JIM DAVIS
GARFIELD! ODIE! WHY DON'T YOU BOYS GO OUTSIDE TO FIGHT
2-14
© 1979 PAWS, INC. All Rights Reserved.
WHILE I LIE HERE AND QUIETLY BLEED TO DEATH

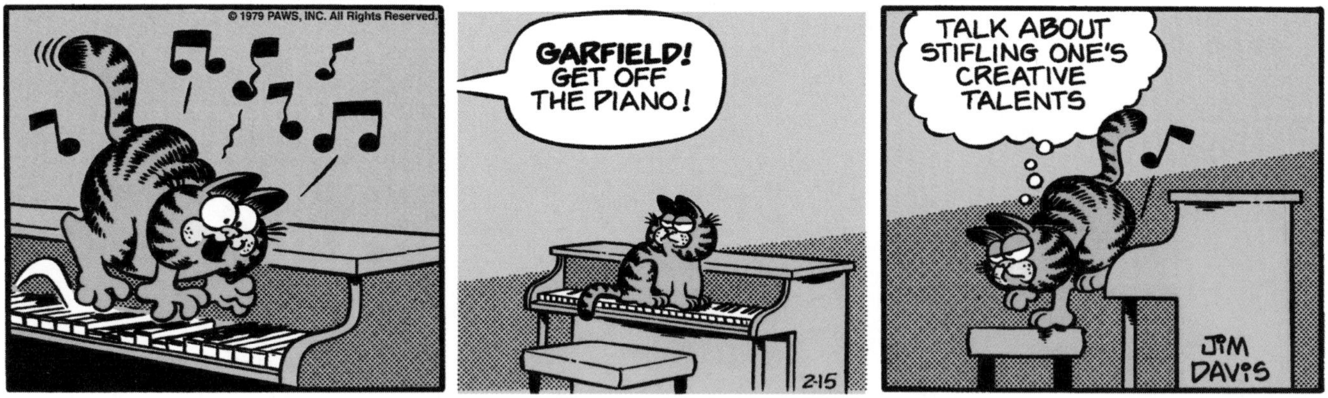
© 1979 PAWS, INC. All Rights Reserved.
GARFIELD! GET OFF THE PIANO!
TALK ABOUT STIFLING ONE'S CREATIVE TALENTS
2-15
JIM DAVIS

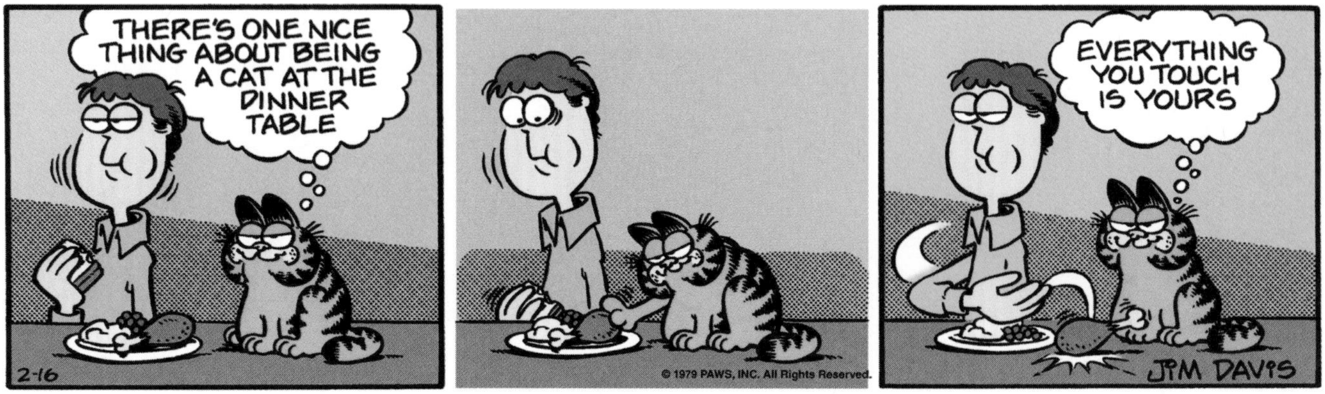
THERE'S ONE NICE THING ABOUT BEING A CAT AT THE DINNER TABLE
2-16
© 1979 PAWS, INC. All Rights Reserved.
EVERYTHING YOU TOUCH IS YOURS
JIM DAVIS

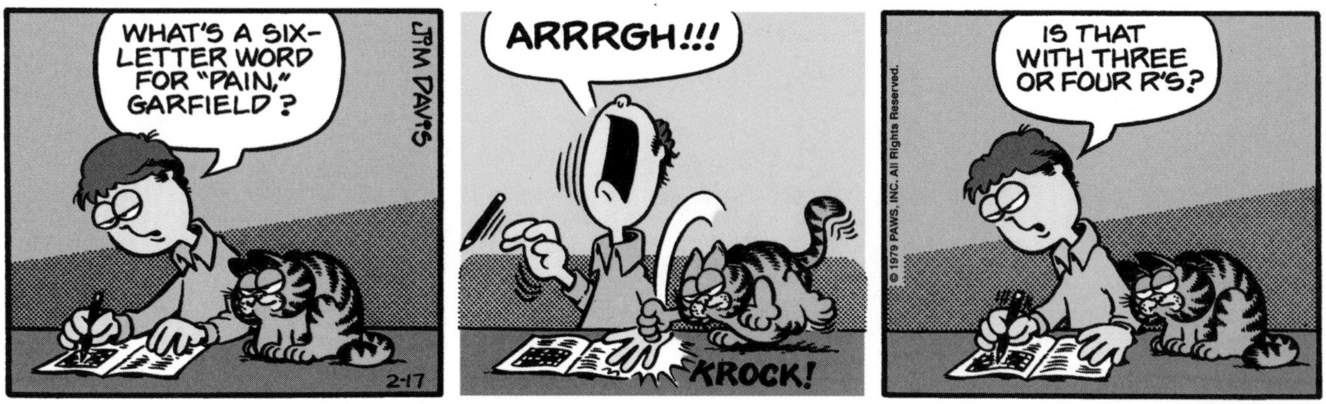
WHAT'S A SIX-LETTER WORD FOR "PAIN," GARFIELD?
JIM DAVIS
2-17
ARRRGH!!!
KROCK!
© 1979 PAWS, INC. All Rights Reserved.
IS THAT WITH THREE OR FOUR R'S?

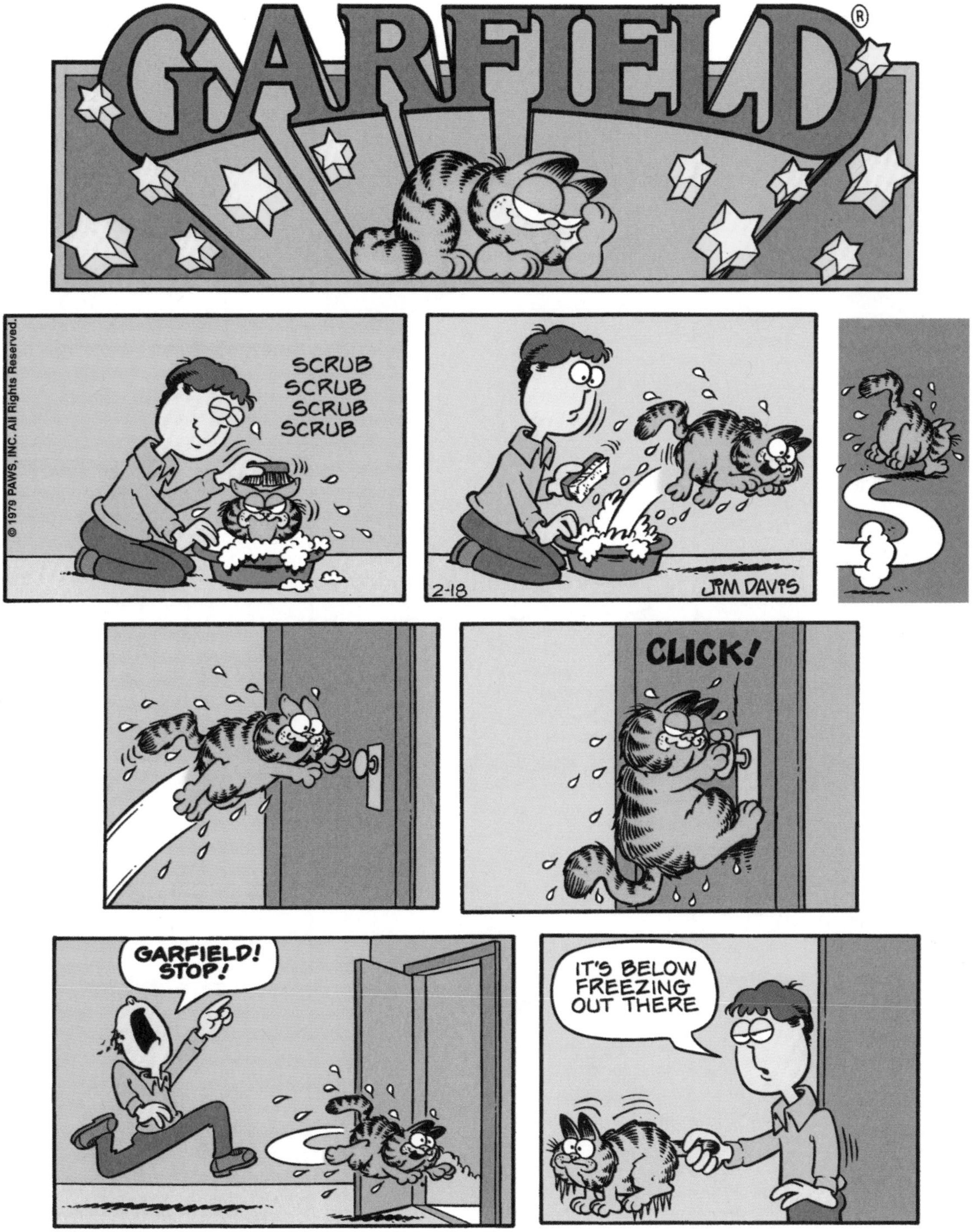
GARFIELD®
© 1979 PAWS, INC. All Rights Reserved.
SCRUB SCRUB SCRUB SCRUB
2-18
JIM DAVIS
CLICK!
GARFIELD! STOP!
IT'S BELOW FREEZING OUT THERE

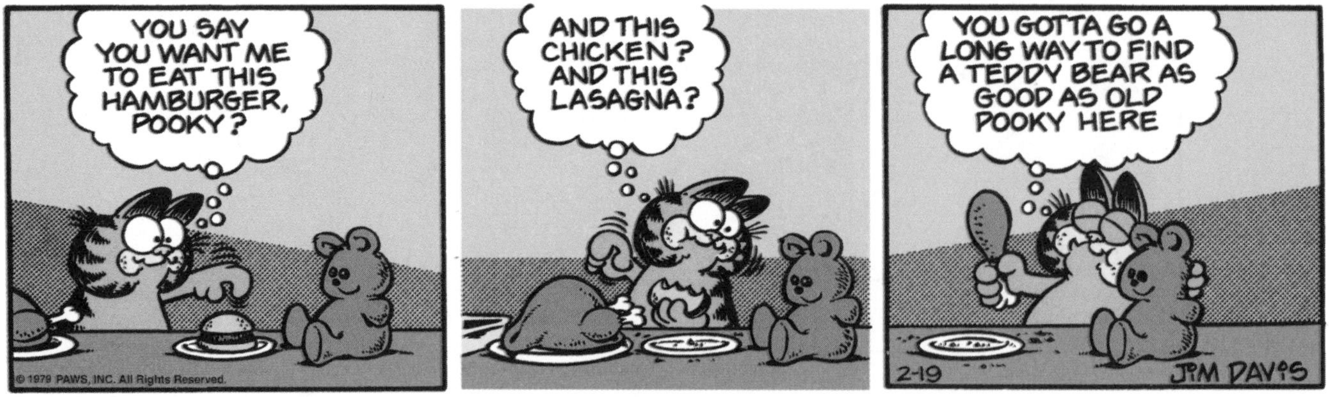
YOU SAY YOU WANT ME TO EAT THIS HAMBURGER, POOKY?
© 1979 PAWS, INC. All Rights Reserved.
AND THIS CHICKEN? AND THIS LASAGNA?
YOU GOTTA GO A LONG WAY TO FIND A TEDDY BEAR AS GOOD AS OLD POOKY HERE
2-19
JIM DAVIS

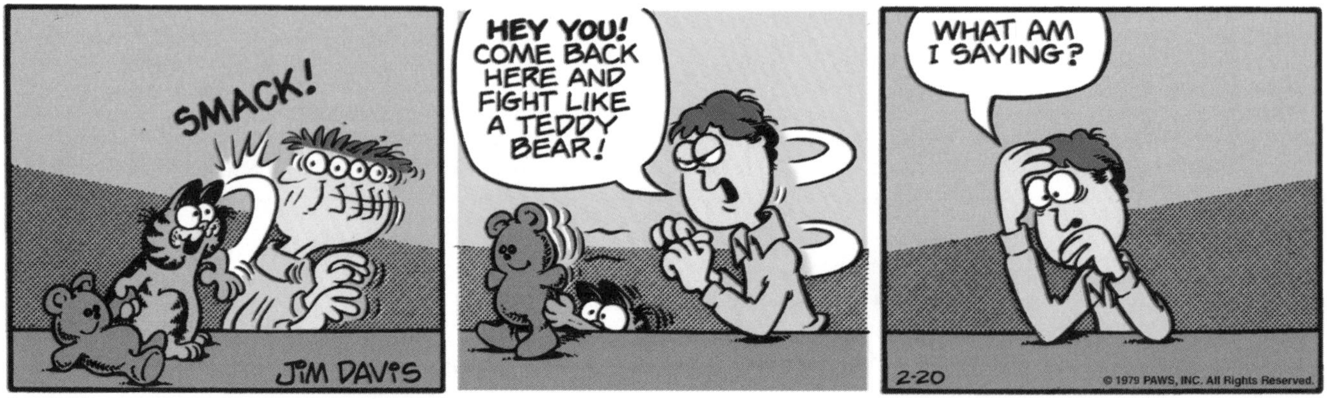
SMACK!
JIM DAVIS
HEY YOU! COME BACK HERE AND FIGHT LIKE A TEDDY BEAR!
WHAT AM I SAYING?
2-20
© 1979 PAWS, INC. All Rights Reserved.

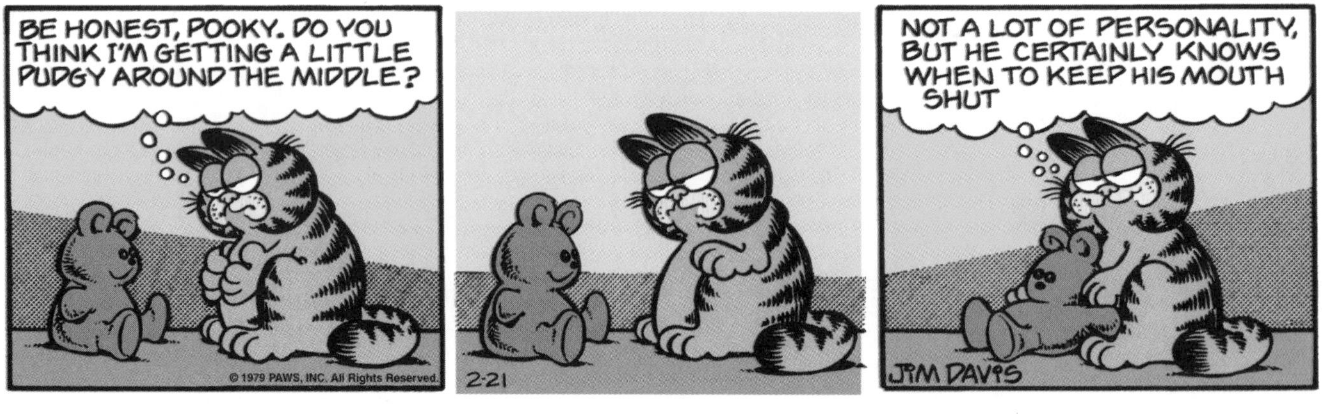
BE HONEST, POOKY. DO YOU THINK I'M GETTING A LITTLE PUDGY AROUND THE MIDDLE?
© 1979 PAWS, INC. All Rights Reserved.
2-21
NOT A LOT OF PERSONALITY, BUT HE CERTAINLY KNOWS WHEN TO KEEP HIS MOUTH SHUT
JIM DAVIS

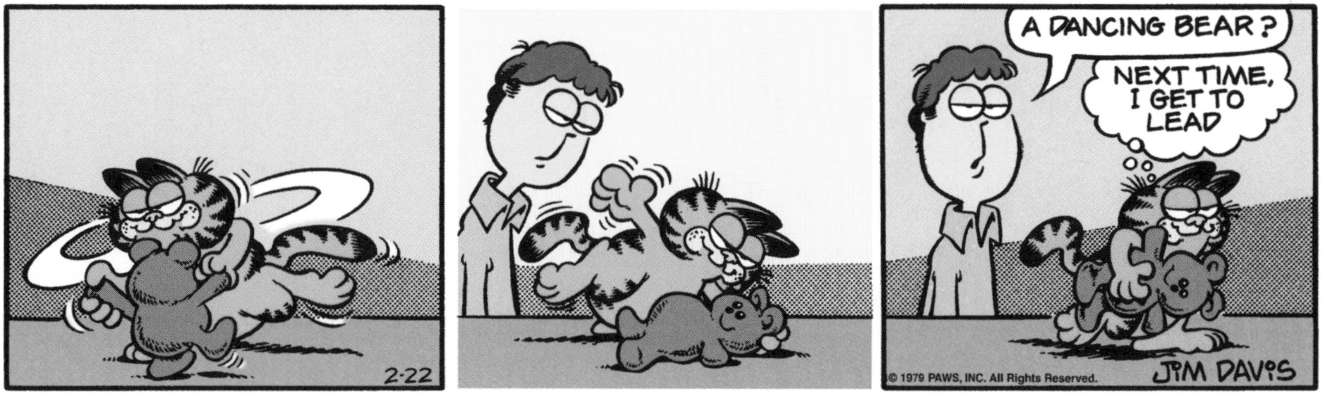
2-22
A DANCING BEAR?
NEXT TIME, I GET TO LEAD
© 1979 PAWS, INC. All Rights Reserved.
JIM DAVIS

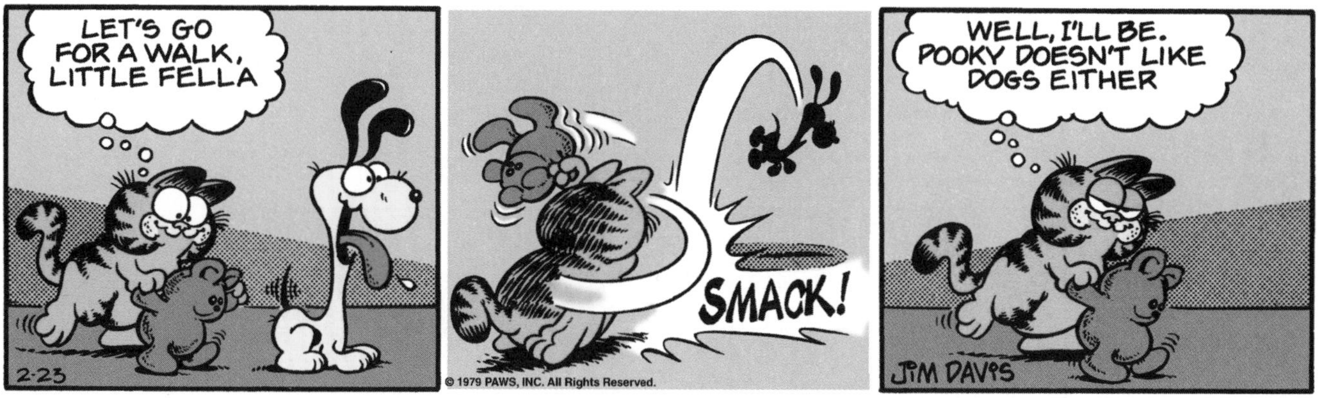
LET'S GO FOR A WALK, LITTLE FELLA
2-23
SMACK!
© 1979 PAWS, INC. All Rights Reserved.
WELL, I'LL BE. POOKY DOESN'T LIKE DOGS EITHER
JIM DAVIS

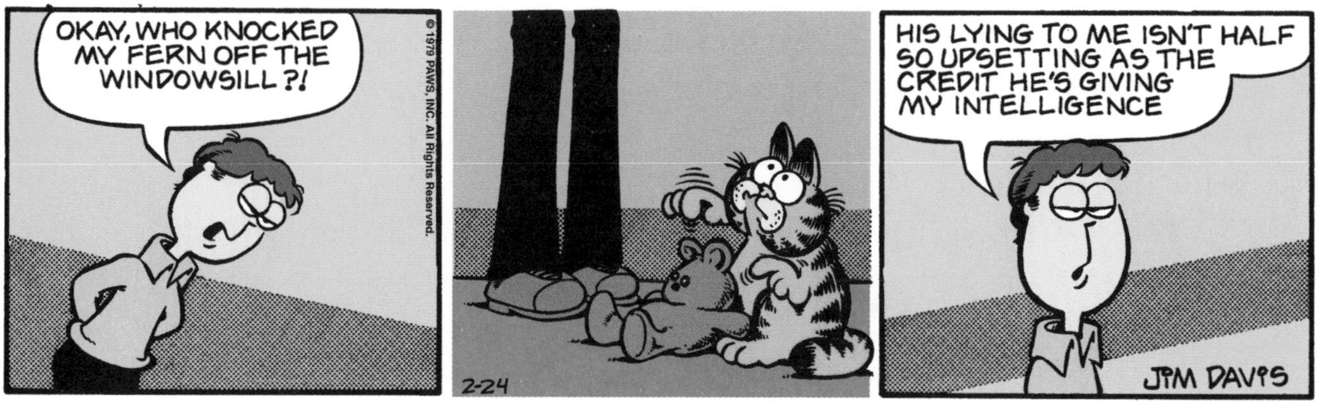
OKAY, WHO KNOCKED MY FERN OFF THE WINDOWSILL?!
© 1979 PAWS, INC. All Rights Reserved.
2-24
HIS LYING TO ME ISN'T HALF SO UPSETTING AS THE CREDIT HE'S GIVING MY INTELLIGENCE
JIM DAVIS

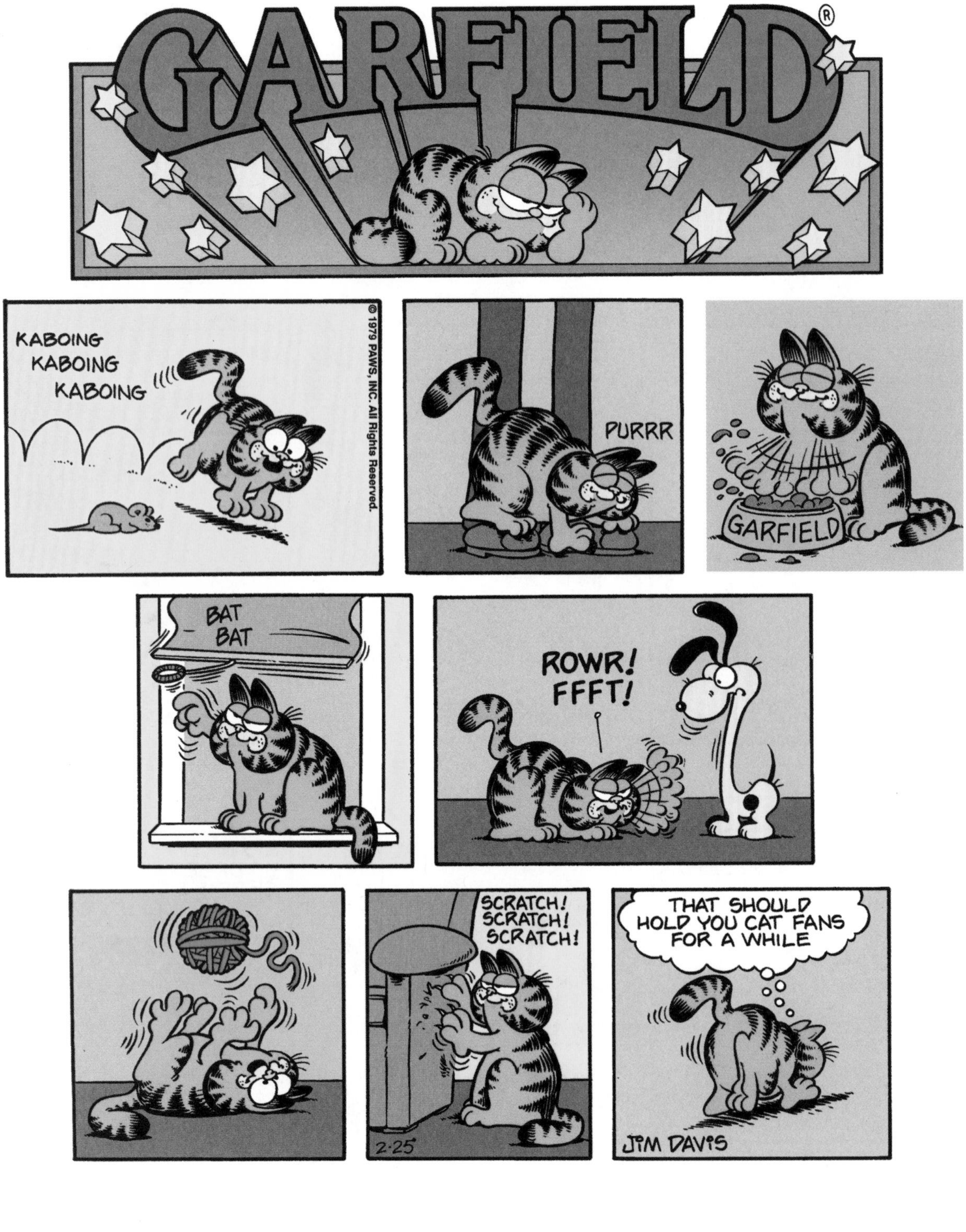
GARFIELD®
© 1979 PAWS, INC. All Rights Reserved.
KABOING
KABOING
KABOING
PURRR
GARFIELD
BAT
BAT
ROWR! FFFT!
SCRATCH! SCRATCH! SCRATCH!
2-25
THAT SHOULD HOLD YOU CAT FANS FOR A WHILE
JIM DAVIS

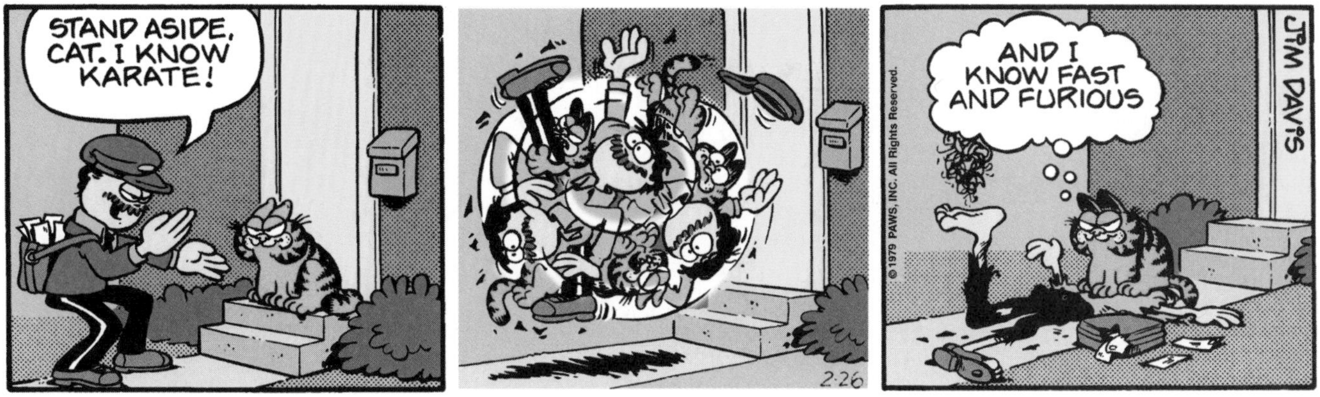
STAND ASIDE, CAT. I KNOW KARATE!
2-26
AND I KNOW FAST AND FURIOUS
© 1979 PAWS, INC. All Rights Reserved.
JIM DAVIS

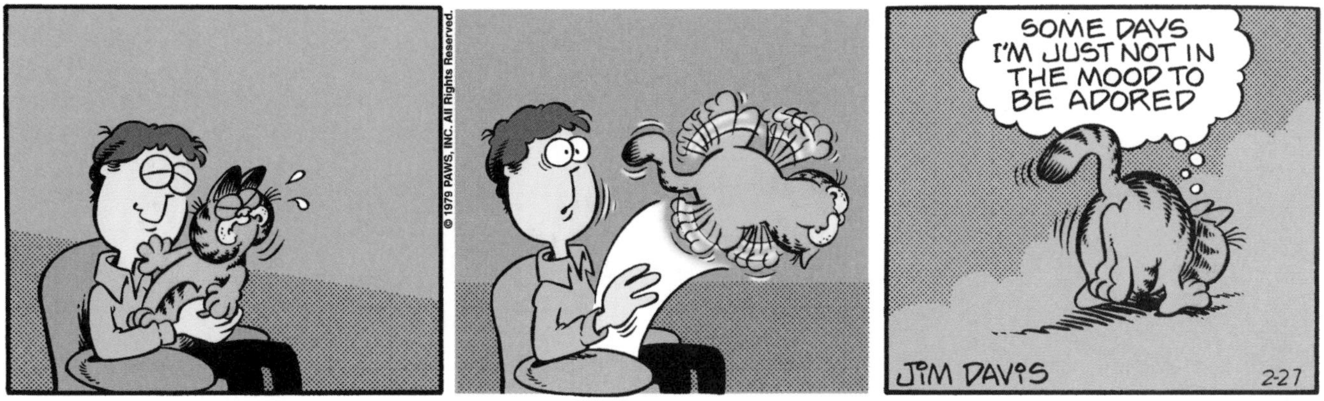
© 1979 PAWS, INC. All Rights Reserved.
SOME DAYS I'M JUST NOT IN THE MOOD TO BE ADORED
JIM DAVIS
2-27

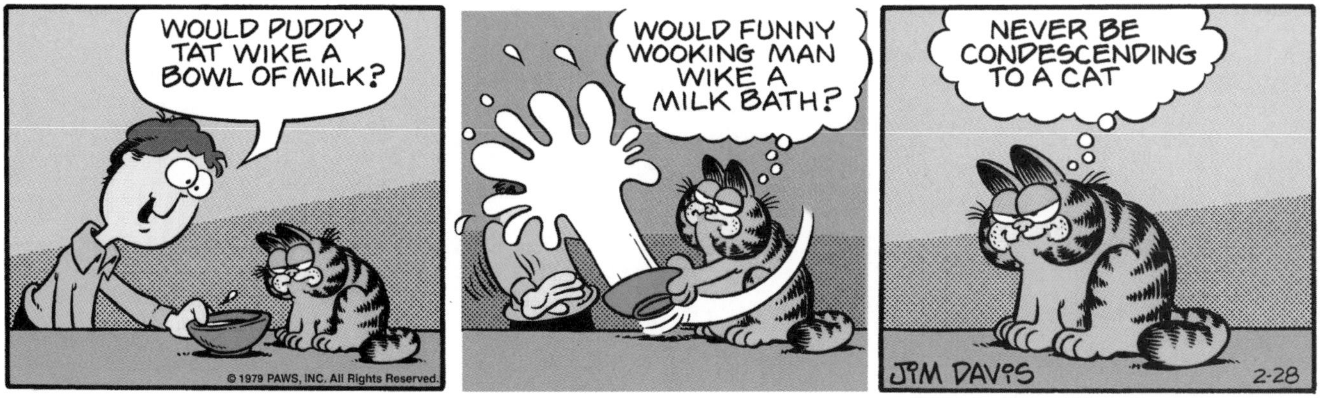
WOULD PUDDY TAT WIKE A BOWL OF MILK?
© 1979 PAWS, INC. All Rights Reserved.
WOULD FUNNY WOOKING MAN WIKE A MILK BATH?
NEVER BE CONDESCENDING TO A CAT
JIM DAVIS
2-28

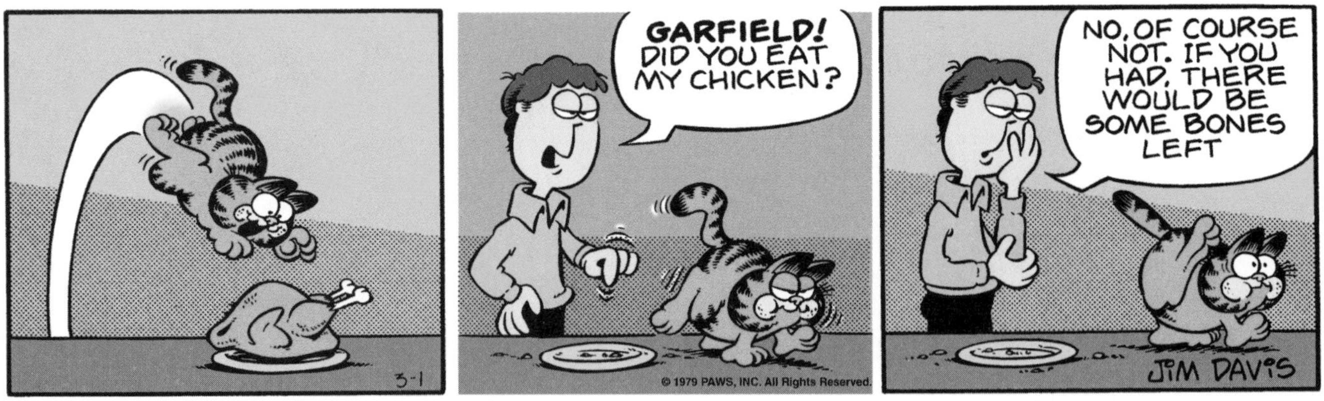
GARFIELD! DID YOU EAT MY CHICKEN?
NO, OF COURSE NOT. IF YOU HAD, THERE WOULD BE SOME BONES LEFT
3-1
© 1979 PAWS, INC. All Rights Reserved.
JIM DAVIS

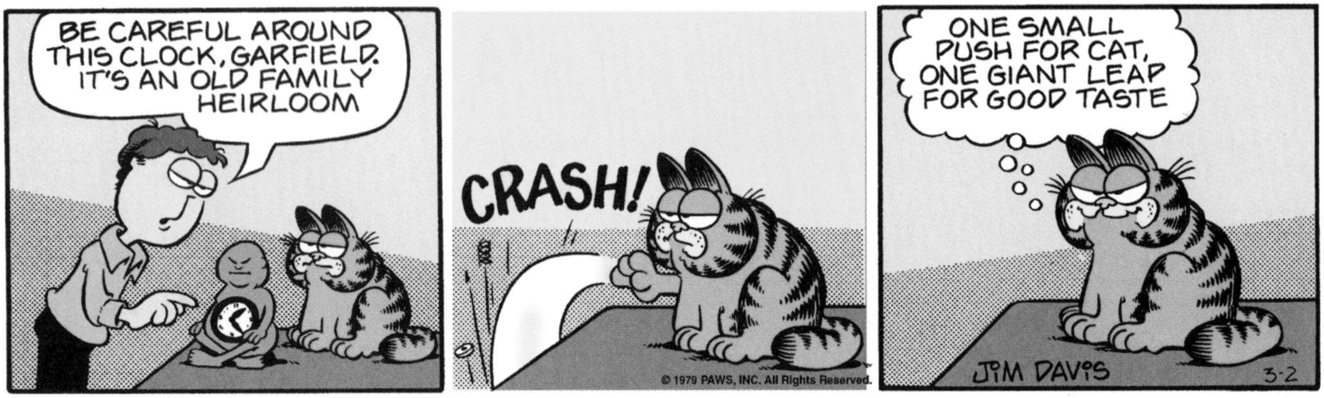
BE CAREFUL AROUND THIS CLOCK, GARFIELD. IT'S AN OLD FAMILY HEIRLOOM
CRASH!
© 1979 PAWS, INC. All Rights Reserved.
ONE SMALL PUSH FOR CAT, ONE GIANT LEAP FOR GOOD TASTE
JIM DAVIS
3-2

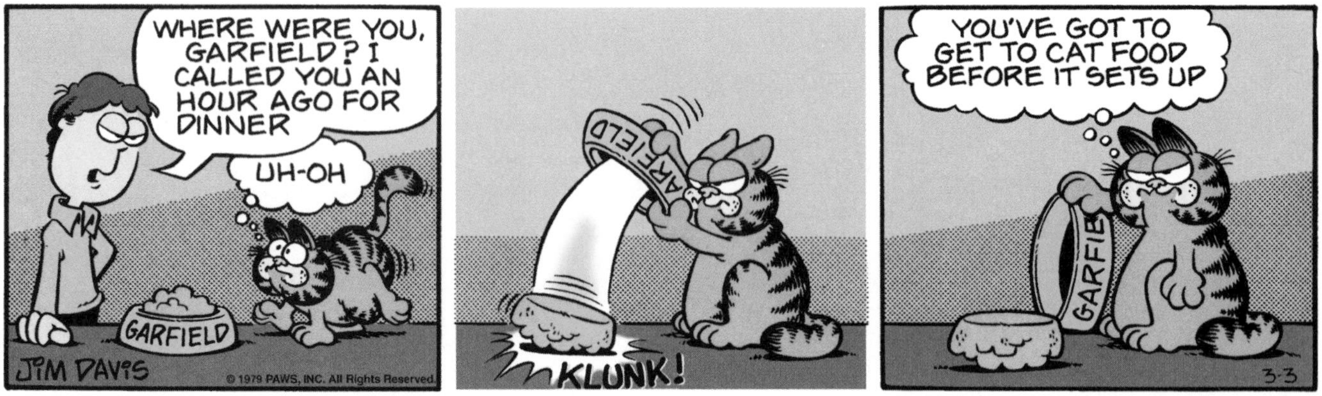
WHERE WERE YOU, GARFIELD? I CALLED YOU AN HOUR AGO FOR DINNER
UH-OH
GARFIELD
JIM DAVIS
© 1979 PAWS, INC. All Rights Reserved.
KLUNK!
YOU'VE GOT TO GET TO CAT FOOD BEFORE IT SETS UP
3-3

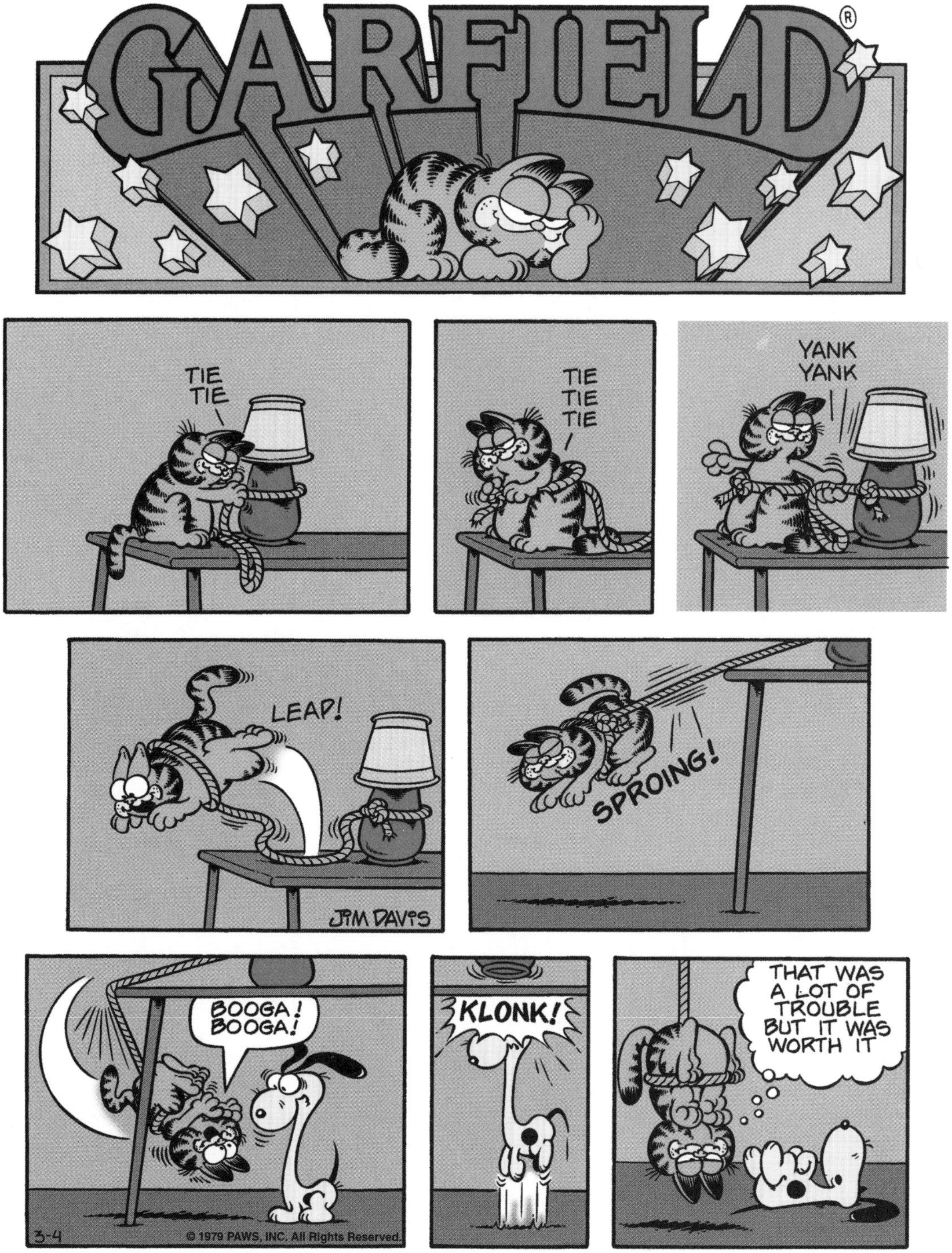
GARFIELD®
TIE TIE
TIE TIE TIE
YANK YANK
LEAP!
JIM DAVIS
SPROING!
BOOGA! BOOGA!
3-4
© 1979 PAWS, INC. All Rights Reserved.
KLONK!
THAT WAS A LOT OF TROUBLE BUT IT WAS WORTH IT

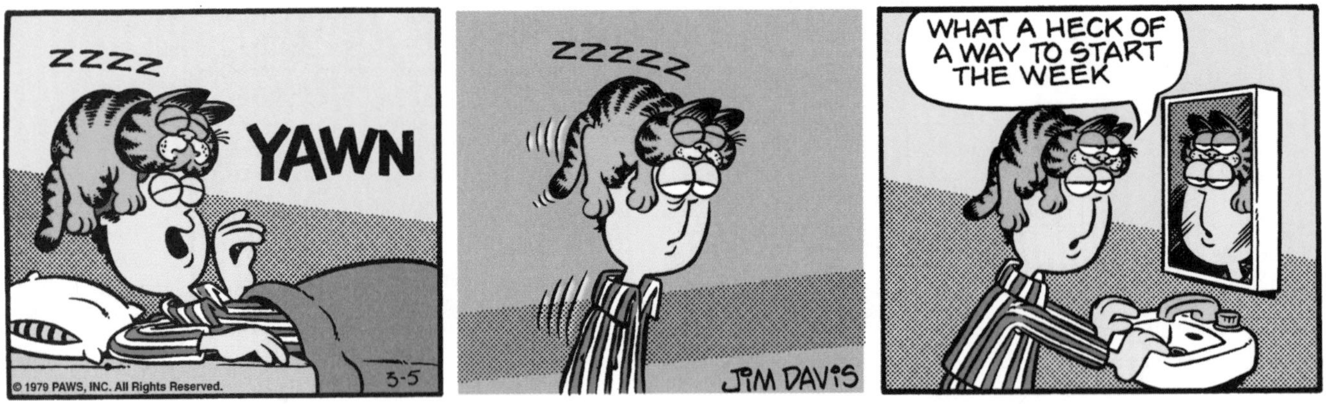
ZZZZ
YAWN
© 1979 PAWS, INC. All Rights Reserved.
3-5
ZZZZZ
JIM DAVIS
WHAT A HECK OF A WAY TO START THE WEEK

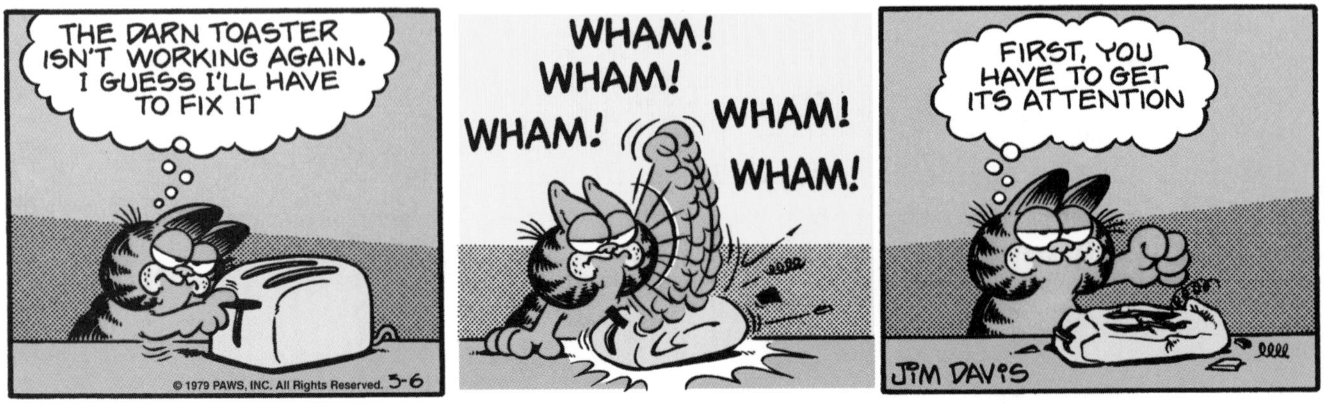
THE DARN TOASTER ISN'T WORKING AGAIN. I GUESS I'LL HAVE TO FIX IT
© 1979 PAWS, INC. All Rights Reserved. 3-6
WHAM!
WHAM!
WHAM!
WHAM!
WHAM!
FIRST, YOU HAVE TO GET ITS ATTENTION
JIM DAVIS

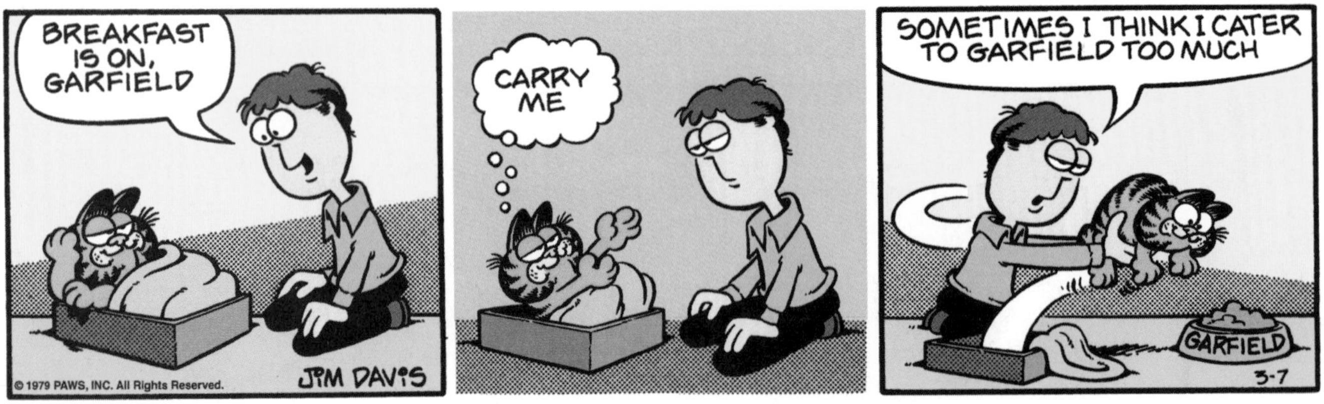
BREAKFAST IS ON, GARFIELD
© 1979 PAWS, INC. All Rights Reserved.
JIM DAVIS
CARRY ME
SOMETIMES I THINK I CATER TO GARFIELD TOO MUCH
GARFIELD
3-7

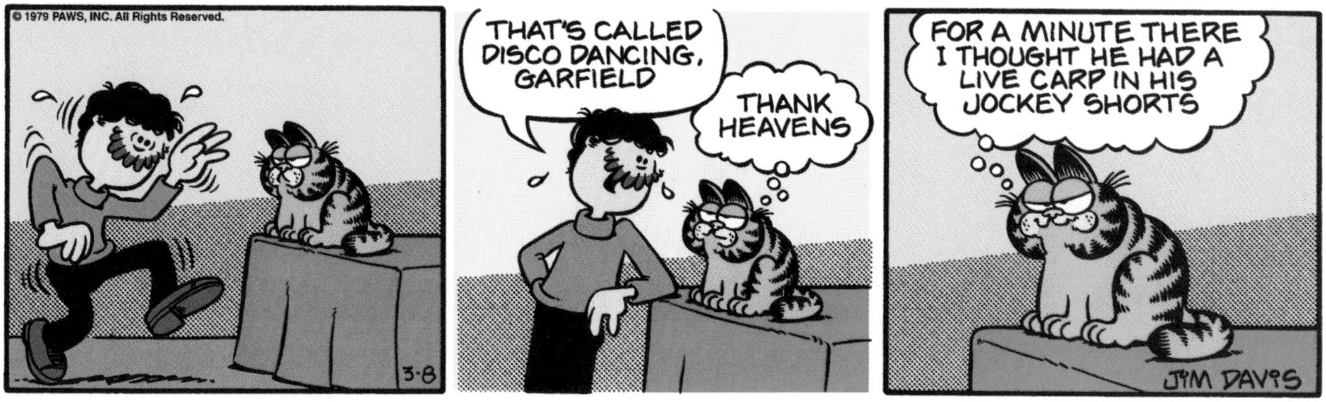
© 1979 PAWS, INC. All Rights Reserved.
3-8
THAT'S CALLED DISCO DANCING, GARFIELD
THANK HEAVENS
FOR A MINUTE THERE I THOUGHT HE HAD A LIVE CARP IN HIS JOCKEY SHORTS
JIM DAVIS

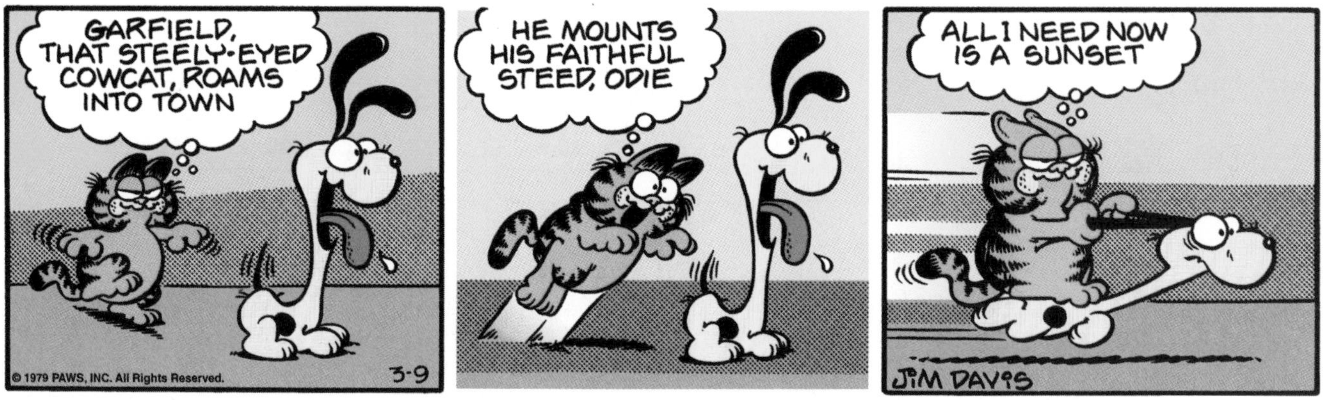
GARFIELD, THAT STEELY-EYED COWCAT, ROAMS INTO TOWN
© 1979 PAWS, INC. All Rights Reserved.
3-9
HE MOUNTS HIS FAITHFUL STEED, ODIE
ALL I NEED NOW IS A SUNSET
JIM DAVIS

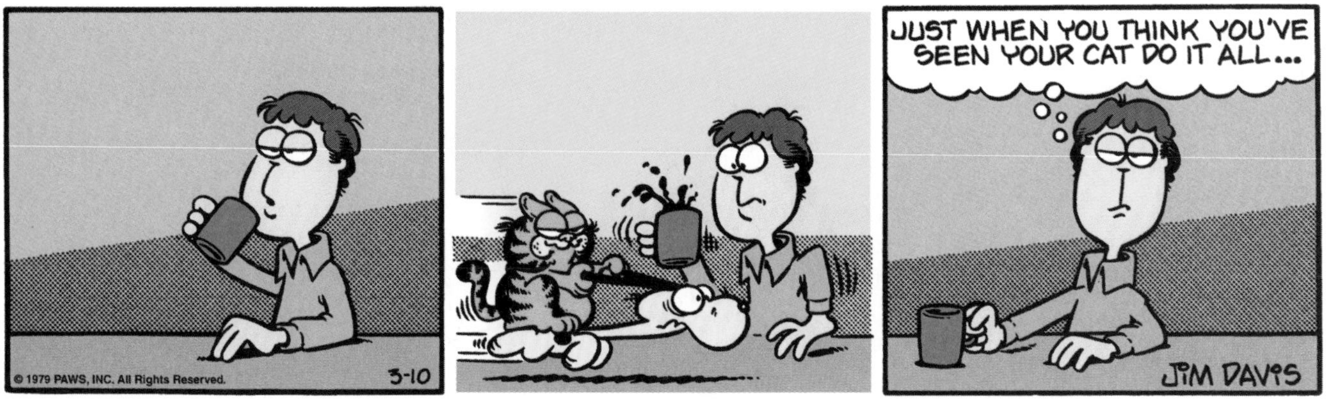
© 1979 PAWS, INC. All Rights Reserved.
3-10
JUST WHEN YOU THINK YOU'VE SEEN YOUR CAT DO IT ALL...
JIM DAVIS

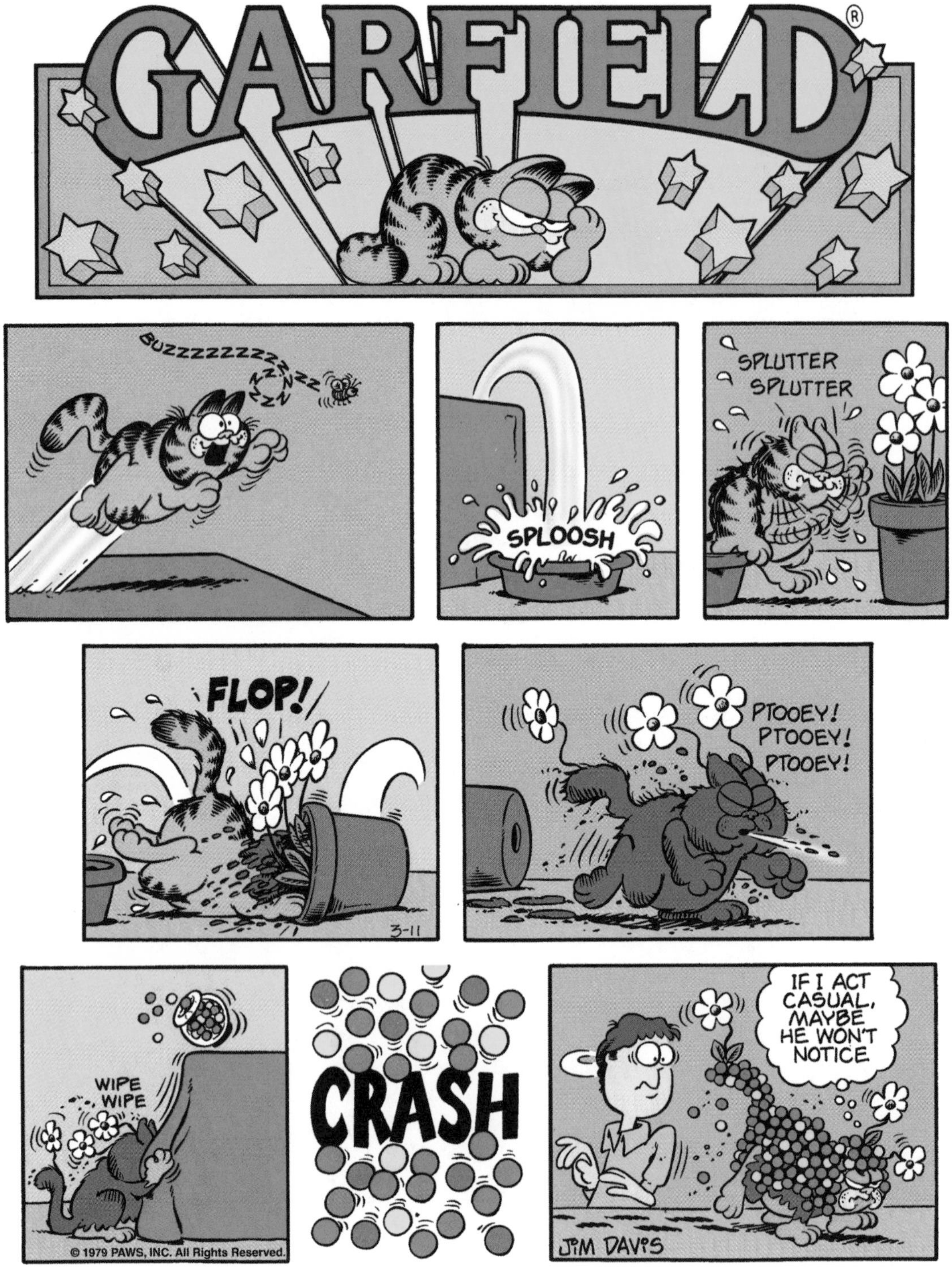
GARFIELD
BUZZZZZZZZZZZZZZZZZZZ
SPLOOSH
SPLUTTER SPLUTTER
FLOP!
3-11
PTOOEY! PTOOEY! PTOOEY!
WIPE WIPE
© 1979 PAWS, INC. All Rights Reserved.
CRASH
IF I ACT CASUAL, MAYBE HE WON'T NOTICE
JIM DAVIS

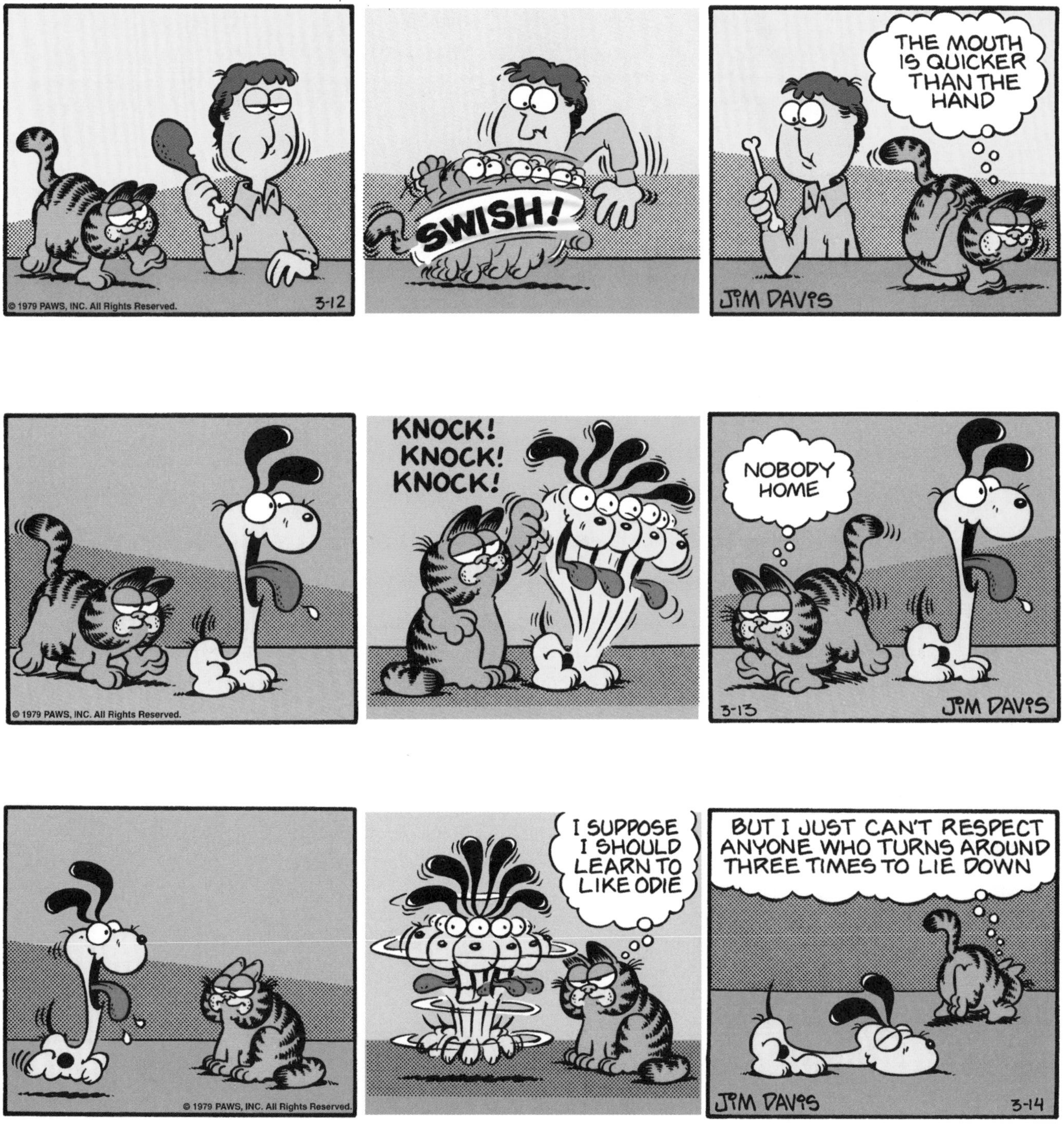
© 1979 PAWS, INC. All Rights Reserved.
3-12
SWISH!
THE MOUTH IS QUICKER THAN THE HAND
JIM DAVIS
© 1979 PAWS, INC. All Rights Reserved.
KNOCK! KNOCK! KNOCK!
NOBODY HOME
3-13
JIM DAVIS
© 1979 PAWS, INC. All Rights Reserved.
I SUPPOSE I SHOULD LEARN TO LIKE ODIE
BUT I JUST CAN'T RESPECT ANYONE WHO TURNS AROUND THREE TIMES TO LIE DOWN
JIM DAVIS
3-14

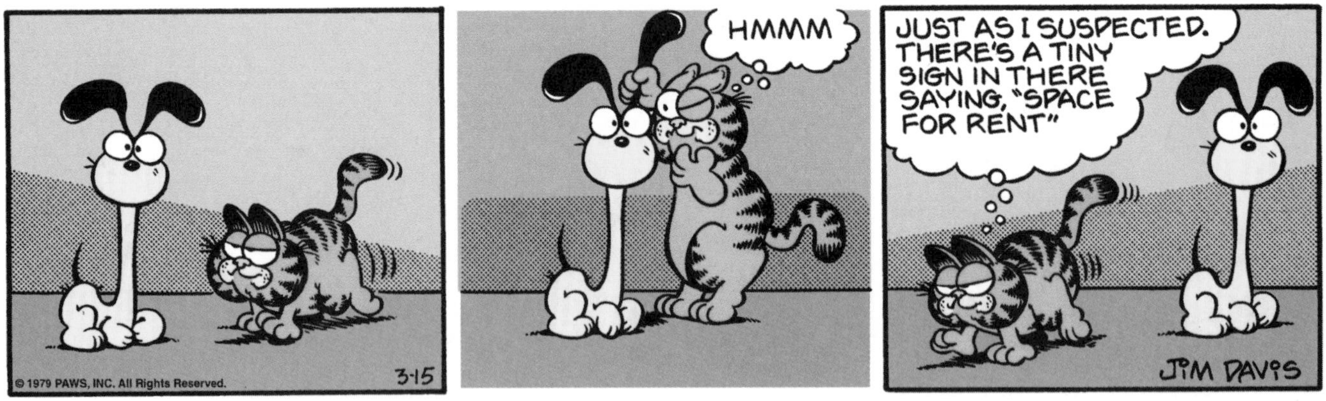
© 1979 PAWS, INC. All Rights Reserved.
3-15
HMMM
JUST AS I SUSPECTED. THERE'S A TINY SIGN IN THERE SAYING, "SPACE FOR RENT"
JIM DAVIS

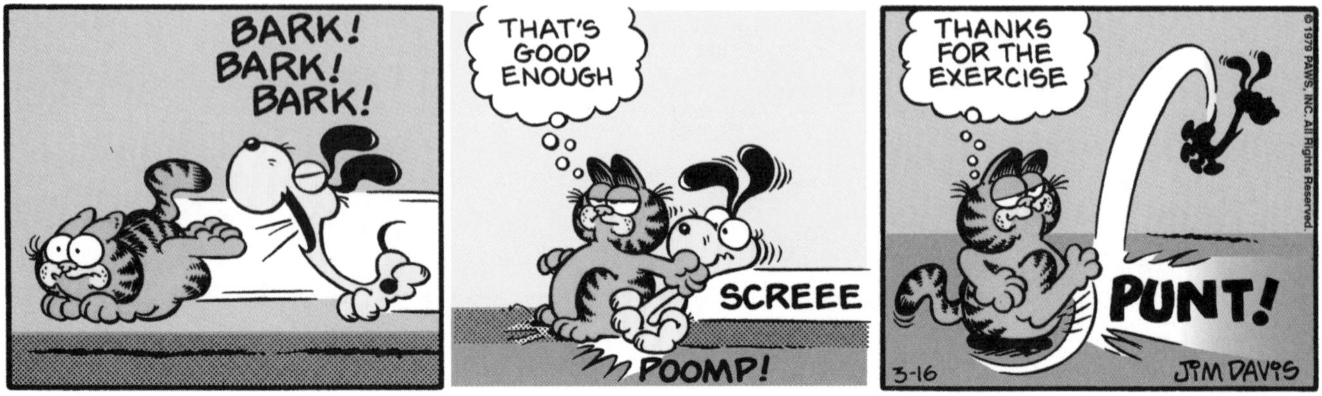
BARK! BARK! BARK!
THAT'S GOOD ENOUGH
SCREEE
POOMP!
THANKS FOR THE EXERCISE
PUNT!
© 1979 PAWS, INC. All Rights Reserved.
3-16
JIM DAVIS

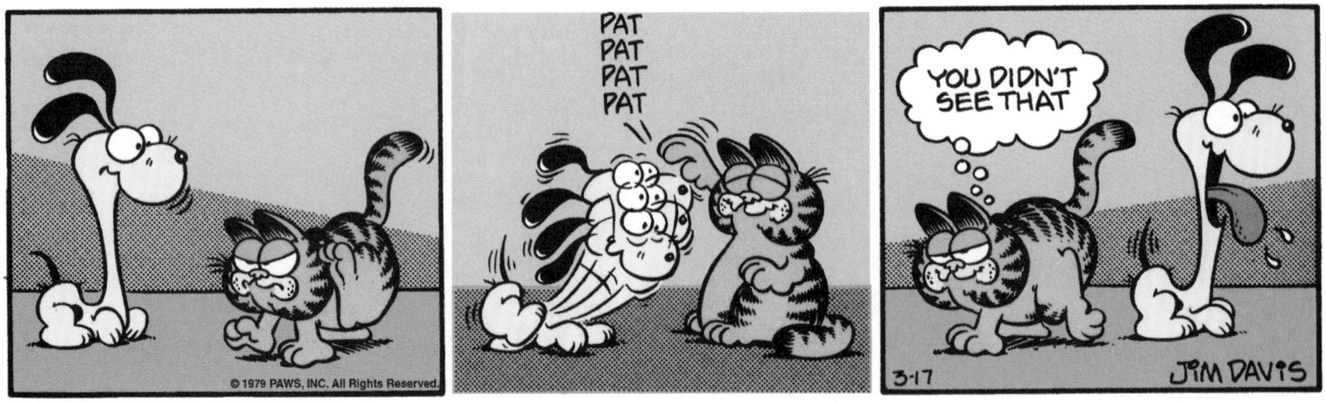
© 1979 PAWS, INC. All Rights Reserved.
PAT PAT PAT PAT
YOU DIDN'T SEE THAT
3-17
JIM DAVIS

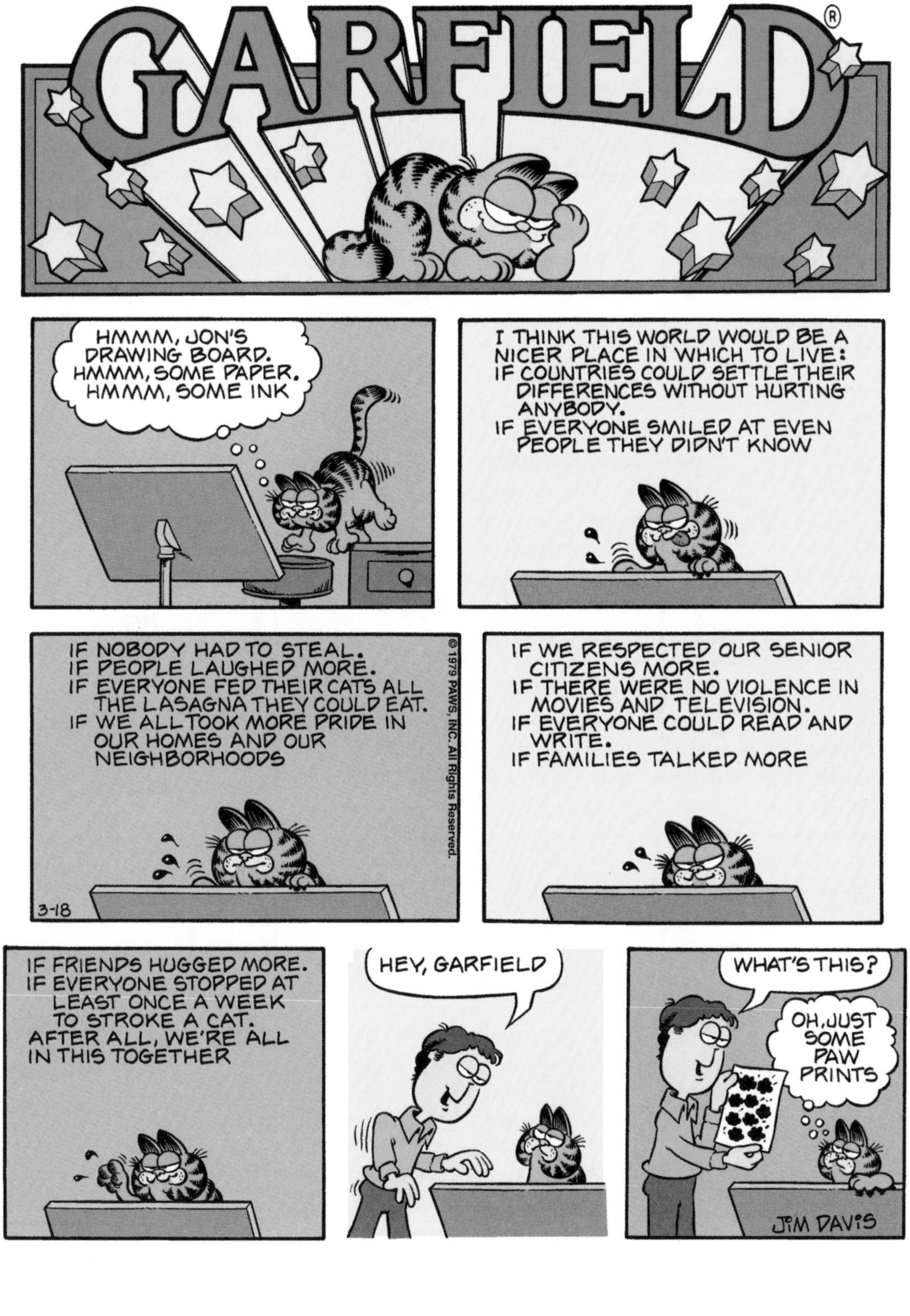
GARFIELD®
HMMM, JON'S DRAWING BOARD. HMMM, SOME PAPER. HMMM, SOME INK
I THINK THIS WORLD WOULD BE A NICER PLACE IN WHICH TO LIVE: IF COUNTRIES COULD SETTLE THEIR DIFFERENCES WITHOUT HURTING ANYBODY. IF EVERYONE SMILED AT EVEN PEOPLE THEY DIDN'T KNOW
IF NOBODY HAD TO STEAL. IF PEOPLE LAUGHED MORE. IF EVERYONE FED THEIR CATS ALL THE LASAGNA THEY COULD EAT. IF WE ALL TOOK MORE PRIDE IN OUR HOMES AND OUR NEIGHBORHOODS
© 1979 PAWS, INC. All Rights Reserved.
3-18
IF WE RESPECTED OUR SENIOR CITIZENS MORE. IF THERE WERE NO VIOLENCE IN MOVIES AND TELEVISION. IF EVERYONE COULD READ AND WRITE. IF FAMILIES TALKED MORE
IF FRIENDS HUGGED MORE. IF EVERYONE STOPPED AT LEAST ONCE A WEEK TO STROKE A CAT. AFTER ALL, WE'RE ALL IN THIS TOGETHER
HEY, GARFIELD
WHAT'S THIS?
OH, JUST SOME PAW PRINTS
JIM DAVIS

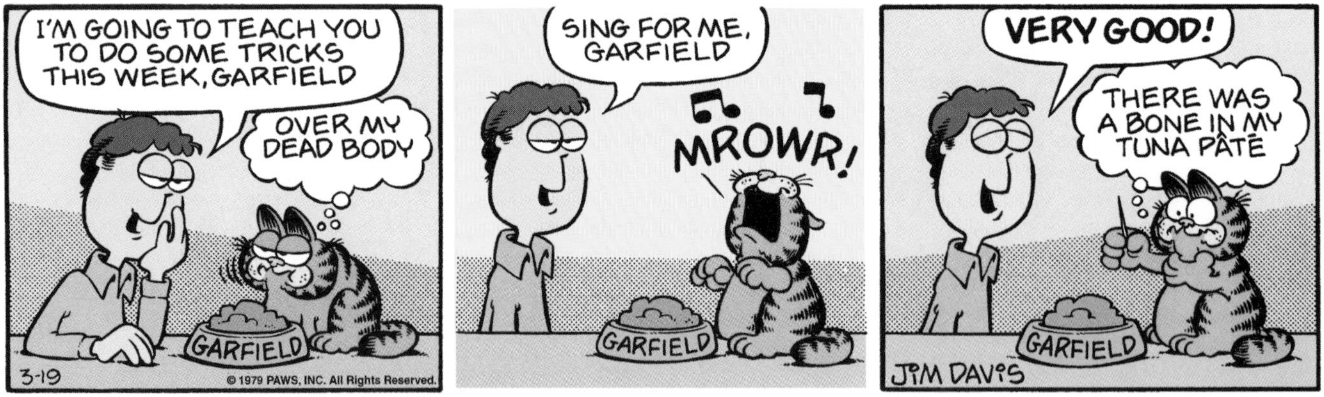
I'M GOING TO TEACH YOU TO DO SOME TRICKS THIS WEEK, GARFIELD
OVER MY DEAD BODY
3-19
© 1979 PAWS, INC. All Rights Reserved.
SING FOR ME, GARFIELD
MROWR!
VERY GOOD!
THERE WAS A BONE IN MY TUNA PÂTÉ
GARFIELD
JIM DAVIS

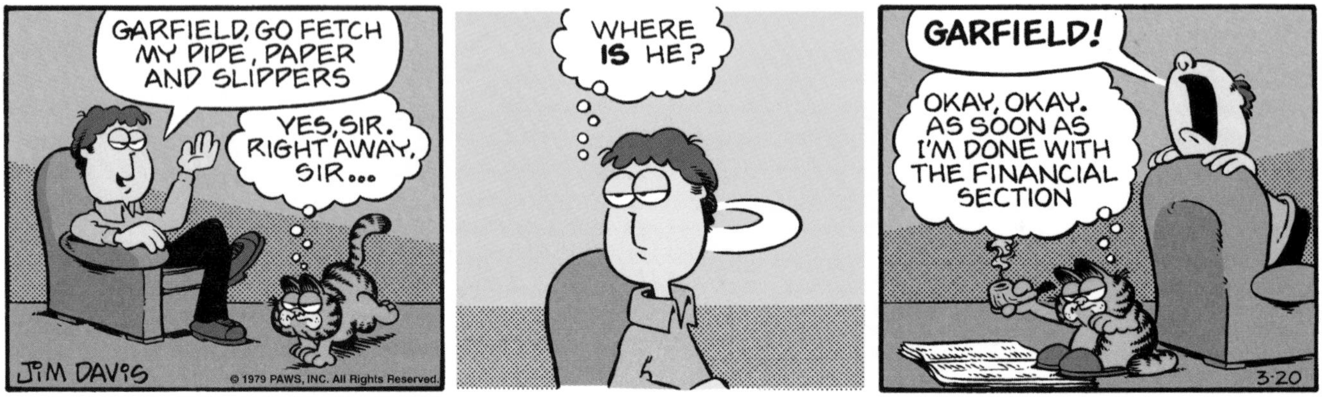
GARFIELD, GO FETCH MY PIPE, PAPER AND SLIPPERS
YES, SIR. RIGHT AWAY, SIR...
JIM DAVIS
© 1979 PAWS, INC. All Rights Reserved.
WHERE **IS** HE?
GARFIELD!
OKAY, OKAY. AS SOON AS I'M DONE WITH THE FINANCIAL SECTION
3-20

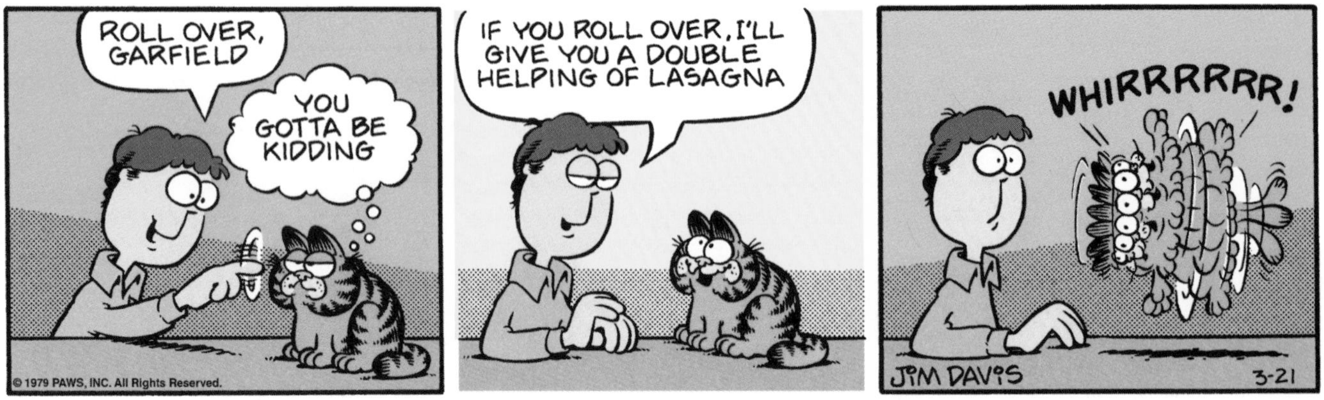
ROLL OVER, GARFIELD
YOU GOTTA BE KIDDING
© 1979 PAWS, INC. All Rights Reserved.
IF YOU ROLL OVER, I'LL GIVE YOU A DOUBLE HELPING OF LASAGNA
WHIRRRRRR!
JIM DAVIS
3-21

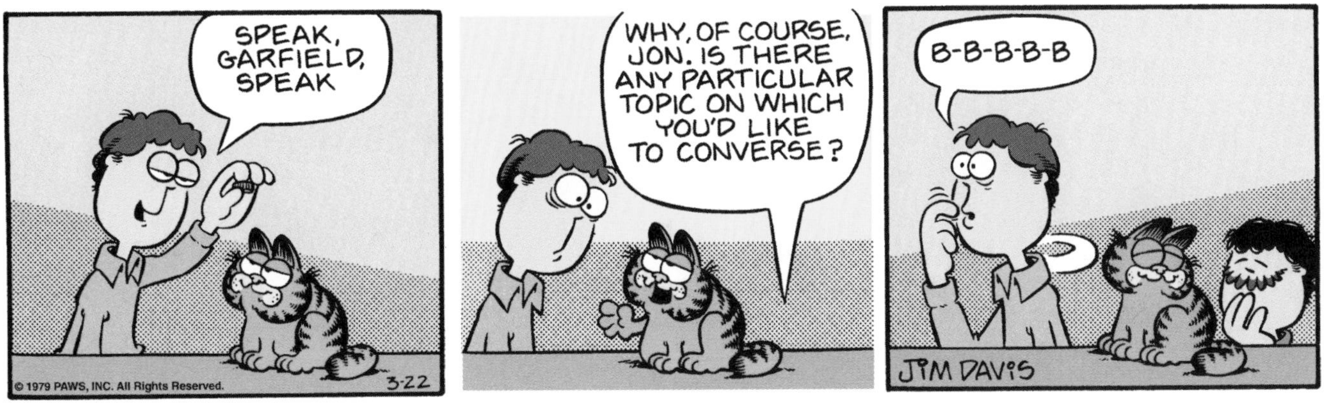
SPEAK, GARFIELD, SPEAK
© 1979 PAWS, INC. All Rights Reserved.
3-22
WHY, OF COURSE, JON. IS THERE ANY PARTICULAR TOPIC ON WHICH YOU'D LIKE TO CONVERSE?
B-B-B-B-B
JIM DAVIS

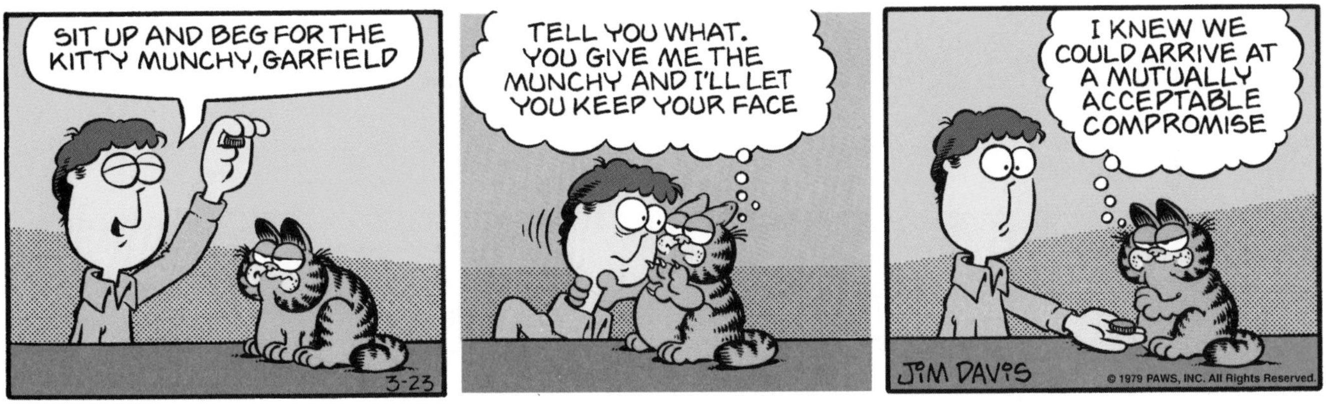
SIT UP AND BEG FOR THE KITTY MUNCHY, GARFIELD
3-23
TELL YOU WHAT. YOU GIVE ME THE MUNCHY AND I'LL LET YOU KEEP YOUR FACE
I KNEW WE COULD ARRIVE AT A MUTUALLY ACCEPTABLE COMPROMISE
JIM DAVIS
© 1979 PAWS, INC. All Rights Reserved.

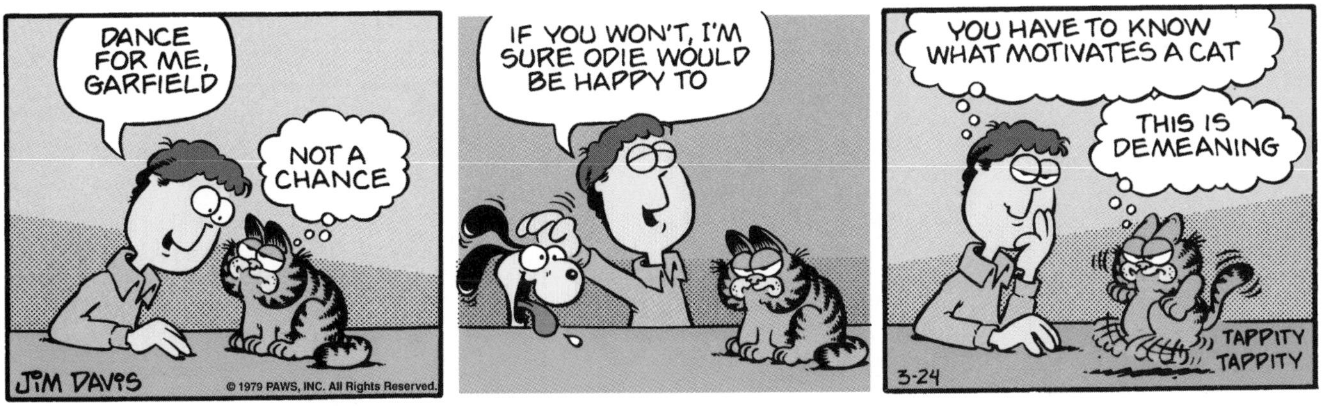
DANCE FOR ME, GARFIELD
NOT A CHANCE
JIM DAVIS
© 1979 PAWS, INC. All Rights Reserved.
IF YOU WON'T, I'M SURE ODIE WOULD BE HAPPY TO
YOU HAVE TO KNOW WHAT MOTIVATES A CAT
THIS IS DEMEANING
TAPPITY TAPPITY
3-24

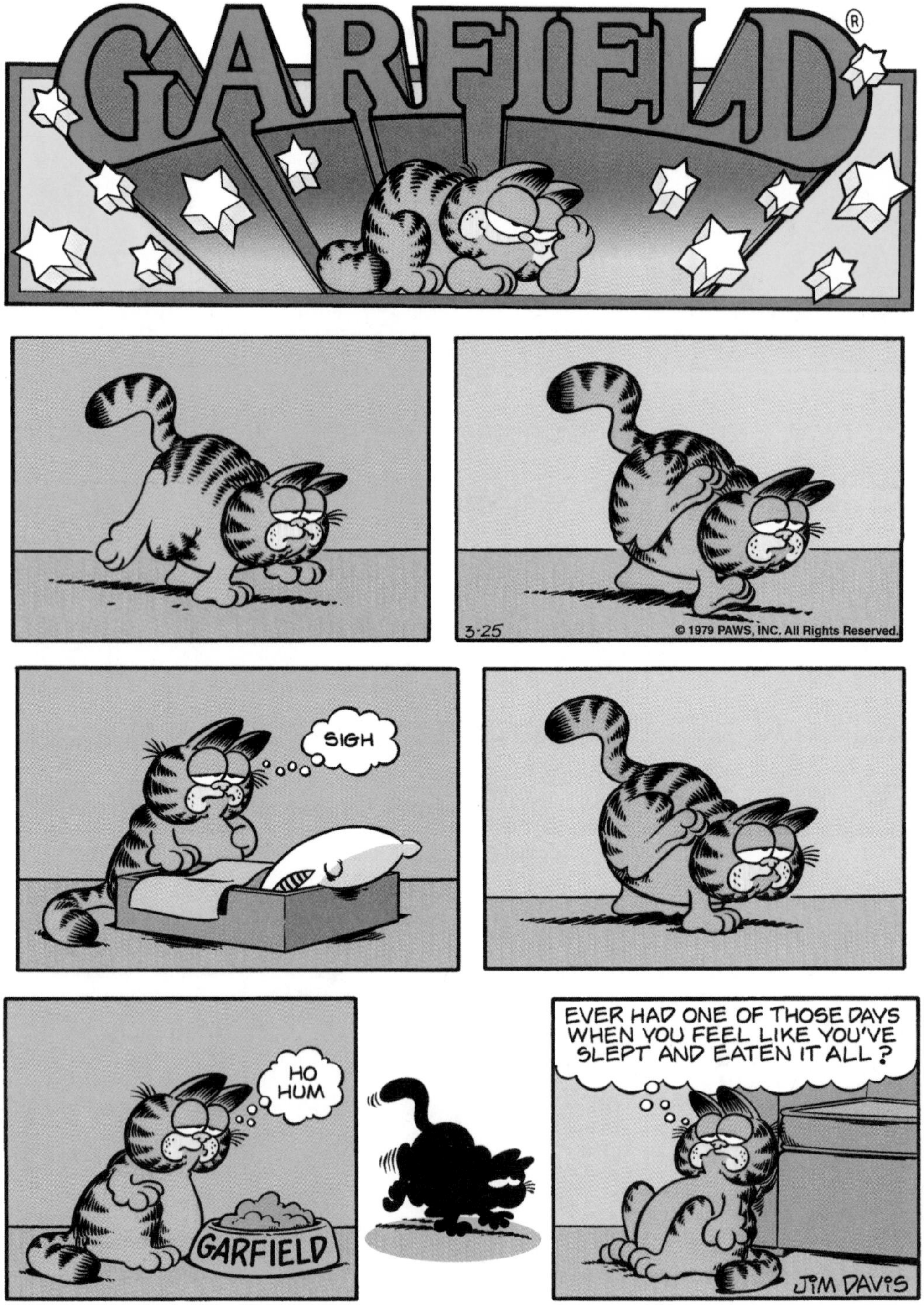
GARFIELD®
3-25
© 1979 PAWS, INC. All Rights Reserved.
SIGH
HO HUM
GARFIELD
EVER HAD ONE OF THOSE DAYS WHEN YOU FEEL LIKE YOU'VE SLEPT AND EATEN IT ALL ?
JIM DAVIS

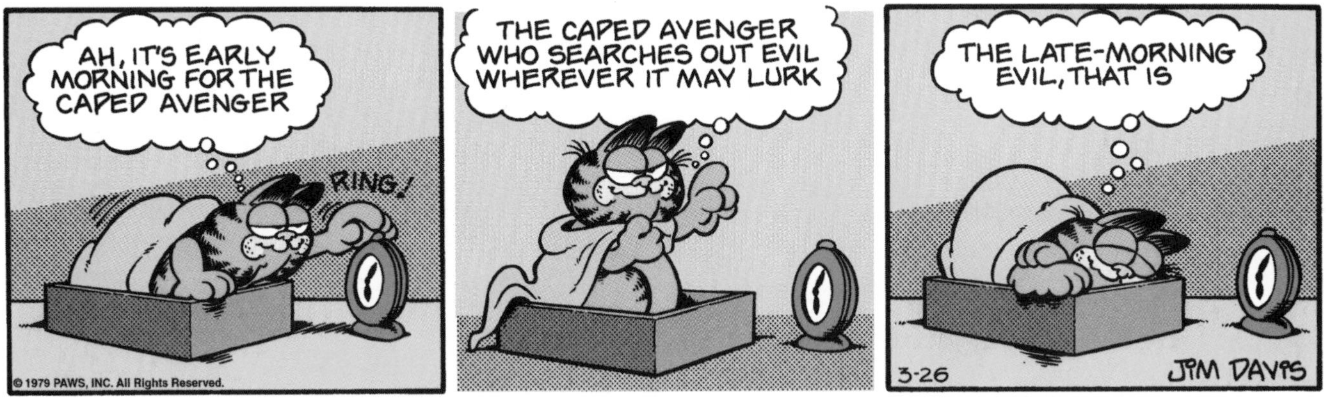
AH, IT'S EARLY MORNING FOR THE CAPED AVENGER
RING!
THE CAPED AVENGER WHO SEARCHES OUT EVIL WHEREVER IT MAY LURK
THE LATE-MORNING EVIL, THAT IS
© 1979 PAWS, INC. All Rights Reserved.
3-26
JIM DAVIS

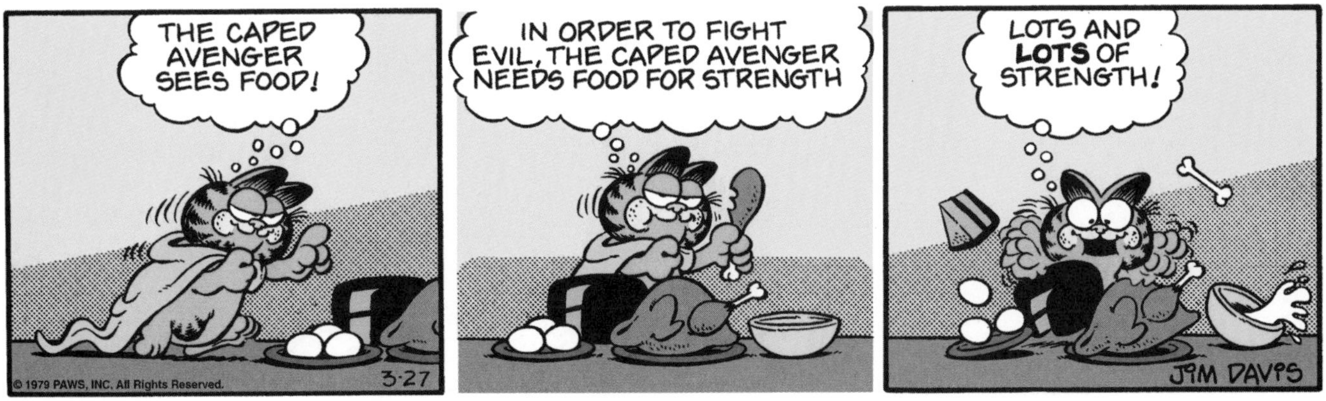
THE CAPED AVENGER SEES FOOD!
IN ORDER TO FIGHT EVIL, THE CAPED AVENGER NEEDS FOOD FOR STRENGTH
LOTS AND **LOTS** OF STRENGTH!
© 1979 PAWS, INC. All Rights Reserved.
3-27
JIM DAVIS

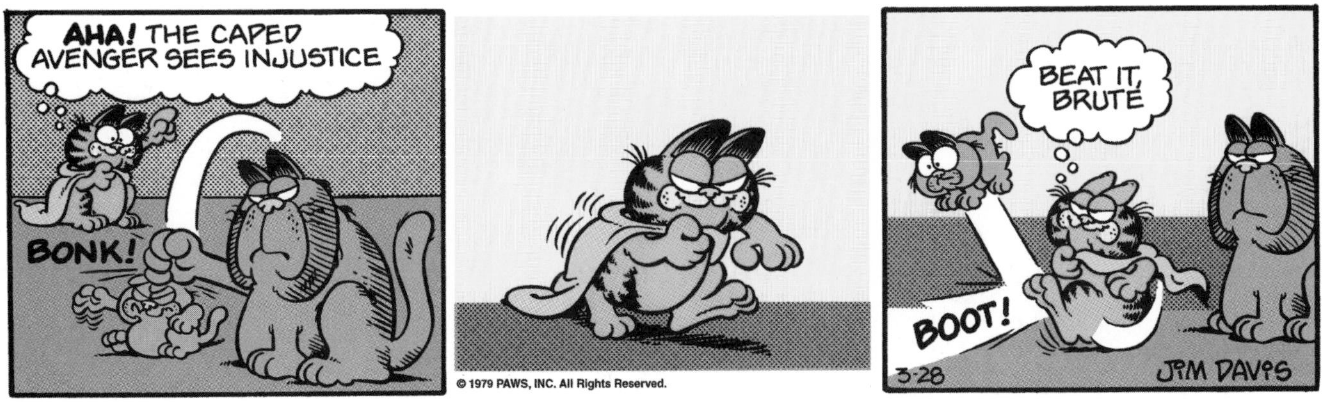
AHA! THE CAPED AVENGER SEES INJUSTICE
BONK!
BEAT IT, BRUTE
BOOT!
© 1979 PAWS, INC. All Rights Reserved.
3-28
JIM DAVIS

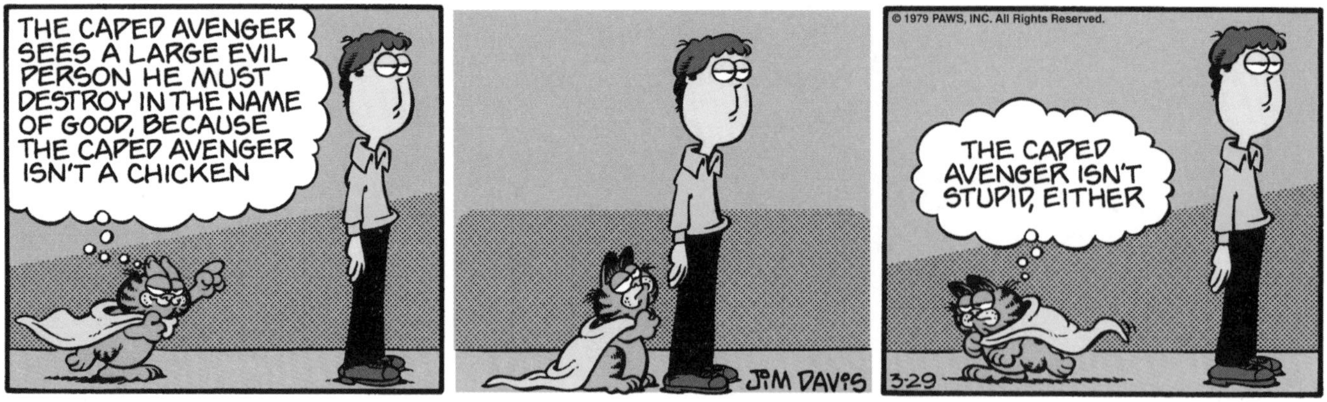
THE CAPED AVENGER SEES A LARGE EVIL PERSON HE MUST DESTROY IN THE NAME OF GOOD, BECAUSE THE CAPED AVENGER ISN'T A CHICKEN
JIM DAVIS
© 1979 PAWS, INC. All Rights Reserved.
THE CAPED AVENGER ISN'T STUPID, EITHER
3-29

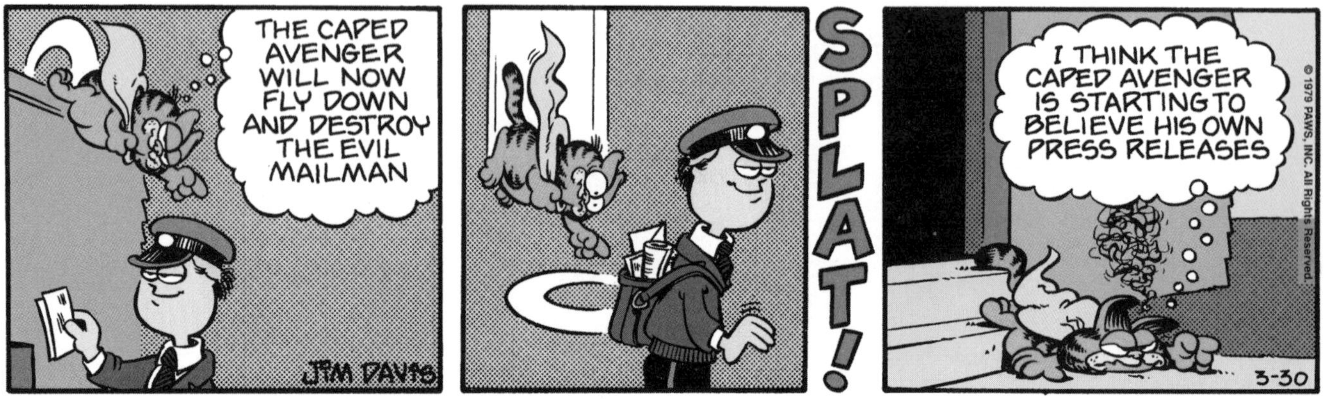
THE CAPED AVENGER WILL NOW FLY DOWN AND DESTROY THE EVIL MAILMAN
JIM DAVIS
SPLAT!
I THINK THE CAPED AVENGER IS STARTING TO BELIEVE HIS OWN PRESS RELEASES
© 1979 PAWS, INC. All Rights Reserved.
3-30

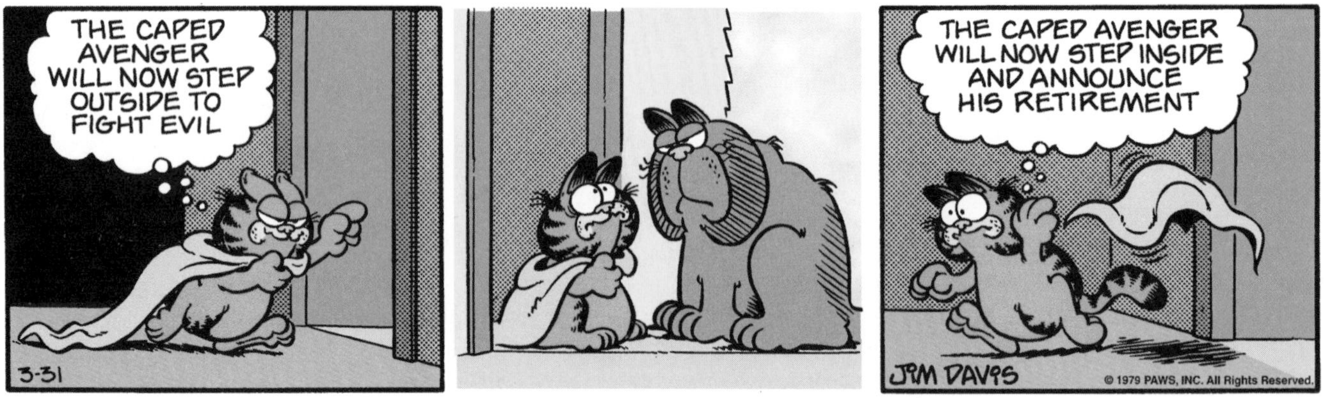
THE CAPED AVENGER WILL NOW STEP OUTSIDE TO FIGHT EVIL
3-31
THE CAPED AVENGER WILL NOW STEP INSIDE AND ANNOUNCE HIS RETIREMENT
JIM DAVIS
© 1979 PAWS, INC. All Rights Reserved.

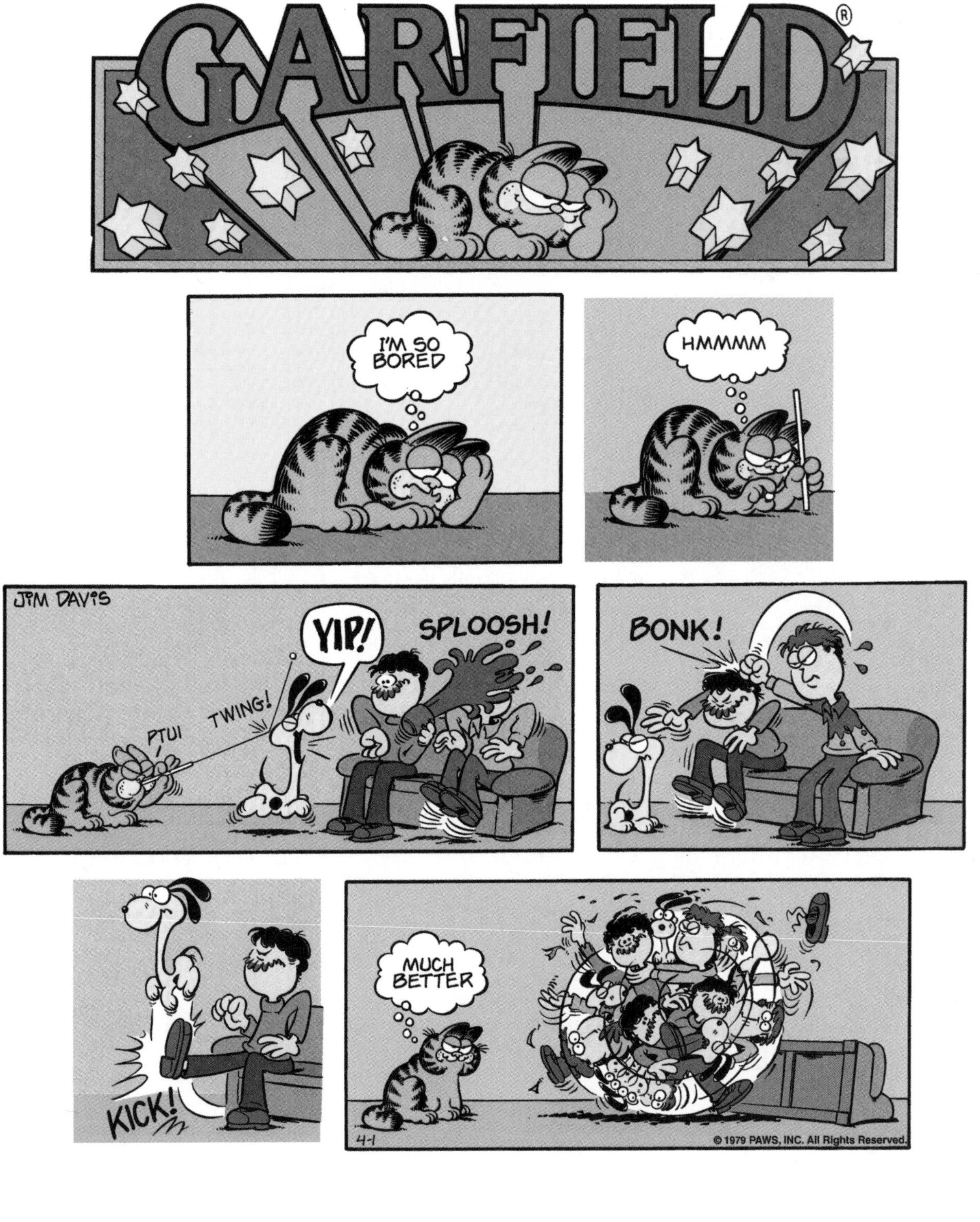
GARFIELD®
I'M SO BORED
HMMMM
JIM DAVIS
PTUI
TWING!
YIP!
SPLOOSH!
BONK!
KICK!
MUCH BETTER
4-1
© 1979 PAWS, INC. All Rights Reserved.

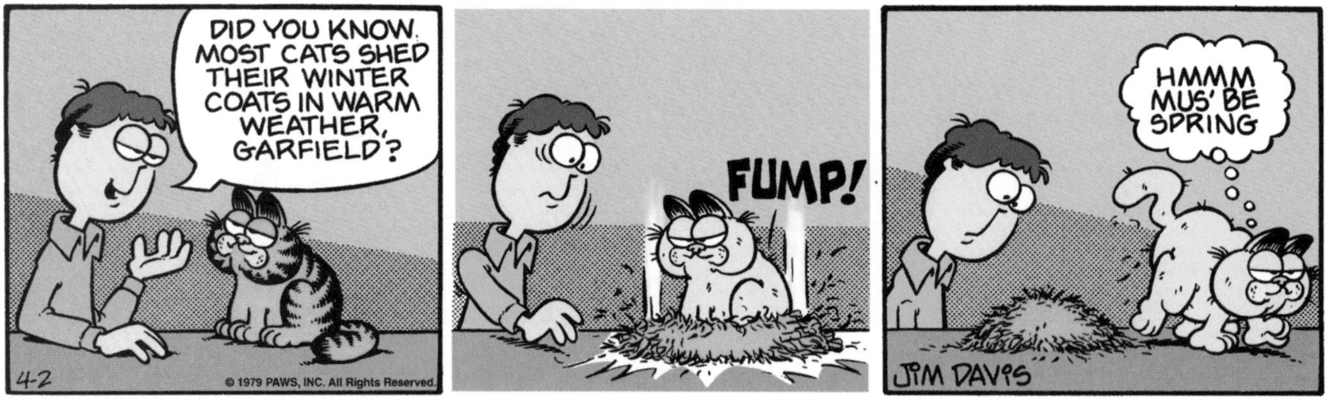
DID YOU KNOW MOST CATS SHED THEIR WINTER COATS IN WARM WEATHER, GARFIELD?
4-2
© 1979 PAWS, INC. All Rights Reserved.
FUMP!
HMMM MUS' BE SPRING
JIM DAVIS

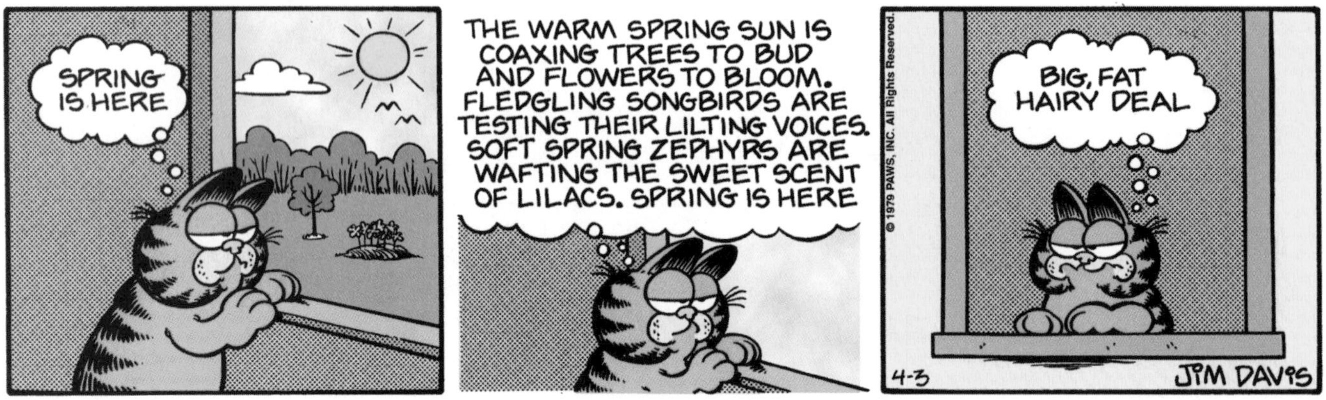
SPRING IS HERE
THE WARM SPRING SUN IS COAXING TREES TO BUD AND FLOWERS TO BLOOM. FLEDGLING SONGBIRDS ARE TESTING THEIR LILTING VOICES. SOFT SPRING ZEPHYRS ARE WAFTING THE SWEET SCENT OF LILACS. SPRING IS HERE
© 1979 PAWS, INC. All Rights Reserved.
BIG, FAT HAIRY DEAL
4-3
JIM DAVIS

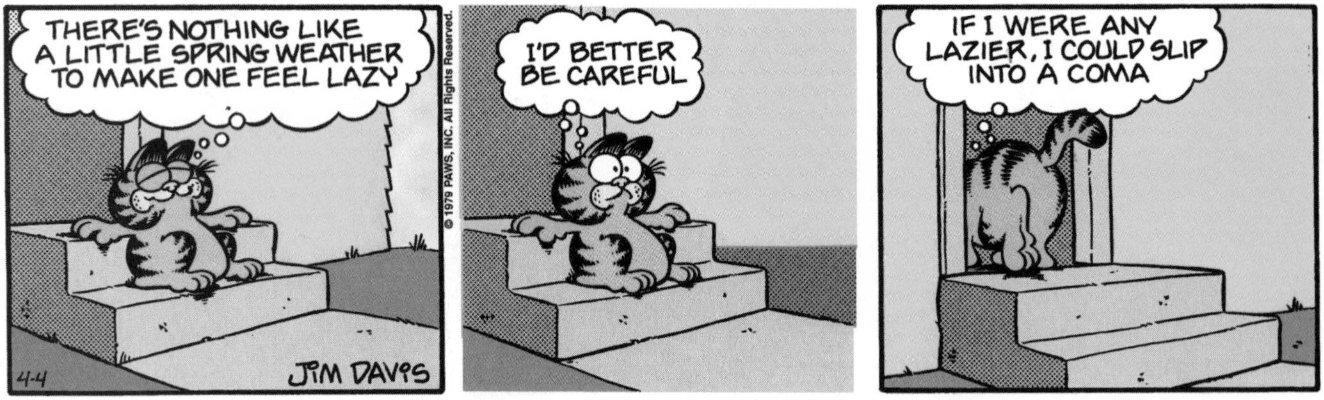
THERE'S NOTHING LIKE A LITTLE SPRING WEATHER TO MAKE ONE FEEL LAZY
4-4
JIM DAVIS
© 1979 PAWS, INC. All Rights Reserved.
I'D BETTER BE CAREFUL
IF I WERE ANY LAZIER, I COULD SLIP INTO A COMA

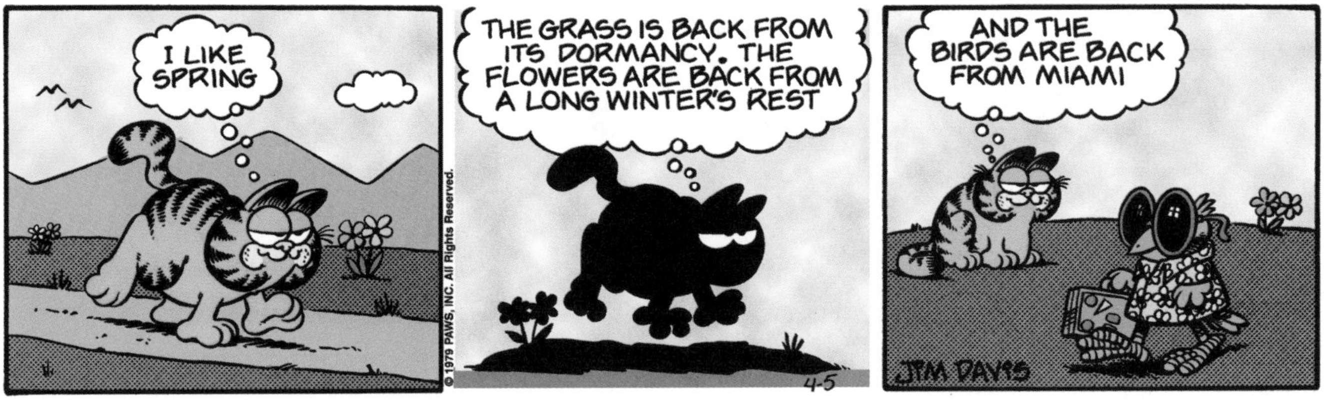
I LIKE SPRING
THE GRASS IS BACK FROM ITS DORMANCY. THE FLOWERS ARE BACK FROM A LONG WINTER'S REST
AND THE BIRDS ARE BACK FROM MIAMI
© 1979 PAWS, INC. All Rights Reserved.
4-5
JIM DAVIS

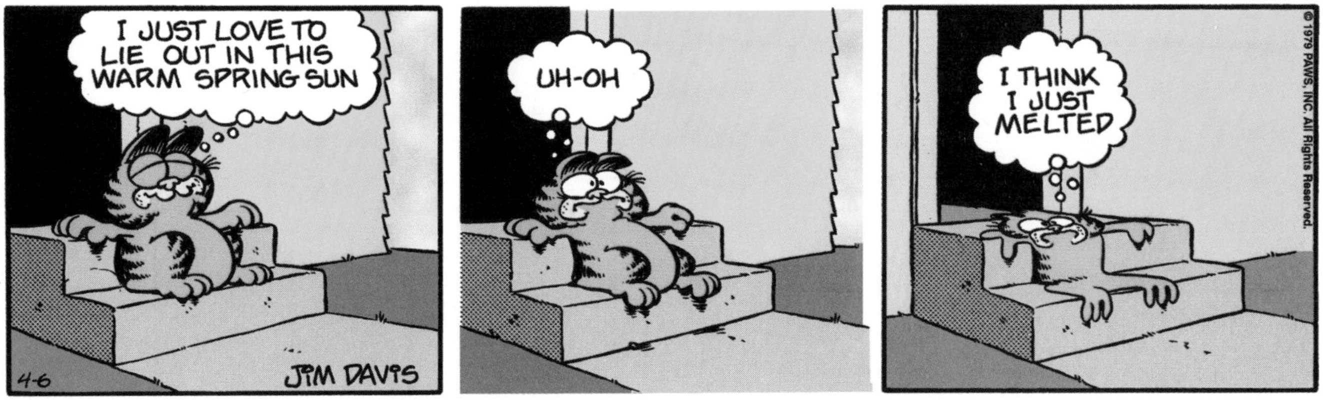
I JUST LOVE TO LIE OUT IN THIS WARM SPRING SUN
4-6
JIM DAVIS
UH-OH
I THINK I JUST MELTED
© 1979 PAWS, INC. All Rights Reserved.

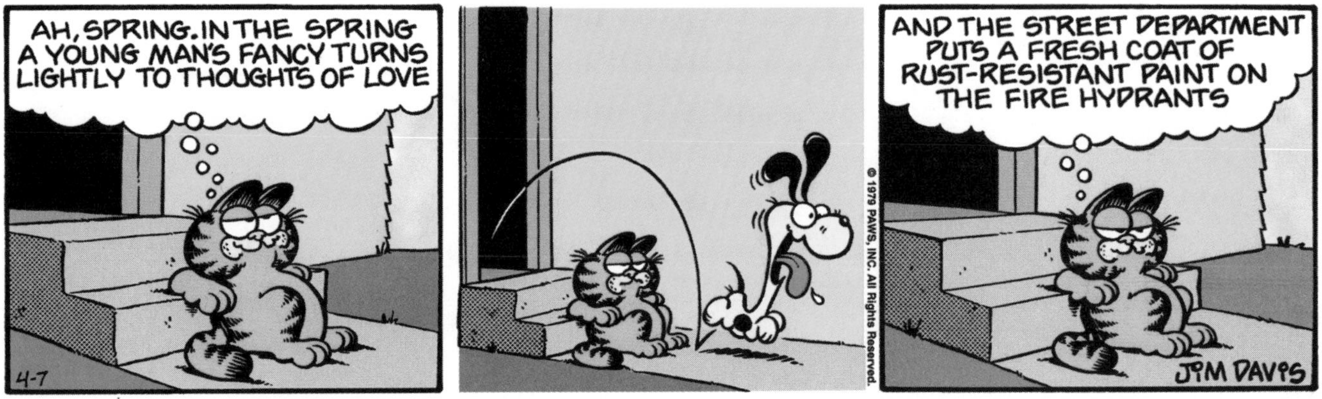
AH, SPRING. IN THE SPRING A YOUNG MAN'S FANCY TURNS LIGHTLY TO THOUGHTS OF LOVE
4-7
© 1979 PAWS, INC. All Rights Reserved.
AND THE STREET DEPARTMENT PUTS A FRESH COAT OF RUST-RESISTANT PAINT ON THE FIRE HYDRANTS
JIM DAVIS

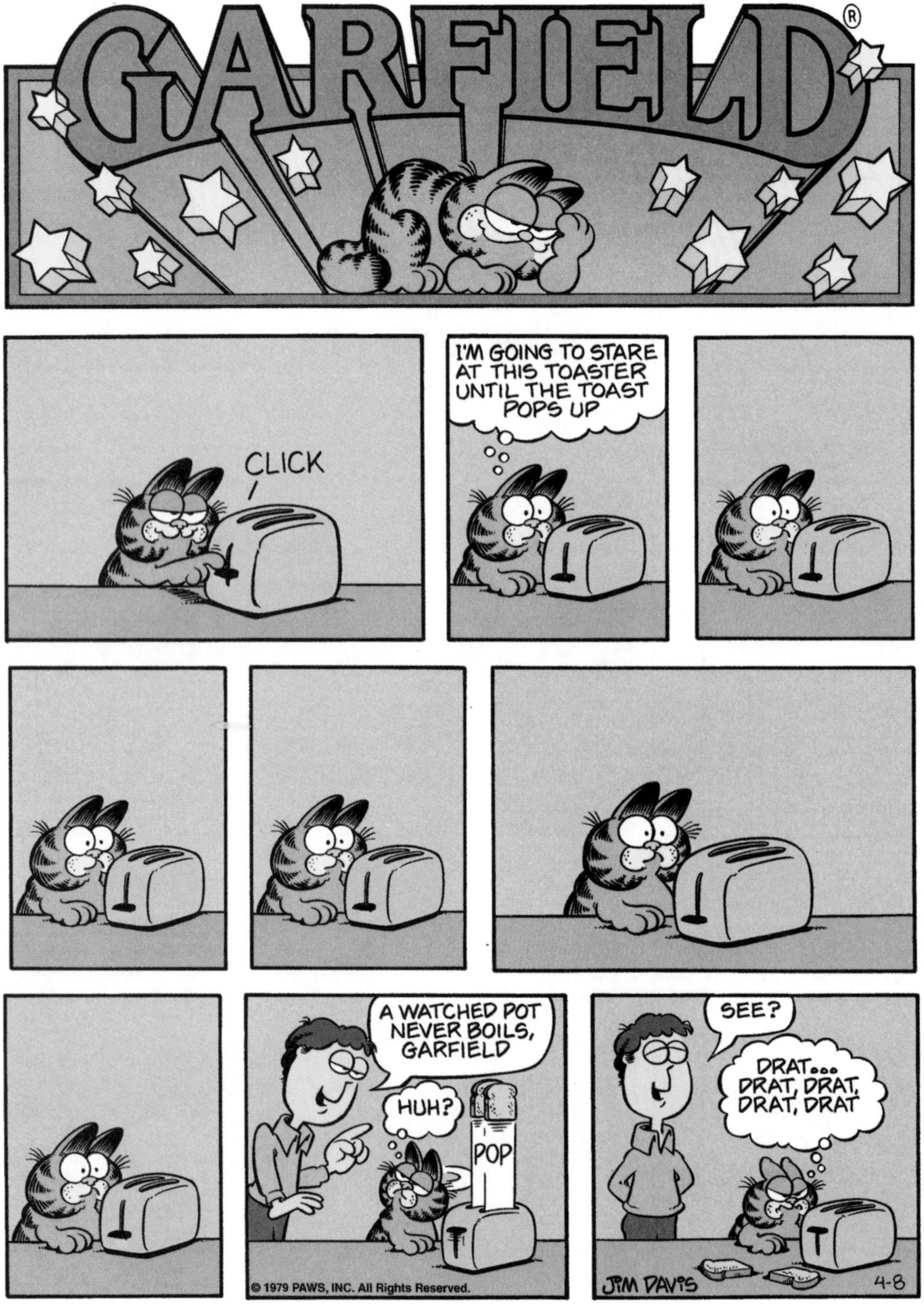
GARFIELD®
CLICK
I'M GOING TO STARE AT THIS TOASTER UNTIL THE TOAST POPS UP
A WATCHED POT NEVER BOILS, GARFIELD
HUH?
POP
SEE?
DRAT... DRAT, DRAT, DRAT, DRAT
© 1979 PAWS, INC. All Rights Reserved.
JIM DAVIS
4-8

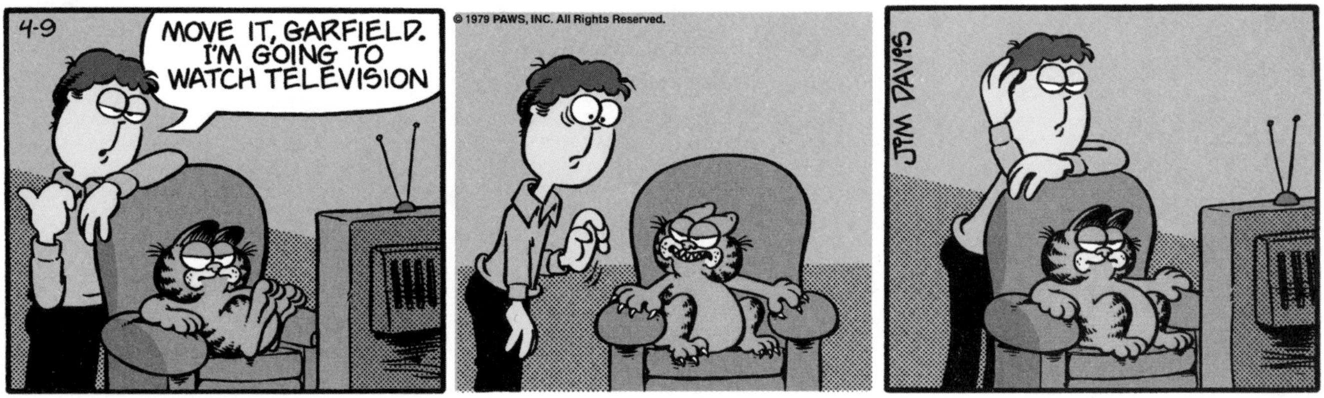
4-9
MOVE IT, GARFIELD. I'M GOING TO WATCH TELEVISION
© 1979 PAWS, INC. All Rights Reserved.
JIM DAVIS

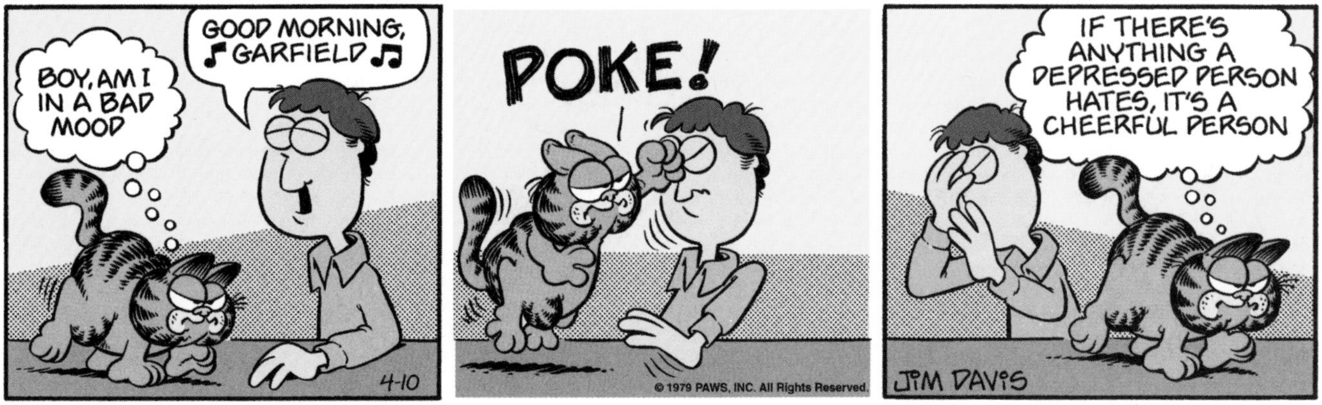
BOY, AM I IN A BAD MOOD
GOOD MORNING, ♪ GARFIELD ♫
4-10
POKE!
© 1979 PAWS, INC. All Rights Reserved.
IF THERE'S ANYTHING A DEPRESSED PERSON HATES, IT'S A CHEERFUL PERSON
JIM DAVIS

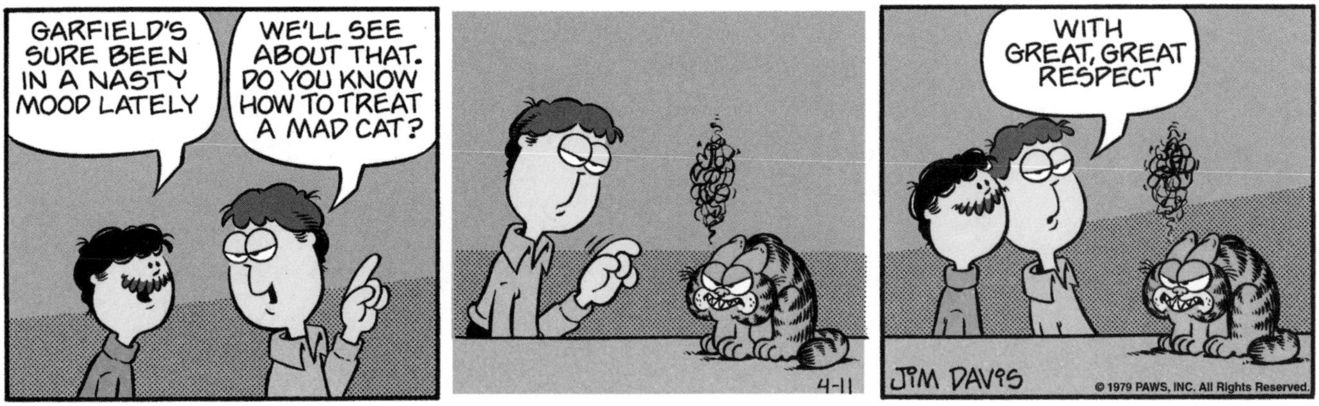
GARFIELD'S SURE BEEN IN A NASTY MOOD LATELY
WE'LL SEE ABOUT THAT. DO YOU KNOW HOW TO TREAT A MAD CAT?
4-11
WITH GREAT, GREAT RESPECT
JIM DAVIS
© 1979 PAWS, INC. All Rights Reserved.

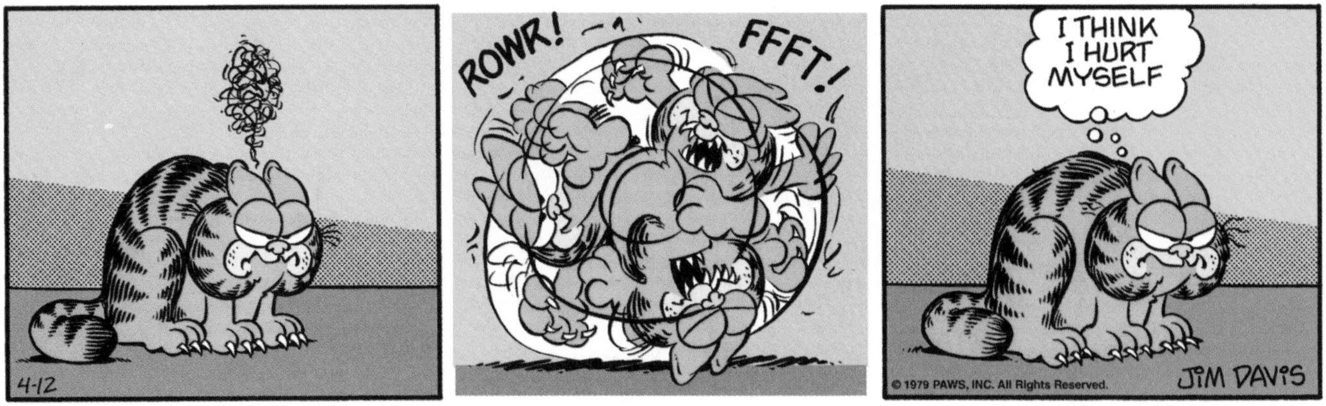
4-12
ROWR!
FFFT!
I THINK I HURT MYSELF
© 1979 PAWS, INC. All Rights Reserved.
JIM DAVIS

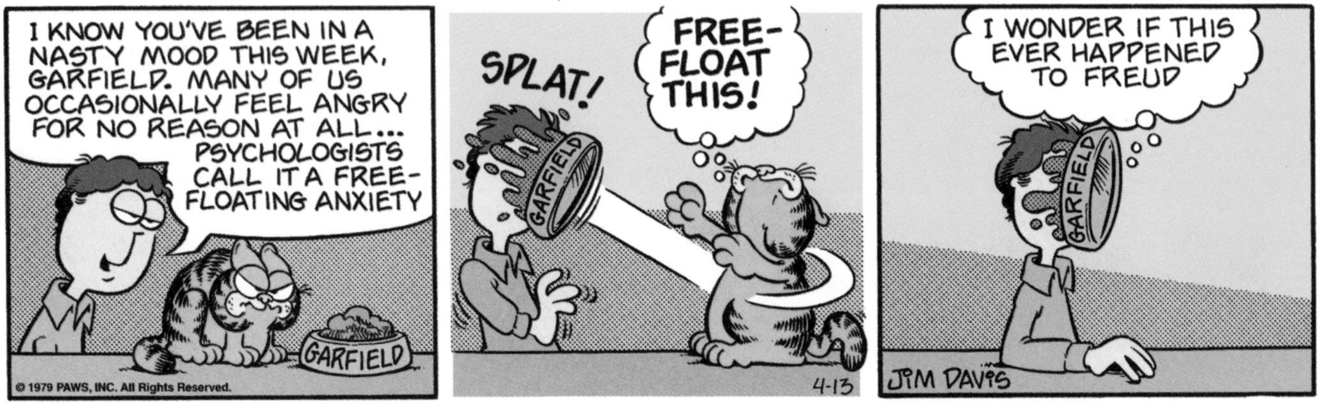
I KNOW YOU'VE BEEN IN A NASTY MOOD THIS WEEK, GARFIELD. MANY OF US OCCASIONALLY FEEL ANGRY FOR NO REASON AT ALL... PSYCHOLOGISTS CALL IT A FREE-FLOATING ANXIETY
GARFIELD
© 1979 PAWS, INC. All Rights Reserved.
SPLAT!
FREE-FLOAT THIS!
GARFIELD
4-13
I WONDER IF THIS EVER HAPPENED TO FREUD
GARFIELD
JIM DAVIS

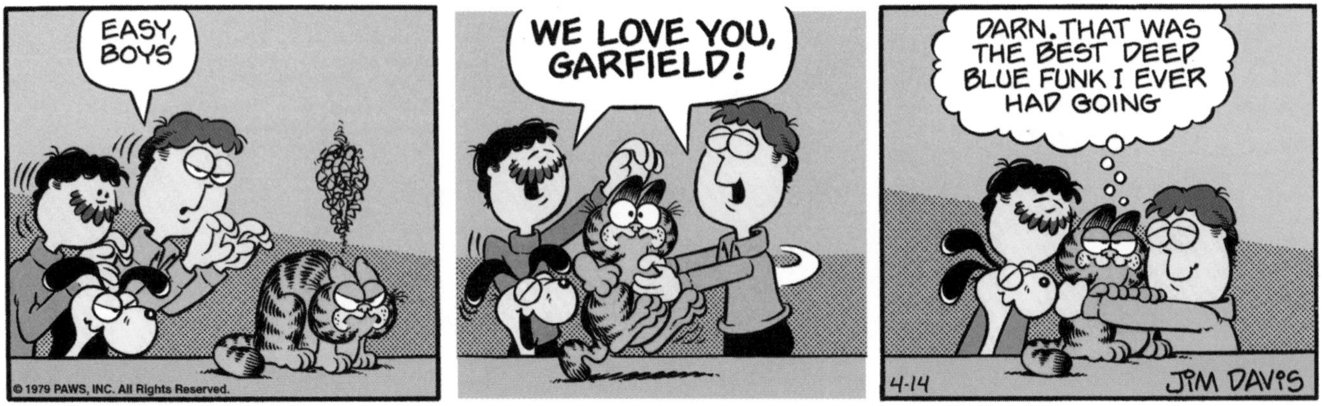
EASY, BOYS
© 1979 PAWS, INC. All Rights Reserved.
WE LOVE YOU, GARFIELD!
DARN. THAT WAS THE BEST DEEP BLUE FUNK I EVER HAD GOING
4-14
JIM DAVIS

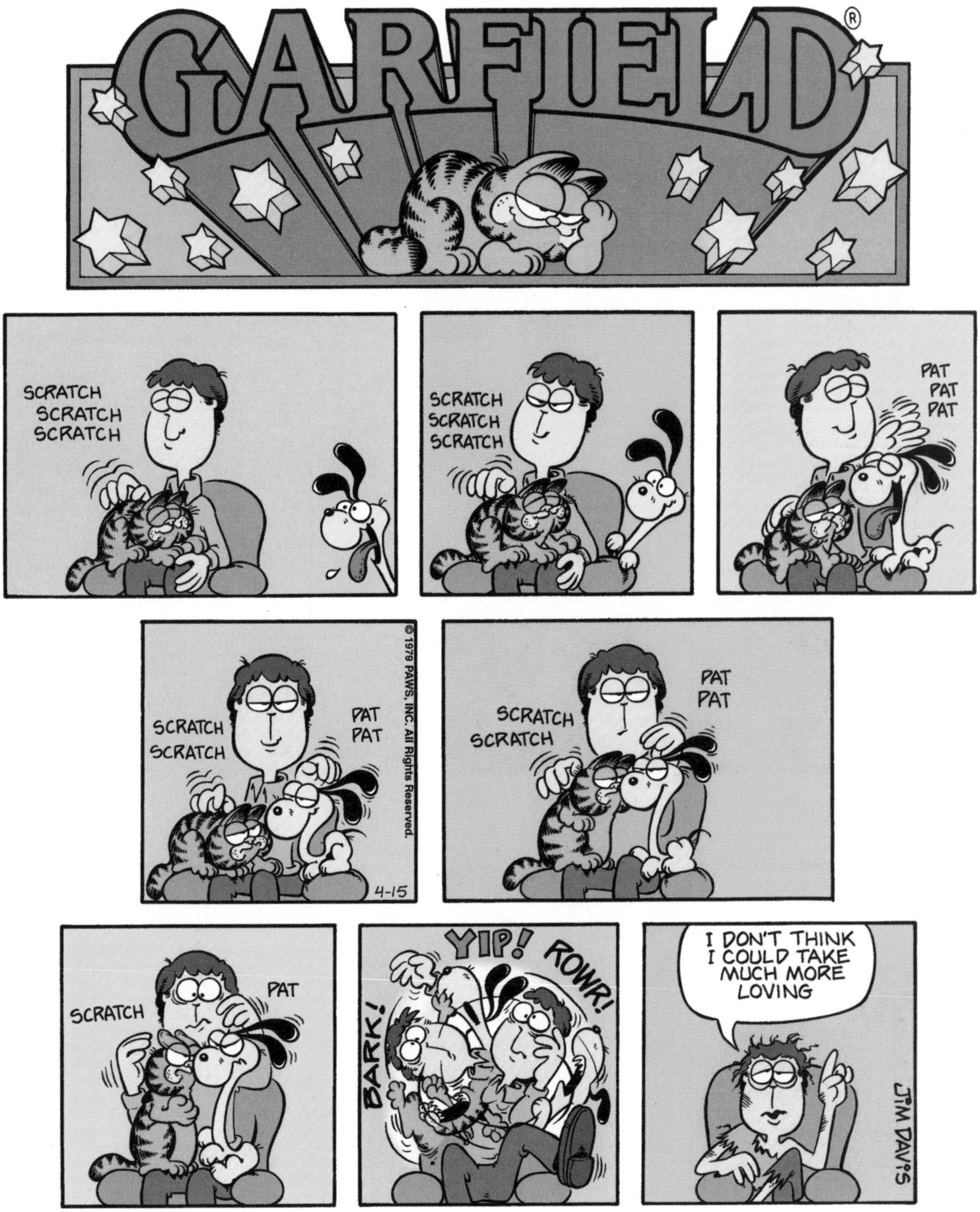
GARFIELD®
SCRATCH SCRATCH SCRATCH
SCRATCH SCRATCH SCRATCH
PAT PAT PAT
SCRATCH SCRATCH
PAT PAT
© 1979 PAWS, INC. All Rights Reserved.
4-15
SCRATCH SCRATCH
PAT PAT
SCRATCH
PAT
YIP! ROWR!
BARK!
I DON'T THINK I COULD TAKE MUCH MORE LOVING
JIM DAVIS

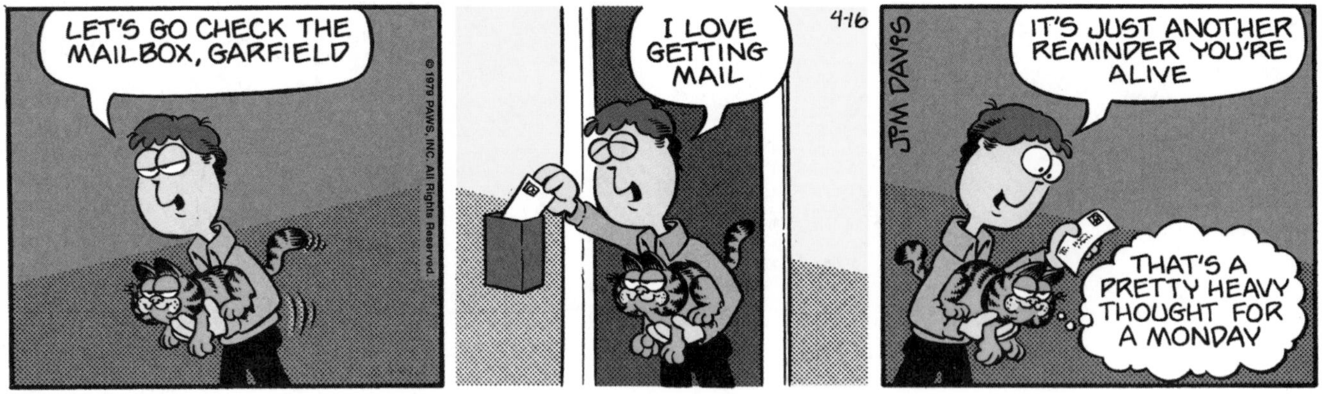
LET'S GO CHECK THE MAILBOX, GARFIELD
© 1979 PAWS, INC. All Rights Reserved.
I LOVE GETTING MAIL
4-16
JIM DAVIS
IT'S JUST ANOTHER REMINDER YOU'RE ALIVE
THAT'S A PRETTY HEAVY THOUGHT FOR A MONDAY

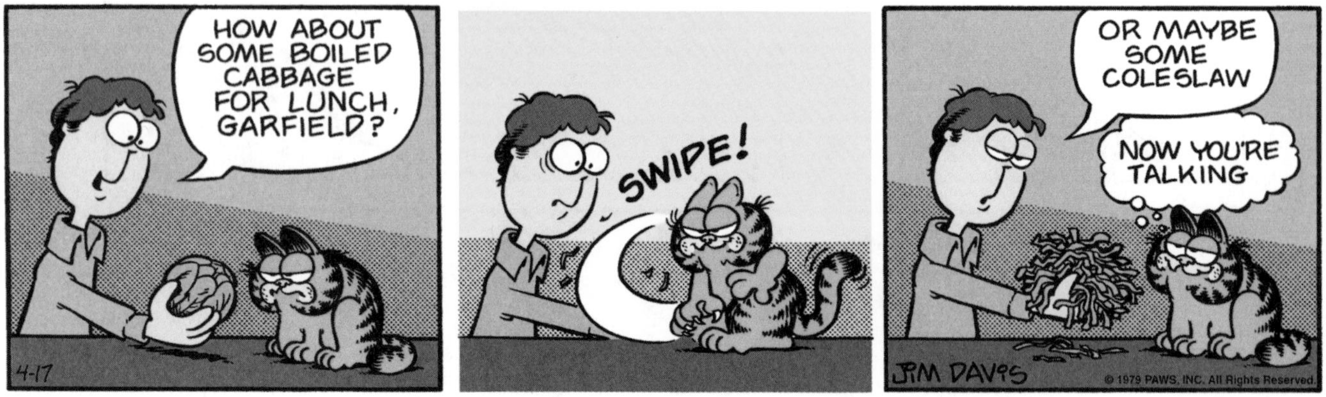
HOW ABOUT SOME BOILED CABBAGE FOR LUNCH, GARFIELD?
4-17
SWIPE!
OR MAYBE SOME COLESLAW
NOW YOU'RE TALKING
JIM DAVIS
© 1979 PAWS, INC. All Rights Reserved.

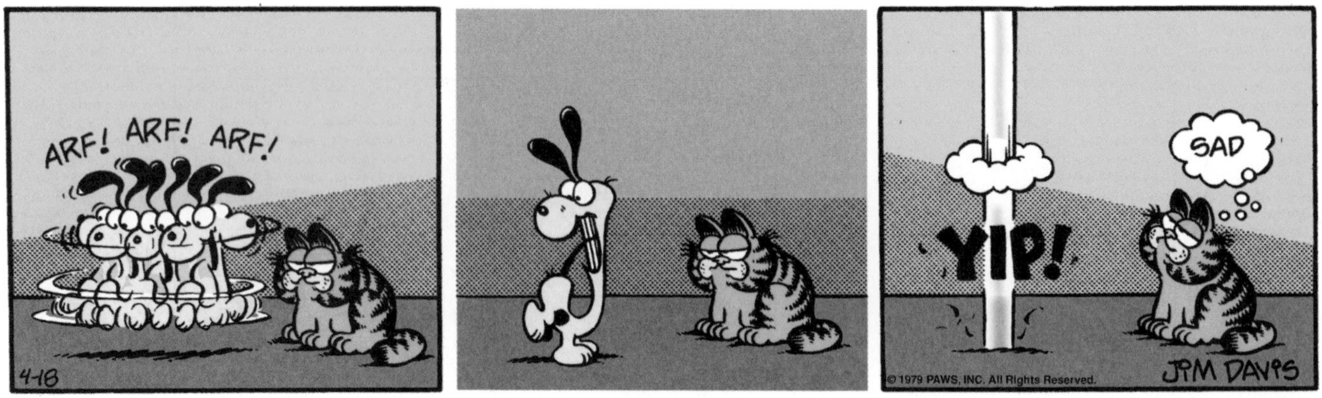
ARF! ARF! ARF!
4-18
YIP!
SAD
© 1979 PAWS, INC. All Rights Reserved.
JIM DAVIS

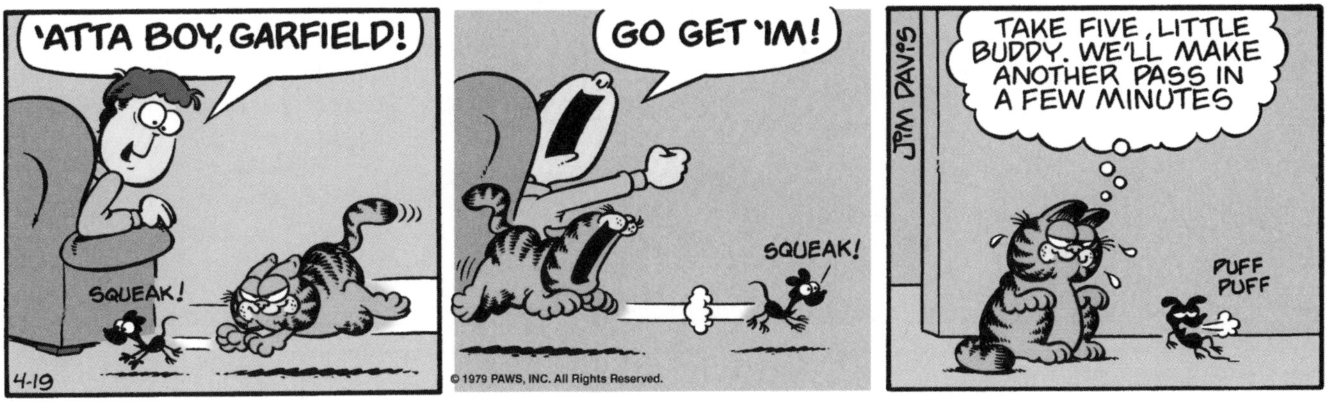
'ATTA BOY, GARFIELD!
SQUEAK!
4-19
GO GET 'IM!
SQUEAK!
© 1979 PAWS, INC. All Rights Reserved.
JIM DAVIS
TAKE FIVE, LITTLE BUDDY. WE'LL MAKE ANOTHER PASS IN A FEW MINUTES
PUFF PUFF

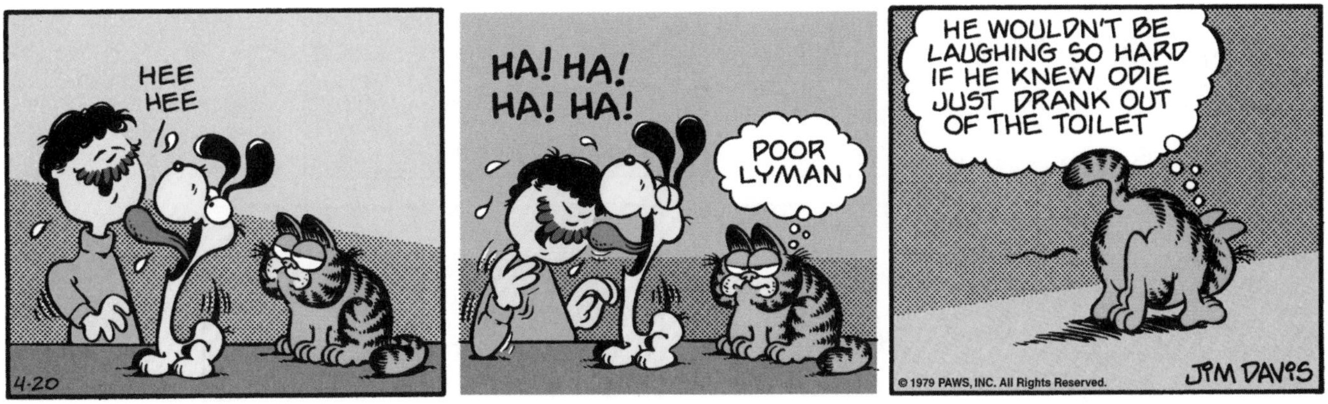
HEE HEE
4-20
HA! HA! HA! HA!
POOR LYMAN
HE WOULDN'T BE LAUGHING SO HARD IF HE KNEW ODIE JUST DRANK OUT OF THE TOILET
© 1979 PAWS, INC. All Rights Reserved.
JIM DAVIS

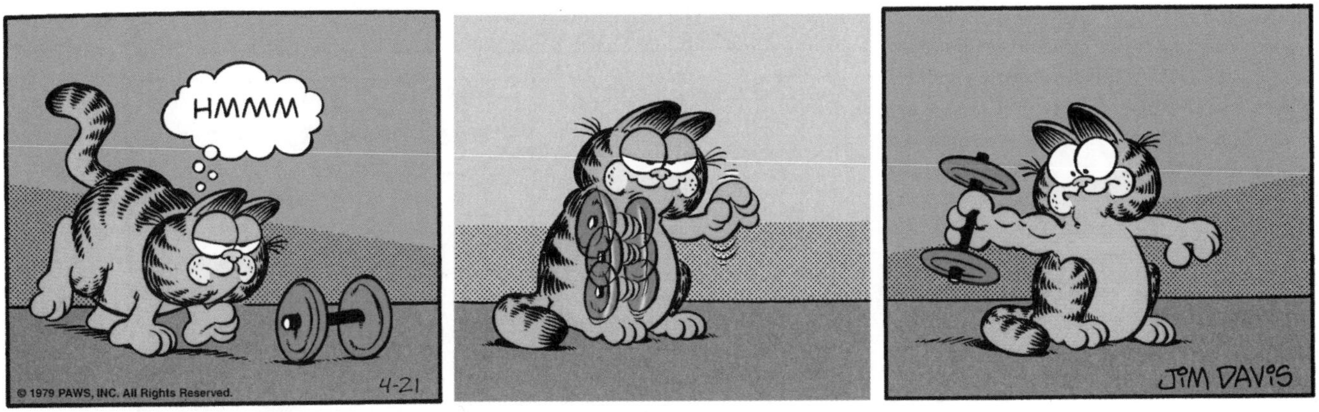
HMMM
© 1979 PAWS, INC. All Rights Reserved.
4-21
JIM DAVIS

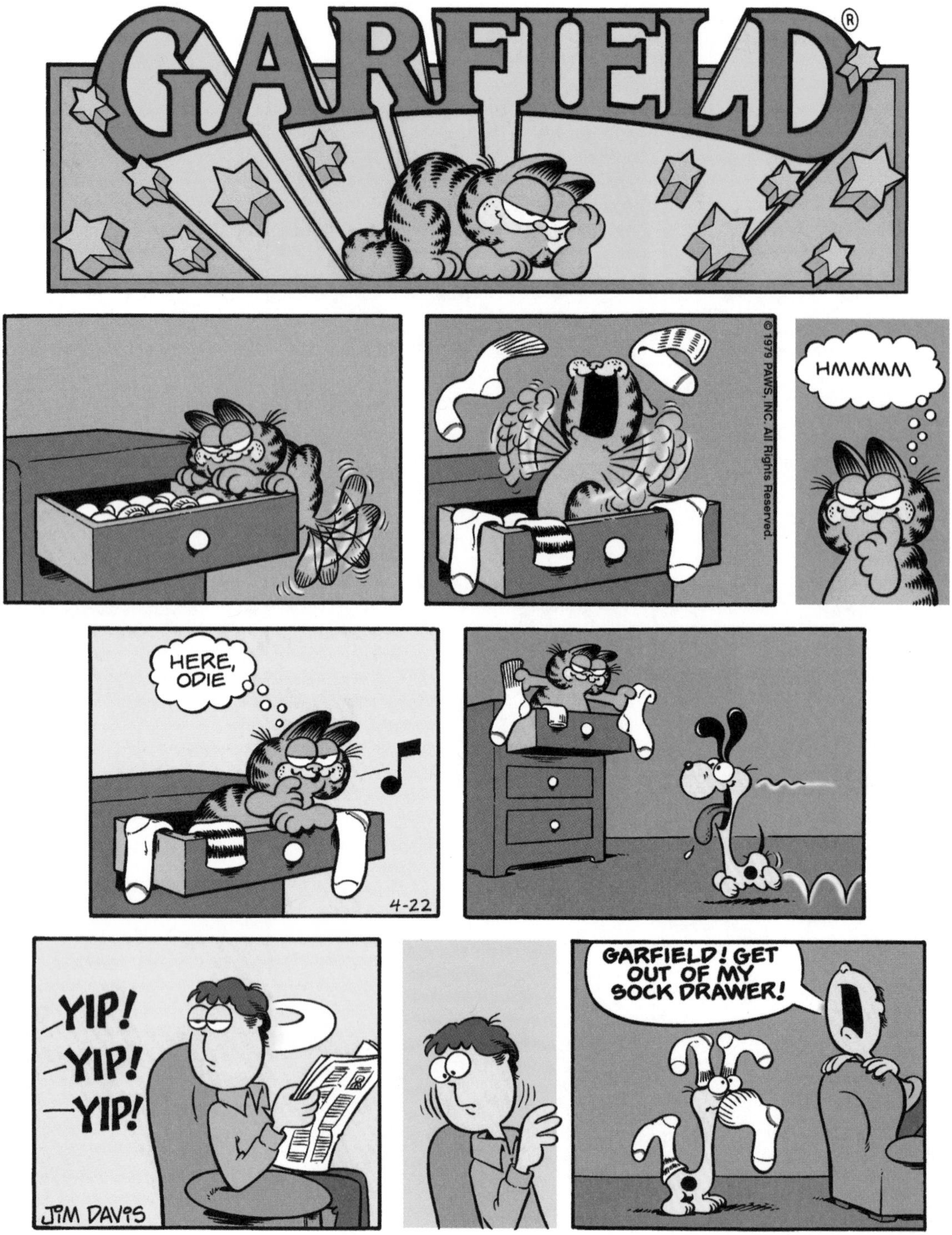
GARFIELD®
© 1979 PAWS, INC. All Rights Reserved.
HMMMM
HERE, ODIE
4-22
YIP!
YIP!
YIP!
JIM DAVIS
GARFIELD! GET OUT OF MY SOCK DRAWER!

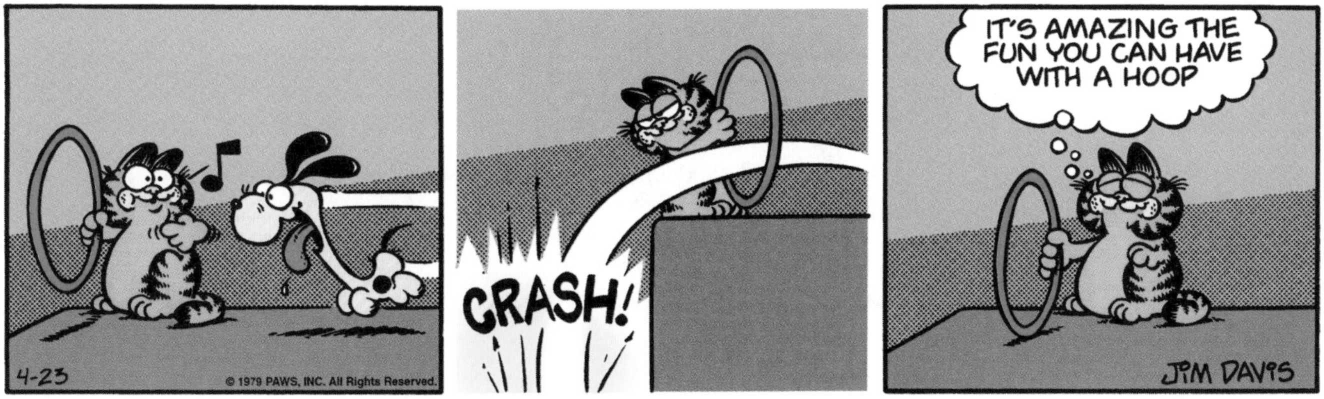
4-23
© 1979 PAWS, INC. All Rights Reserved.
CRASH!
IT'S AMAZING THE FUN YOU CAN HAVE WITH A HOOP
JIM DAVIS

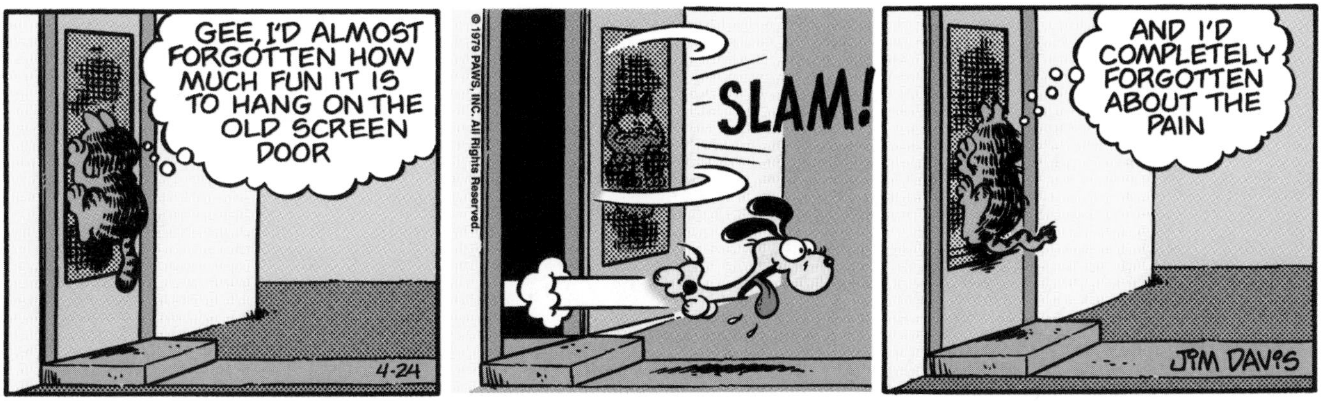
GEE, I'D ALMOST FORGOTTEN HOW MUCH FUN IT IS TO HANG ON THE OLD SCREEN DOOR
4-24
© 1979 PAWS, INC. All Rights Reserved.
SLAM!
AND I'D COMPLETELY FORGOTTEN ABOUT THE PAIN
JIM DAVIS

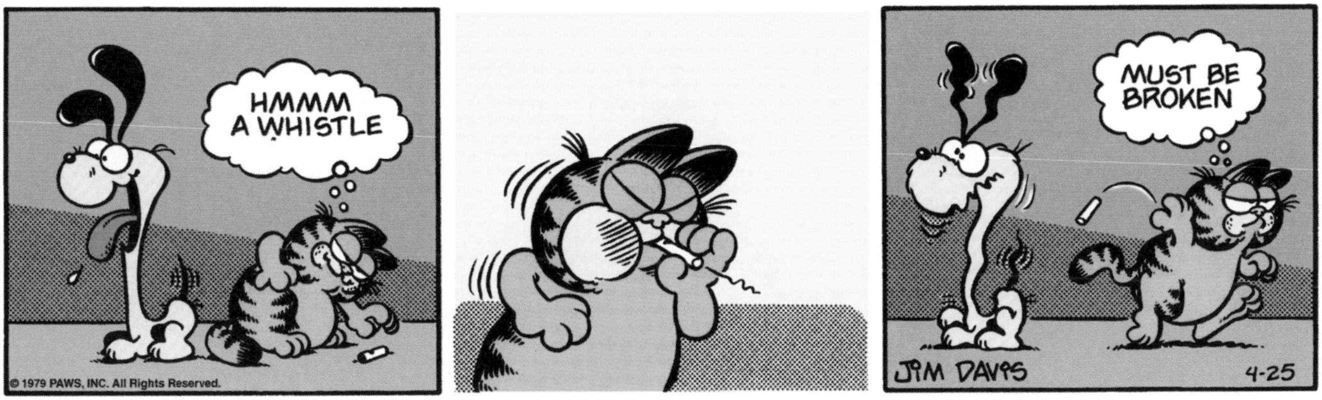
HMMM A WHISTLE
© 1979 PAWS, INC. All Rights Reserved.
MUST BE BROKEN
JIM DAVIS
4-25

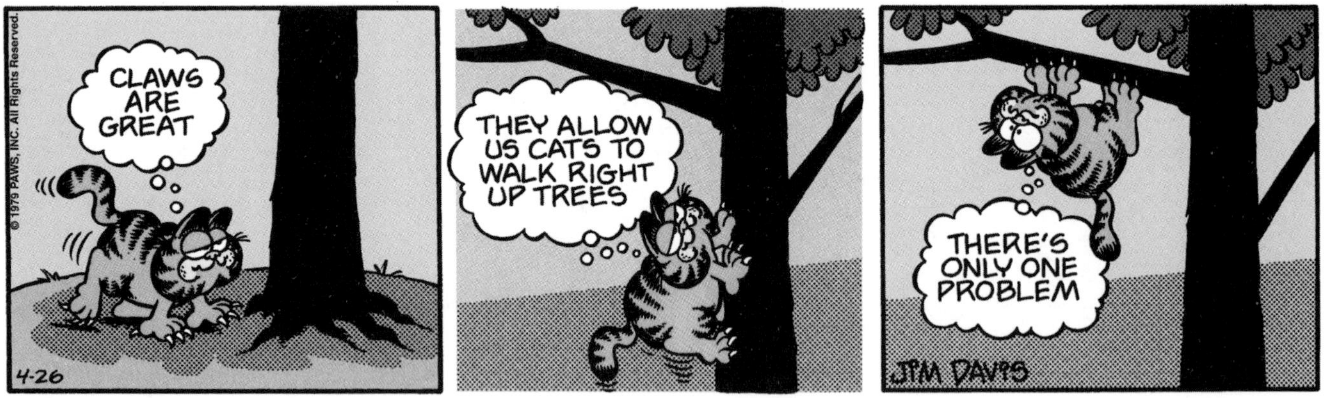
© 1979 PAWS, INC. All Rights Reserved.
CLAWS ARE GREAT
4-26
THEY ALLOW US CATS TO WALK RIGHT UP TREES
THERE'S ONLY ONE PROBLEM
JIM DAVIS

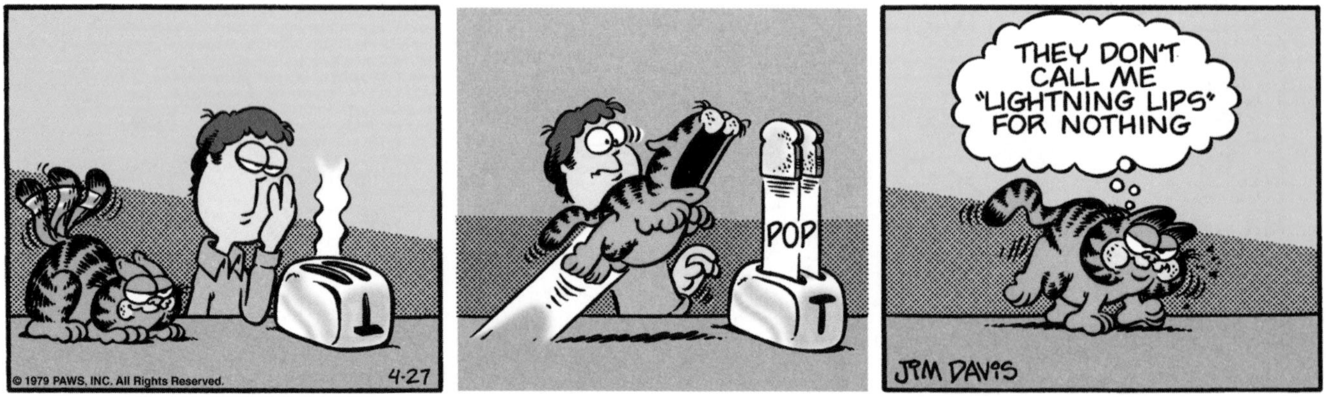
© 1979 PAWS, INC. All Rights Reserved.
4-27
POP
THEY DON'T CALL ME "LIGHTNING LIPS" FOR NOTHING
JIM DAVIS

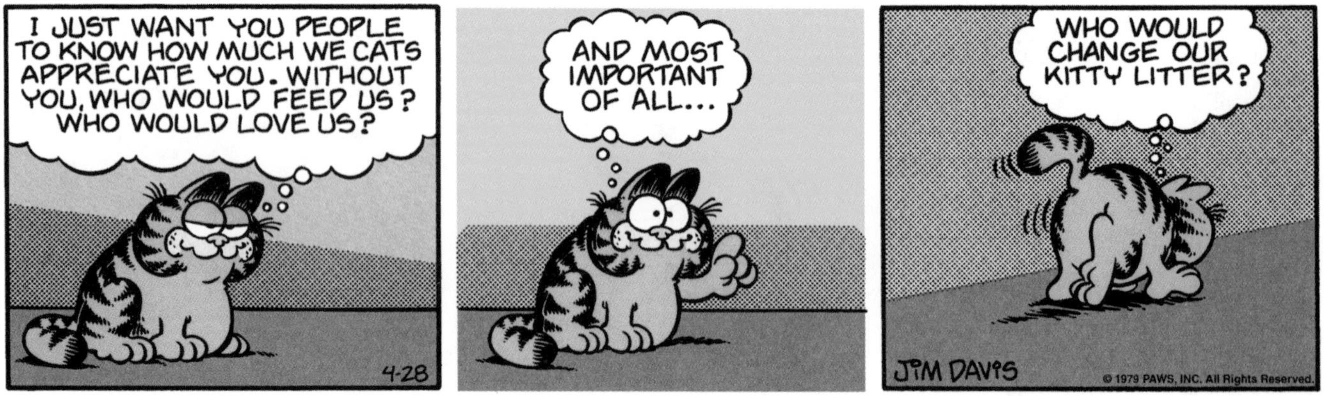
I JUST WANT YOU PEOPLE TO KNOW HOW MUCH WE CATS APPRECIATE YOU. WITHOUT YOU, WHO WOULD FEED US? WHO WOULD LOVE US?
4-28
AND MOST IMPORTANT OF ALL...
WHO WOULD CHANGE OUR KITTY LITTER?
JIM DAVIS
© 1979 PAWS, INC. All Rights Reserved.

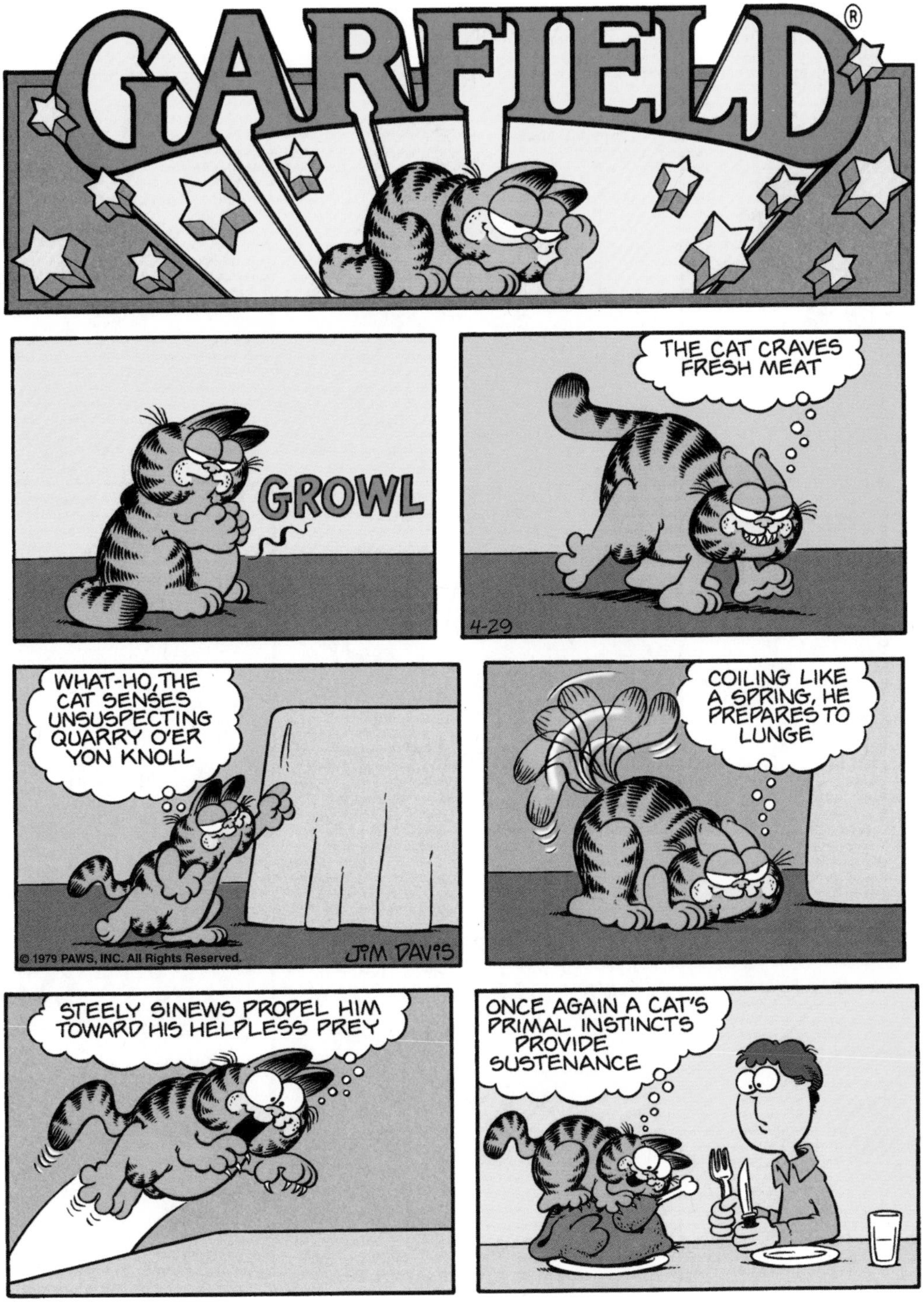
GARFIELD®
GROWL
THE CAT CRAVES FRESH MEAT
4-29
WHAT-HO, THE CAT SENSES UNSUSPECTING QUARRY O'ER YON KNOLL
© 1979 PAWS, INC. All Rights Reserved.
JIM DAVIS
COILING LIKE A SPRING, HE PREPARES TO LUNGE
STEELY SINEWS PROPEL HIM TOWARD HIS HELPLESS PREY
ONCE AGAIN A CAT'S PRIMAL INSTINCTS PROVIDE SUSTENANCE

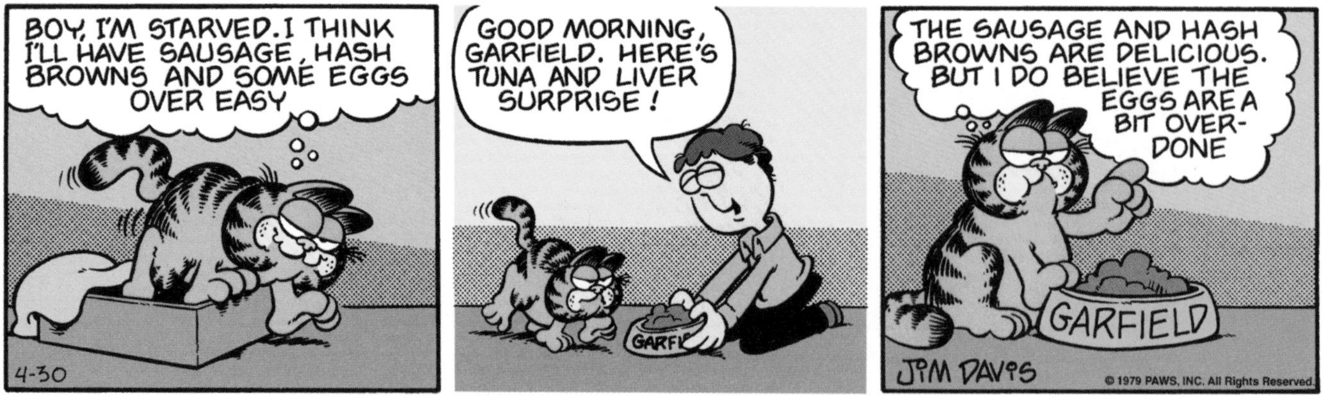
BOY, I'M STARVED. I THINK I'LL HAVE SAUSAGE, HASH BROWNS AND SOME EGGS OVER EASY
4-30
GOOD MORNING, GARFIELD. HERE'S TUNA AND LIVER SURPRISE!
THE SAUSAGE AND HASH BROWNS ARE DELICIOUS. BUT I DO BELIEVE THE EGGS ARE A BIT OVER-DONE
GARFIELD
JIM DAVIS
© 1979 PAWS, INC. All Rights Reserved.

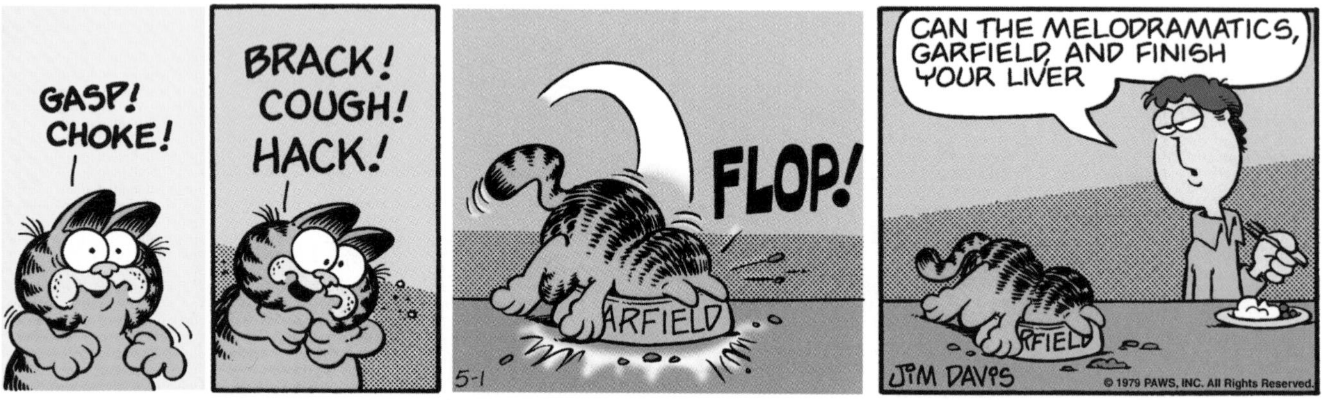
GASP! CHOKE!
BRACK! COUGH! HACK!
FLOP!
5-1
CAN THE MELODRAMATICS, GARFIELD, AND FINISH YOUR LIVER
JIM DAVIS
© 1979 PAWS, INC. All Rights Reserved.

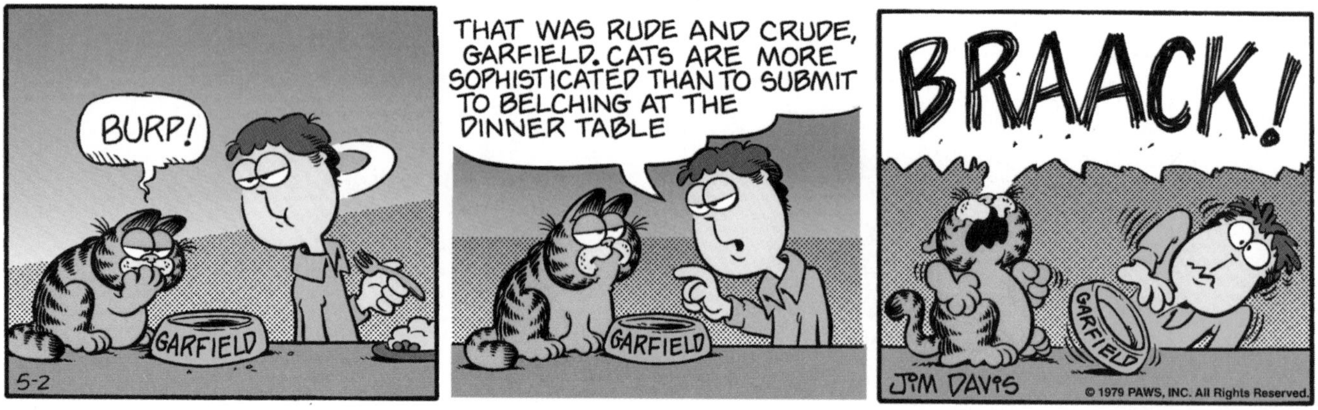
BURP!
GARFIELD
5-2
THAT WAS RUDE AND CRUDE, GARFIELD. CATS ARE MORE SOPHISTICATED THAN TO SUBMIT TO BELCHING AT THE DINNER TABLE
GARFIELD
BRAACK!
GARFIELD
JIM DAVIS
© 1979 PAWS, INC. All Rights Reserved.

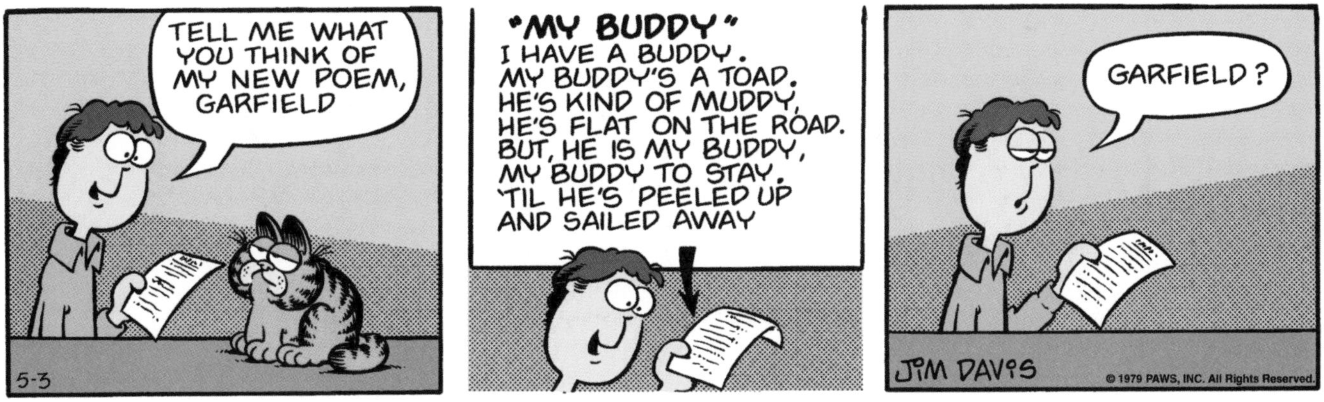
TELL ME WHAT YOU THINK OF MY NEW POEM, GARFIELD
5-3
"MY BUDDY"
I HAVE A BUDDY.
MY BUDDY'S A TOAD.
HE'S KIND OF MUDDY,
HE'S FLAT ON THE ROAD.
BUT, HE IS MY BUDDY,
MY BUDDY TO STAY.
'TIL HE'S PEELED UP
AND SAILED AWAY
GARFIELD ?
JIM DAVIS
© 1979 PAWS, INC. All Rights Reserved.

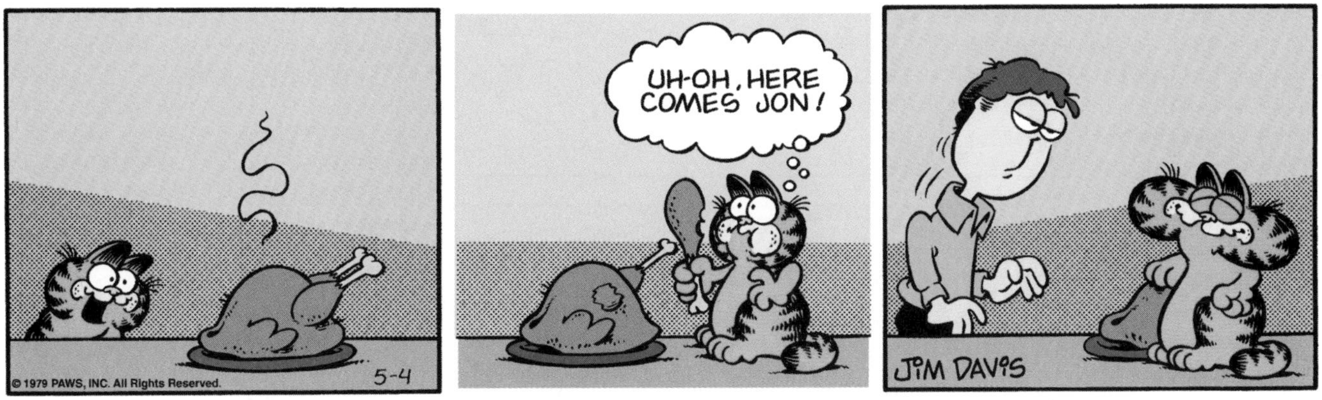
© 1979 PAWS, INC. All Rights Reserved.
5-4
UH-OH, HERE COMES JON!
JIM DAVIS

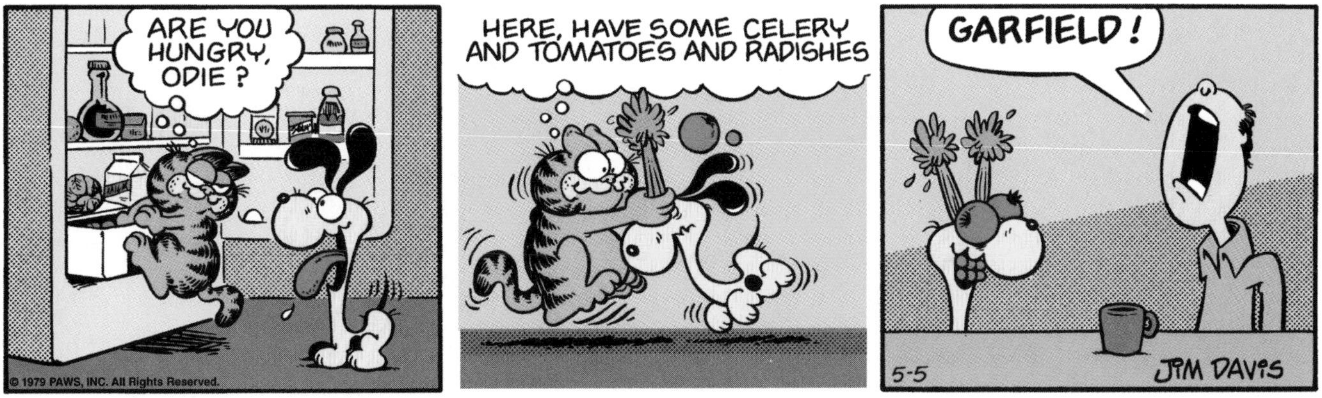
ARE YOU HUNGRY, ODIE ?
© 1979 PAWS, INC. All Rights Reserved.
HERE, HAVE SOME CELERY AND TOMATOES AND RADISHES
GARFIELD!
5-5
JIM DAVIS

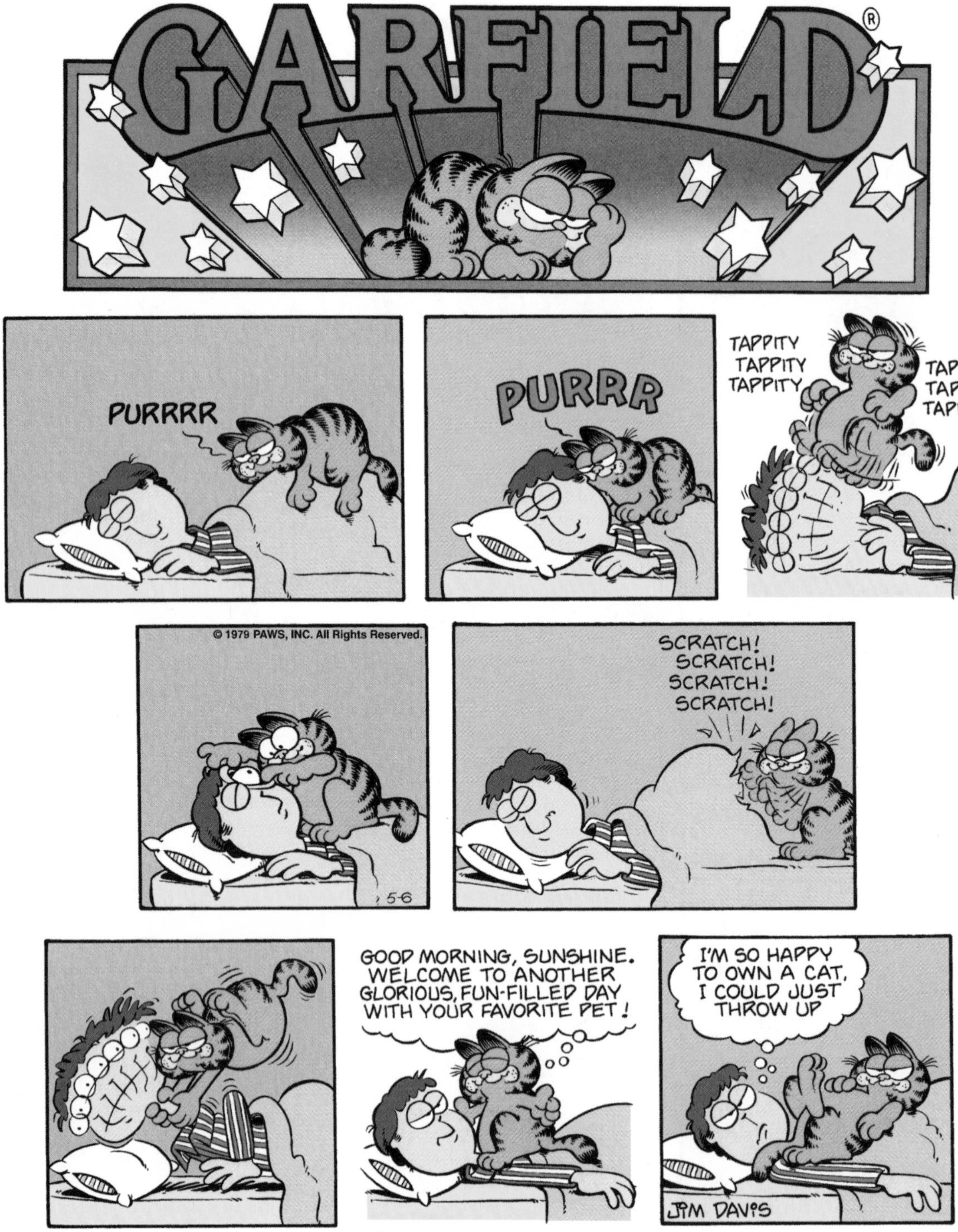
GARFIELD®
PURRRR
PURRR
TAPPITY TAPPITY TAPPITY
TAPPITY TAPPITY TAPPITY
© 1979 PAWS, INC. All Rights Reserved.
5-6
SCRATCH! SCRATCH! SCRATCH! SCRATCH!
GOOD MORNING, SUNSHINE. WELCOME TO ANOTHER GLORIOUS, FUN-FILLED DAY WITH YOUR FAVORITE PET!
I'M SO HAPPY TO OWN A CAT, I COULD JUST THROW UP
JIM DAVIS

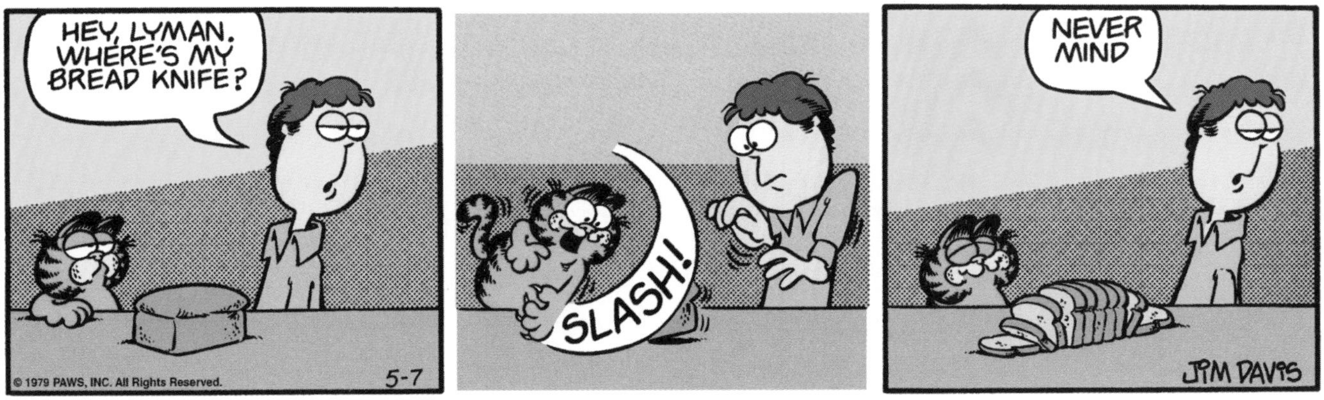
HEY, LYMAN. WHERE'S MY BREAD KNIFE?
SLASH!
NEVER MIND
© 1979 PAWS, INC. All Rights Reserved.
5-7
JIM DAVIS

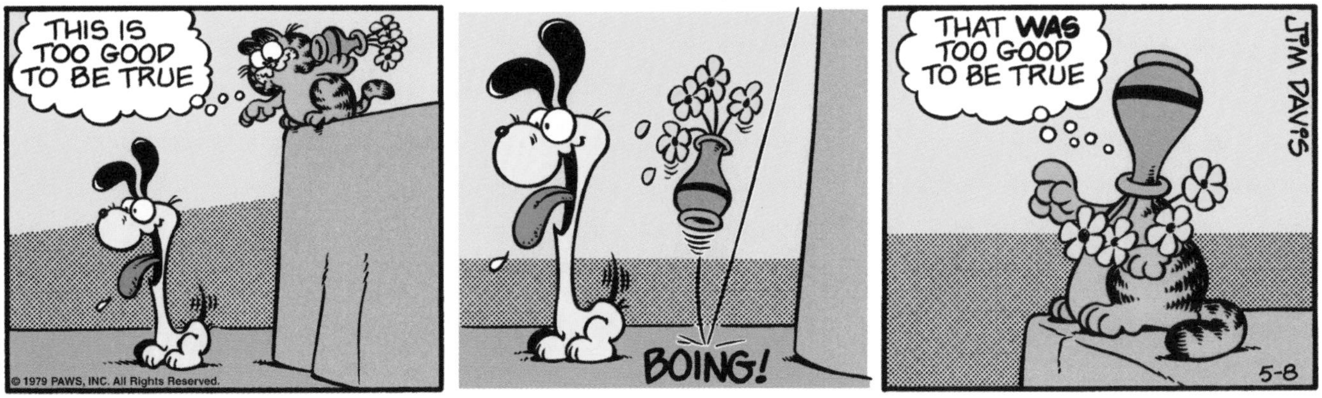
THIS IS TOO GOOD TO BE TRUE
BOING!
THAT **WAS** TOO GOOD TO BE TRUE
JIM DAVIS
© 1979 PAWS, INC. All Rights Reserved.
5-8

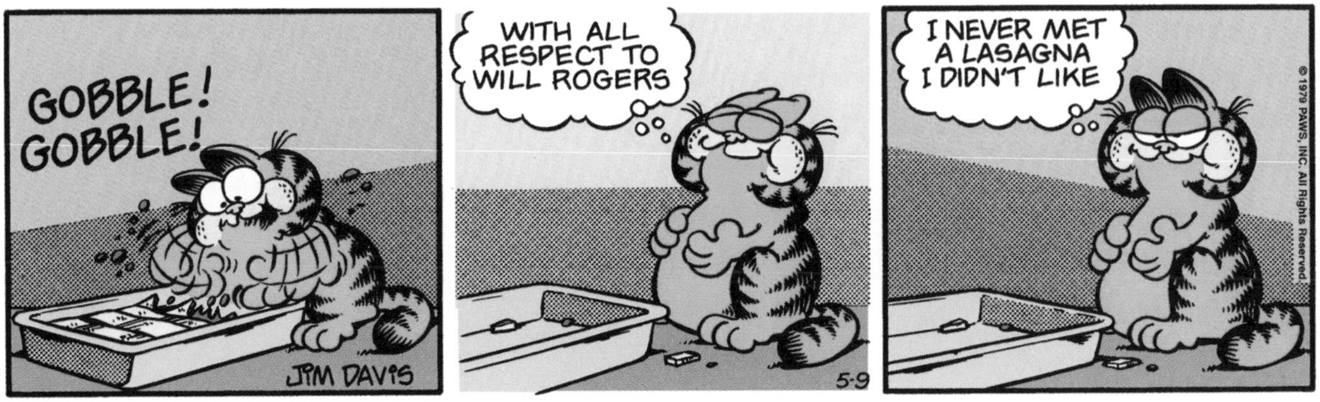
GOBBLE! GOBBLE!
JIM DAVIS
WITH ALL RESPECT TO WILL ROGERS
5-9
I NEVER MET A LASAGNA I DIDN'T LIKE
© 1979 PAWS, INC. All Rights Reserved.

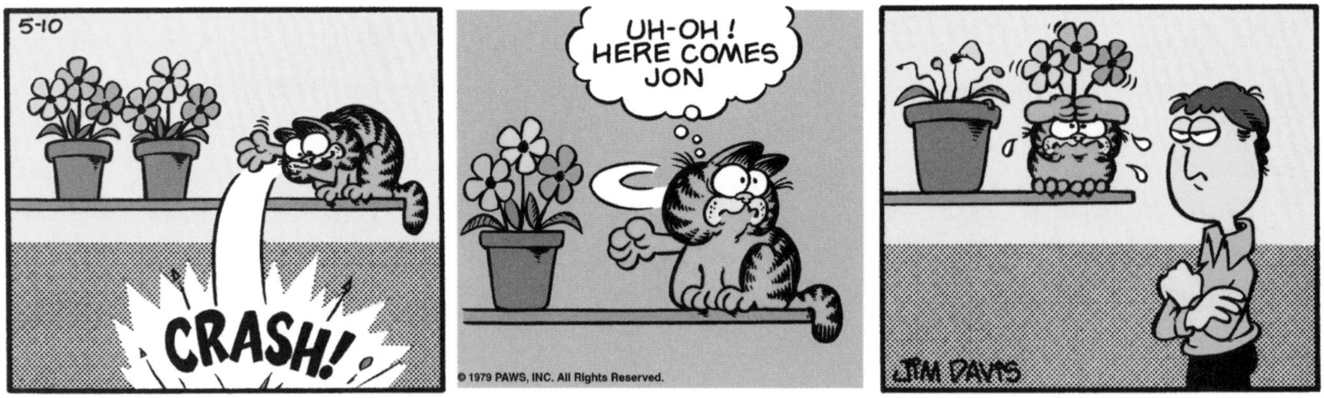
5-10
CRASH!
UH-OH! HERE COMES JON
© 1979 PAWS, INC. All Rights Reserved.
JIM DAVIS

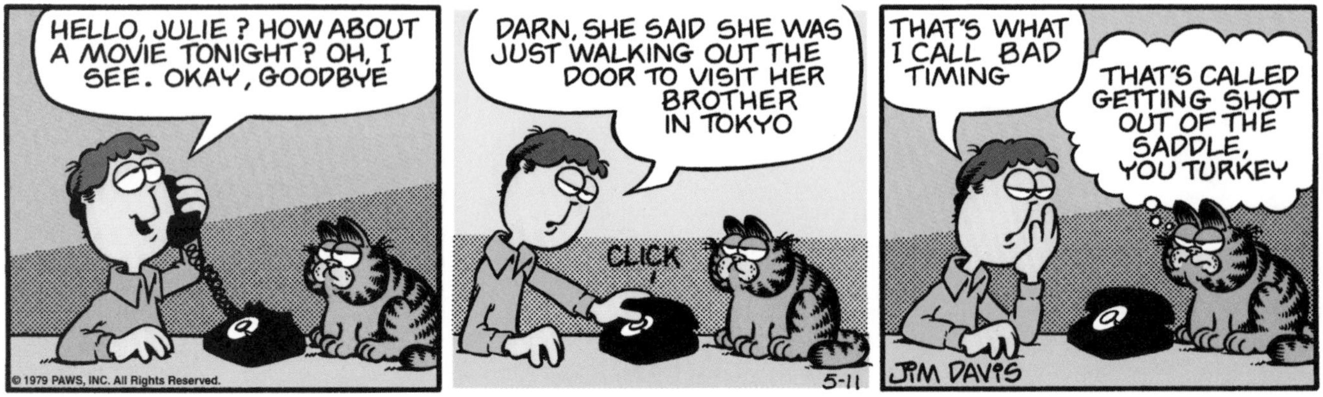
HELLO, JULIE ? HOW ABOUT A MOVIE TONIGHT? OH, I SEE. OKAY, GOODBYE
© 1979 PAWS, INC. All Rights Reserved.
DARN, SHE SAID SHE WAS JUST WALKING OUT THE DOOR TO VISIT HER BROTHER IN TOKYO
CLICK
5-11
THAT'S WHAT I CALL BAD TIMING
THAT'S CALLED GETTING SHOT OUT OF THE SADDLE, YOU TURKEY
JIM DAVIS

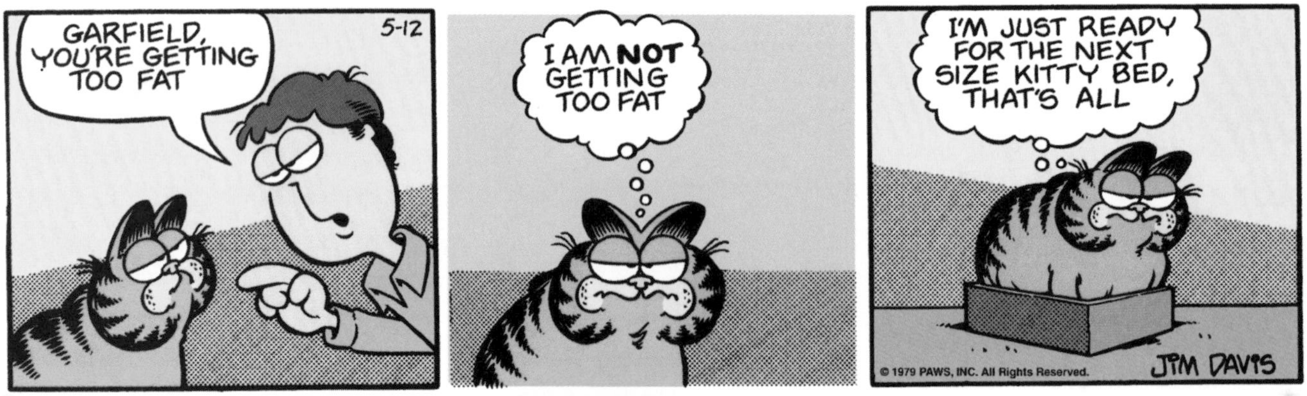
5-12
GARFIELD, YOU'RE GETTING TOO FAT
I AM **NOT** GETTING TOO FAT
I'M JUST READY FOR THE NEXT SIZE KITTY BED, THAT'S ALL
© 1979 PAWS, INC. All Rights Reserved.
JIM DAVIS

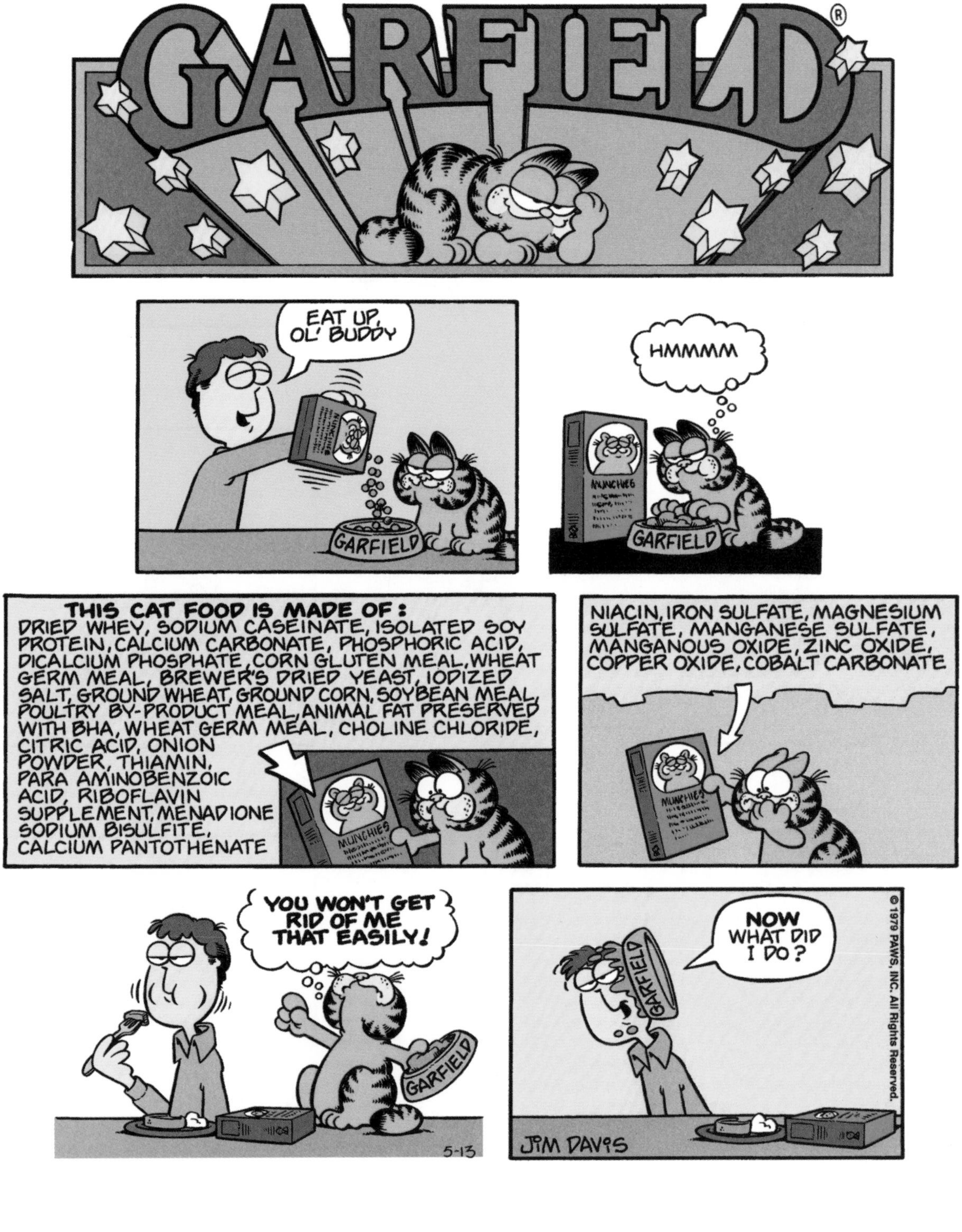
GARFIELD®
EAT UP, OL' BUDDY
GARFIELD
HMMMM
MUNCHIES
GARFIELD
THIS CAT FOOD IS MADE OF:
DRIED WHEY, SODIUM CASEINATE, ISOLATED SOY PROTEIN, CALCIUM CARBONATE, PHOSPHORIC ACID, DICALCIUM PHOSPHATE, CORN GLUTEN MEAL, WHEAT GERM MEAL, BREWER'S DRIED YEAST, IODIZED SALT, GROUND WHEAT, GROUND CORN, SOYBEAN MEAL, POULTRY BY-PRODUCT MEAL, ANIMAL FAT PRESERVED WITH BHA, WHEAT GERM MEAL, CHOLINE CHLORIDE, CITRIC ACID, ONION POWDER, THIAMIN, PARA AMINOBENZOIC ACID, RIBOFLAVIN SUPPLEMENT, MENADIONE SODIUM BISULFITE, CALCIUM PANTOTHENATE
MUNCHIES
NIACIN, IRON SULFATE, MAGNESIUM SULFATE, MANGANESE SULFATE, MANGANOUS OXIDE, ZINC OXIDE, COPPER OXIDE, COBALT CARBONATE
MUNCHIES
YOU WON'T GET RID OF ME THAT EASILY!
GARFIELD
5-13
NOW WHAT DID I DO?
GARFIELD
JIM DAVIS
© 1979 PAWS, INC. All Rights Reserved.

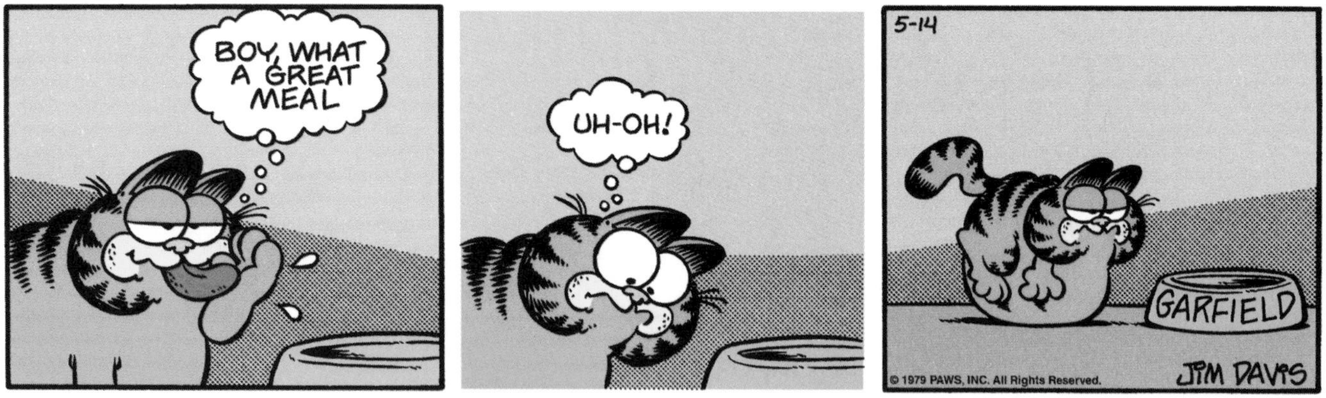
BOY, WHAT A GREAT MEAL
UH-OH!
5-14
GARFIELD
© 1979 PAWS, INC. All Rights Reserved.
JIM DAVIS

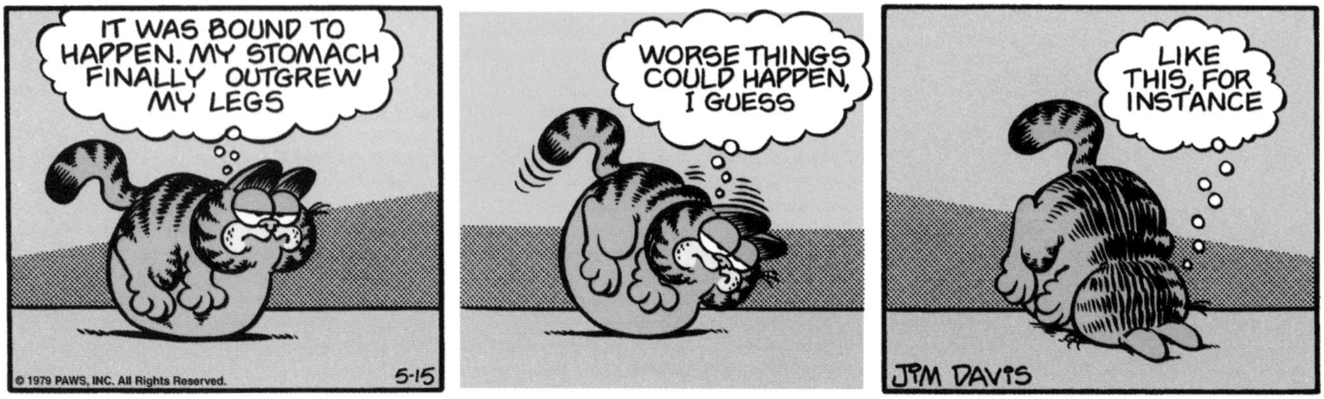
IT WAS BOUND TO HAPPEN. MY STOMACH FINALLY OUTGREW MY LEGS
© 1979 PAWS, INC. All Rights Reserved.
5-15
WORSE THINGS COULD HAPPEN, I GUESS
LIKE THIS, FOR INSTANCE
JIM DAVIS

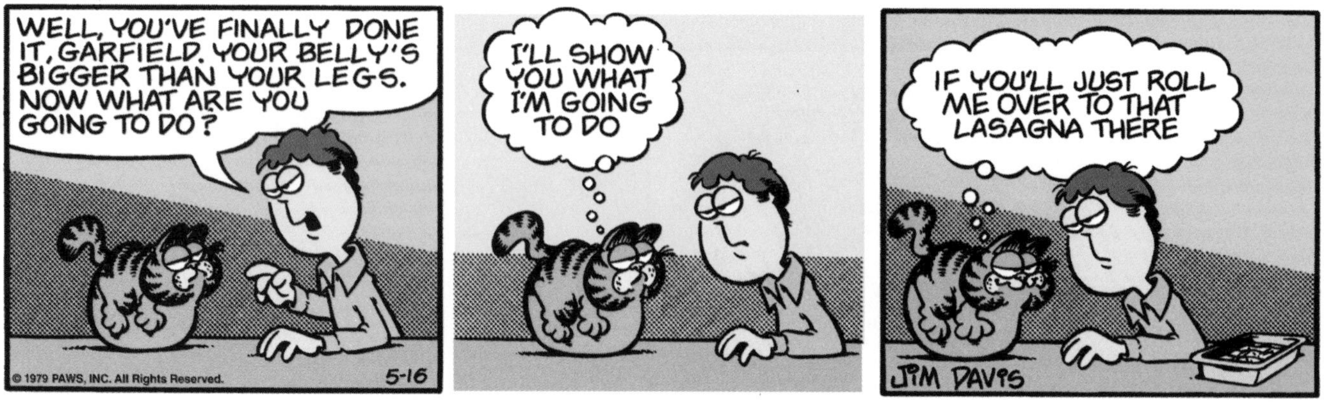
WELL, YOU'VE FINALLY DONE IT, GARFIELD. YOUR BELLY'S BIGGER THAN YOUR LEGS. NOW WHAT ARE YOU GOING TO DO?
© 1979 PAWS, INC. All Rights Reserved.
5-16
I'LL SHOW YOU WHAT I'M GOING TO DO
IF YOU'LL JUST ROLL ME OVER TO THAT LASAGNA THERE
JIM DAVIS

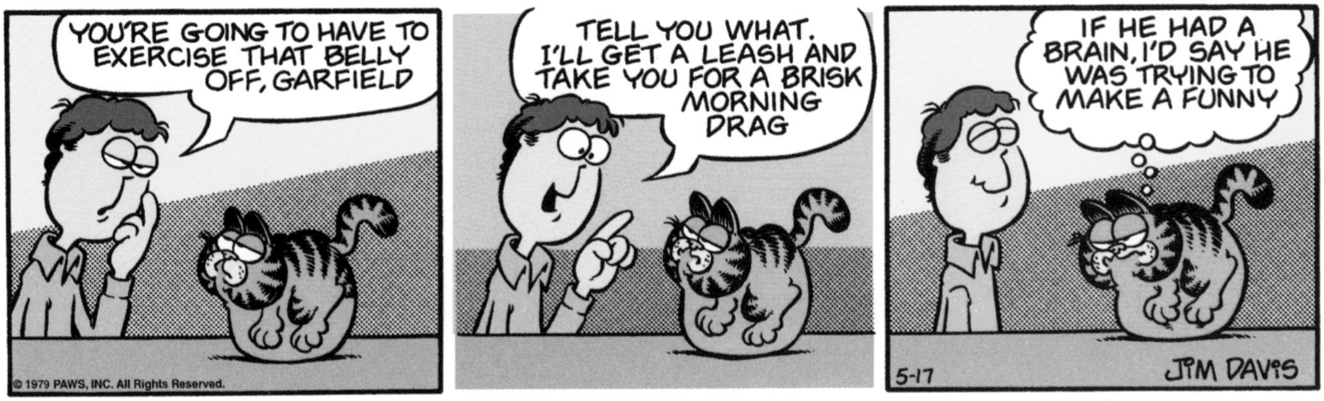
YOU'RE GOING TO HAVE TO EXERCISE THAT BELLY OFF, GARFIELD
TELL YOU WHAT. I'LL GET A LEASH AND TAKE YOU FOR A BRISK MORNING DRAG
IF HE HAD A BRAIN, I'D SAY HE WAS TRYING TO MAKE A FUNNY
© 1979 PAWS, INC. All Rights Reserved.
5-17
JIM DAVIS

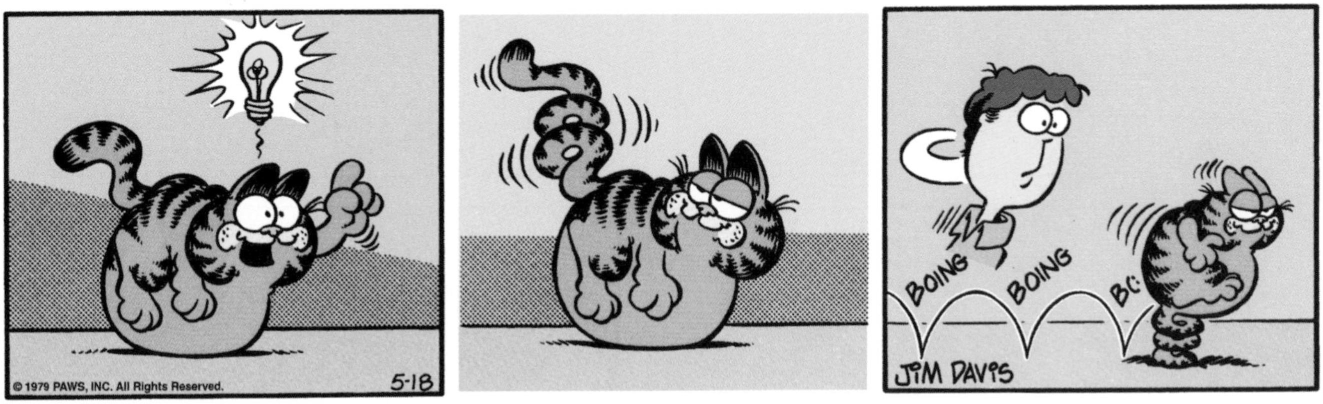
BOING
BOING
BO
© 1979 PAWS, INC. All Rights Reserved.
5-18
JIM DAVIS

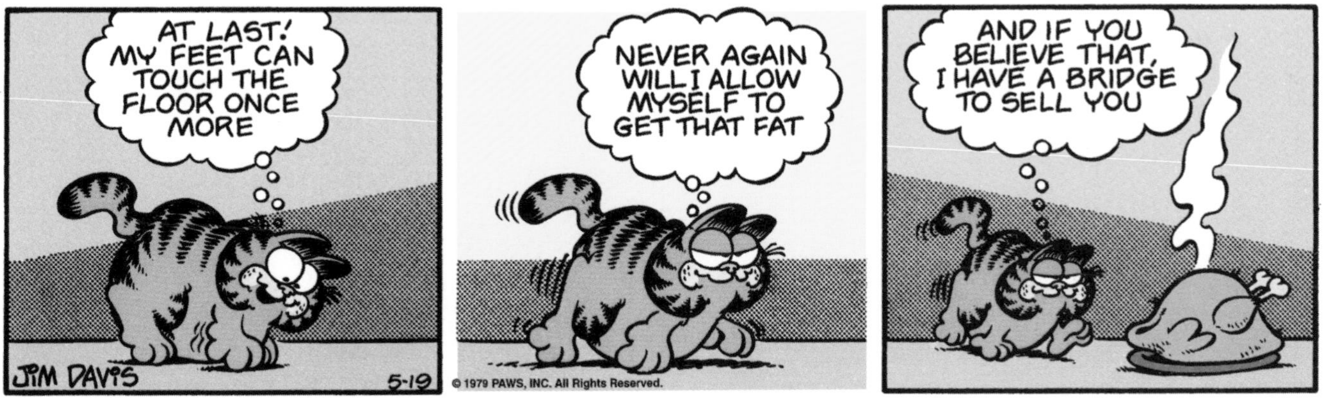
AT LAST! MY FEET CAN TOUCH THE FLOOR ONCE MORE
NEVER AGAIN WILL I ALLOW MYSELF TO GET THAT FAT
AND IF YOU BELIEVE THAT, I HAVE A BRIDGE TO SELL YOU
JIM DAVIS
5-19
© 1979 PAWS, INC. All Rights Reserved.

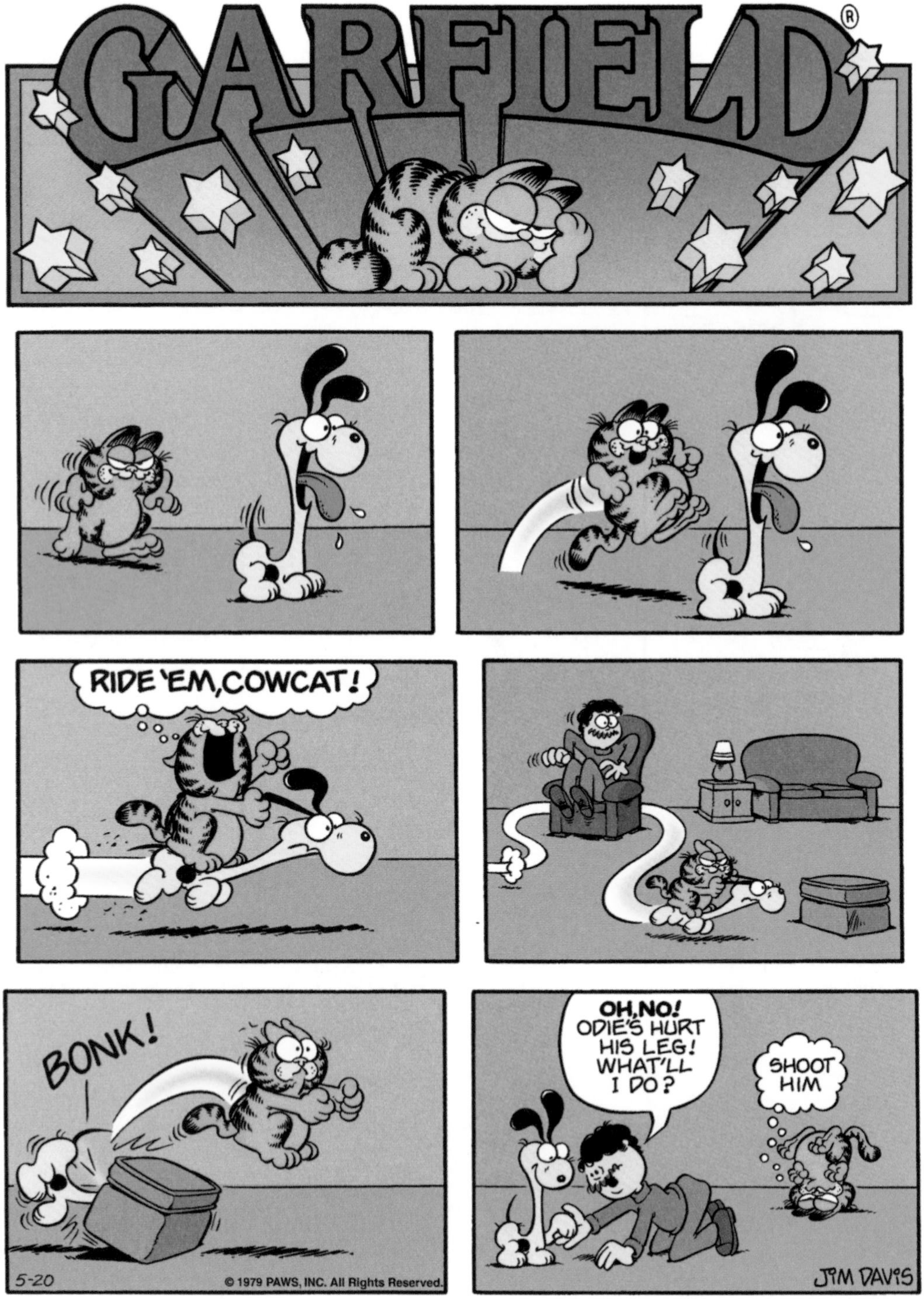
GARFIELD®
RIDE 'EM, COWCAT!
BONK!
5-20
© 1979 PAWS, INC. All Rights Reserved.
OH, NO! ODIE'S HURT HIS LEG! WHAT'LL I DO?
SHOOT HIM
JIM DAVIS

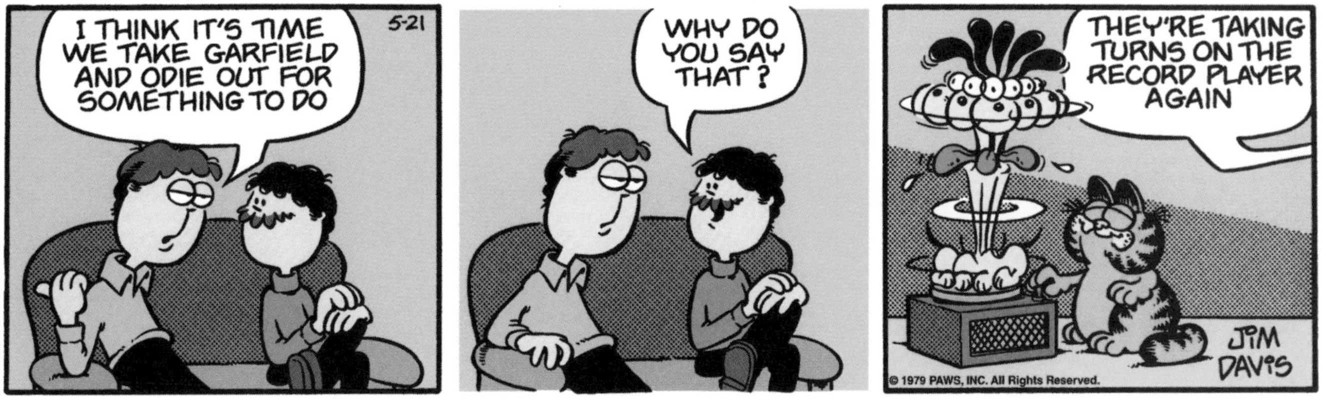
5-21
I THINK IT'S TIME WE TAKE GARFIELD AND ODIE OUT FOR SOMETHING TO DO
WHY DO YOU SAY THAT?
THEY'RE TAKING TURNS ON THE RECORD PLAYER AGAIN
© 1979 PAWS, INC. All Rights Reserved.
JIM DAVIS

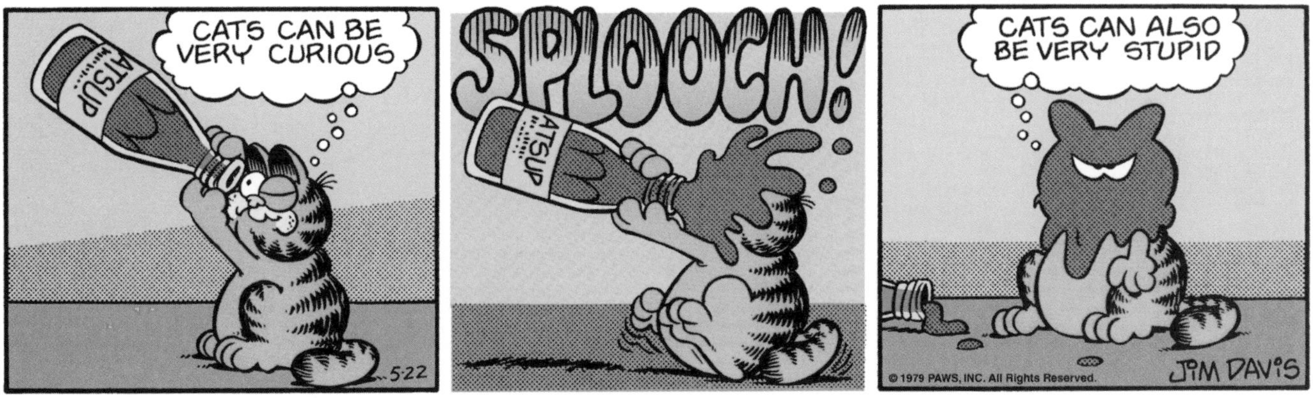
CATS CAN BE VERY CURIOUS
ATSUP
5-22
SPLOOCH!
ATSUP
CATS CAN ALSO BE VERY STUPID
© 1979 PAWS, INC. All Rights Reserved.
JIM DAVIS

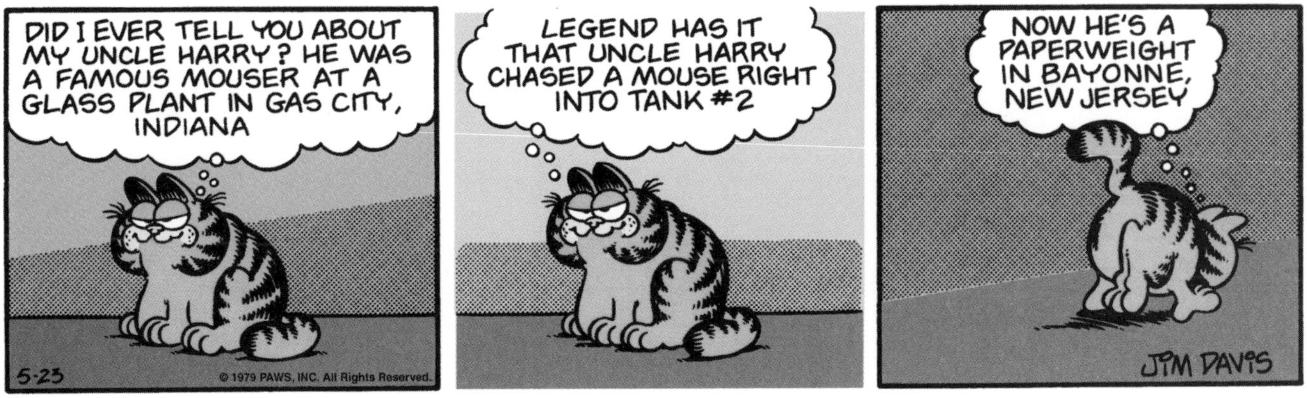
DID I EVER TELL YOU ABOUT MY UNCLE HARRY? HE WAS A FAMOUS MOUSER AT A GLASS PLANT IN GAS CITY, INDIANA
5-23
© 1979 PAWS, INC. All Rights Reserved.
LEGEND HAS IT THAT UNCLE HARRY CHASED A MOUSE RIGHT INTO TANK #2
NOW HE'S A PAPERWEIGHT IN BAYONNE, NEW JERSEY
JIM DAVIS

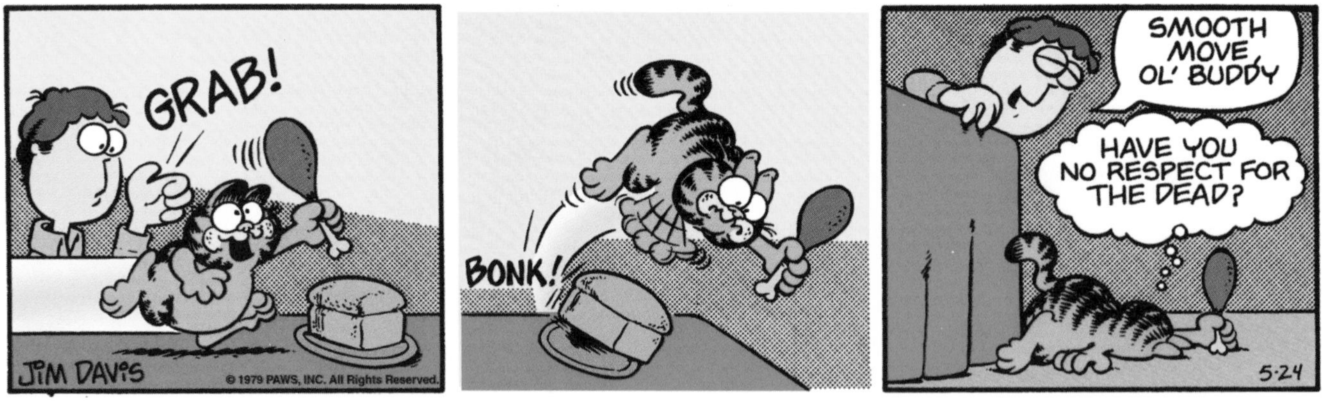
GRAB!
BONK!
SMOOTH MOVE, OL' BUDDY
HAVE YOU NO RESPECT FOR THE DEAD?
JIM DAVIS
© 1979 PAWS, INC. All Rights Reserved.
5·24

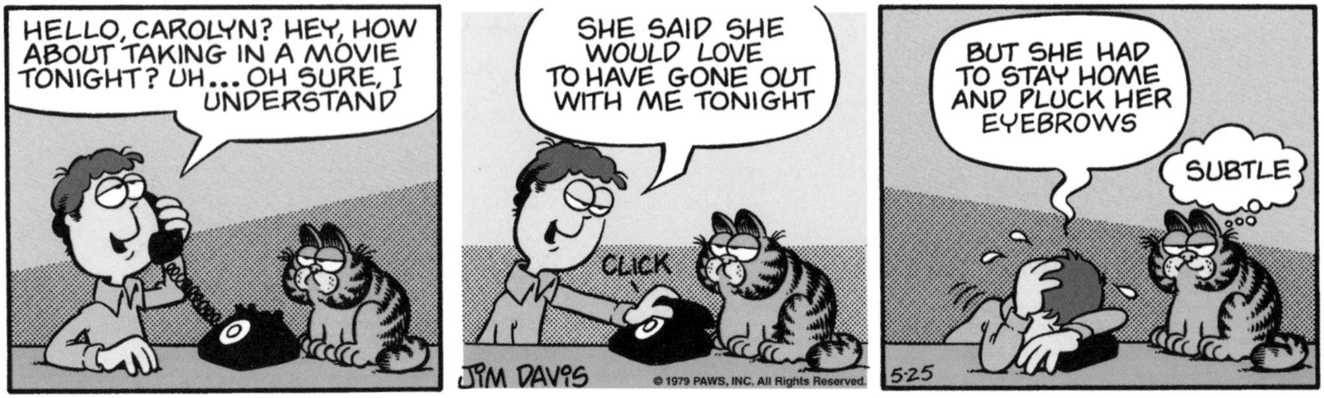
HELLO, CAROLYN? HEY, HOW ABOUT TAKING IN A MOVIE TONIGHT? UH... OH SURE, I UNDERSTAND
SHE SAID SHE WOULD LOVE TO HAVE GONE OUT WITH ME TONIGHT
CLICK
BUT SHE HAD TO STAY HOME AND PLUCK HER EYEBROWS
SUBTLE
JIM DAVIS
© 1979 PAWS, INC. All Rights Reserved.
5·25

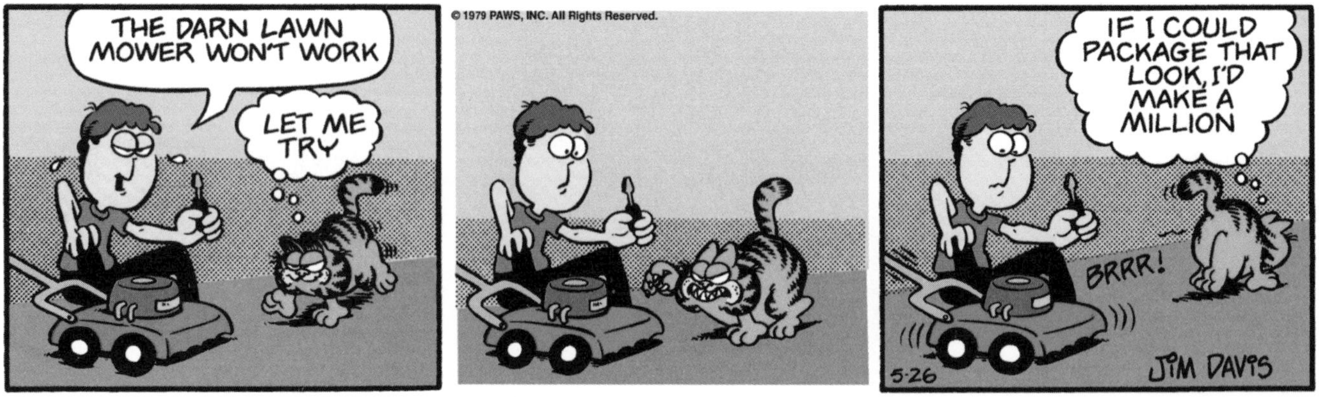
THE DARN LAWN MOWER WON'T WORK
LET ME TRY
© 1979 PAWS, INC. All Rights Reserved.
IF I COULD PACKAGE THAT LOOK, I'D MAKE A MILLION
BRRR!
5·26
JIM DAVIS

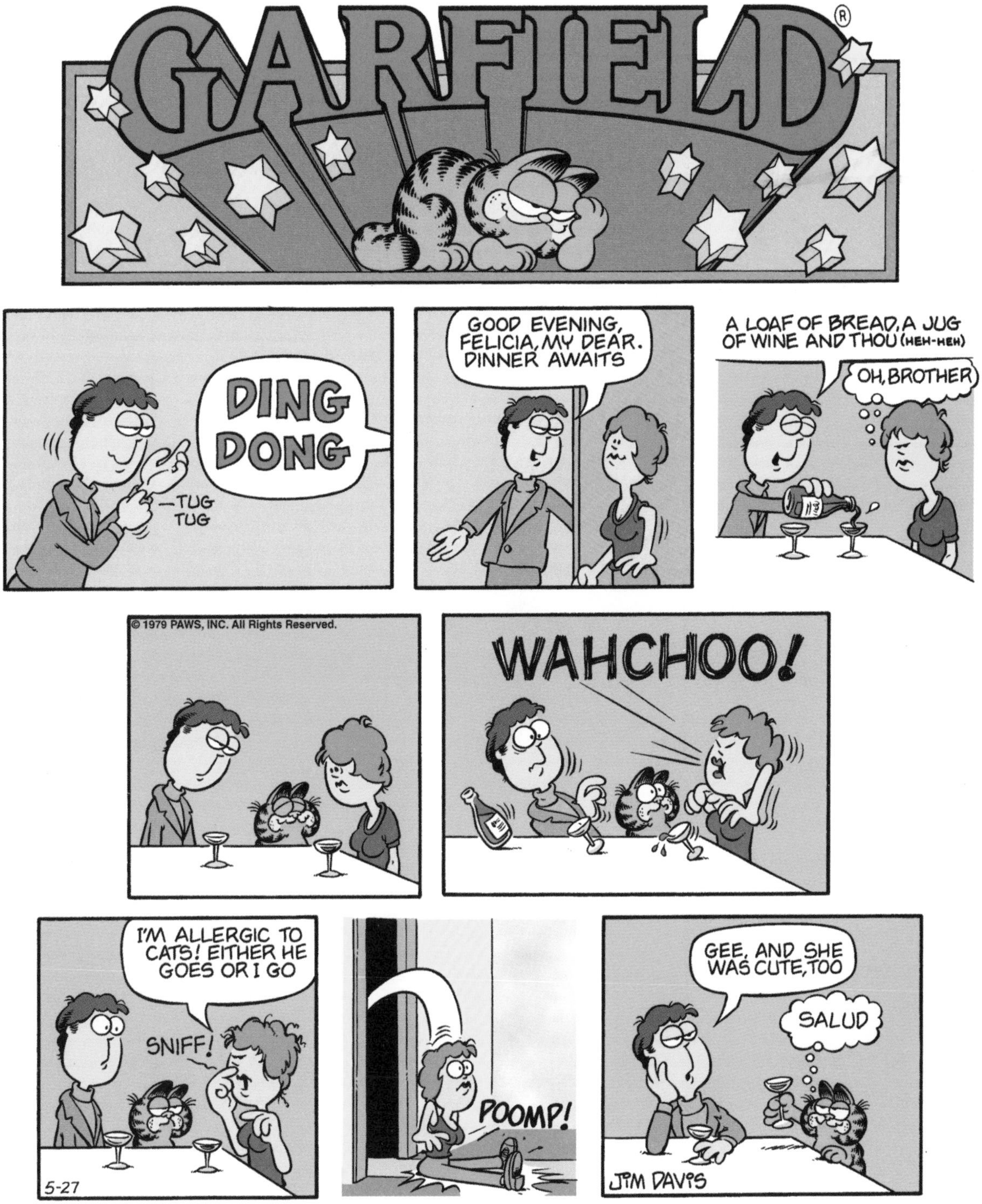

GARFIELD®
DING DONG
—TUG TUG
GOOD EVENING, FELICIA, MY DEAR. DINNER AWAITS
A LOAF OF BREAD, A JUG OF WINE AND THOU (HEH-HEH)
OH, BROTHER
© 1979 PAWS, INC. All Rights Reserved.
WAHCHOO!
I'M ALLERGIC TO CATS! EITHER HE GOES OR I GO
SNIFF!
5-27
POOMP!
GEE, AND SHE WAS CUTE, TOO
SALUD
JIM DAVIS

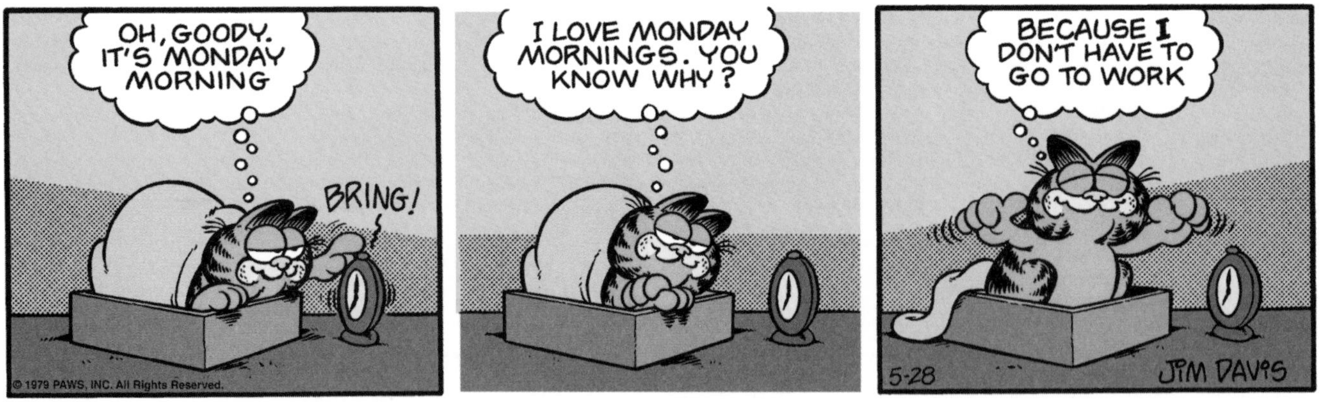
OH, GOODY. IT'S MONDAY MORNING
BRING!
© 1979 PAWS, INC. All Rights Reserved.
I LOVE MONDAY MORNINGS. YOU KNOW WHY?
BECAUSE I DON'T HAVE TO GO TO WORK
5-28
JIM DAVIS

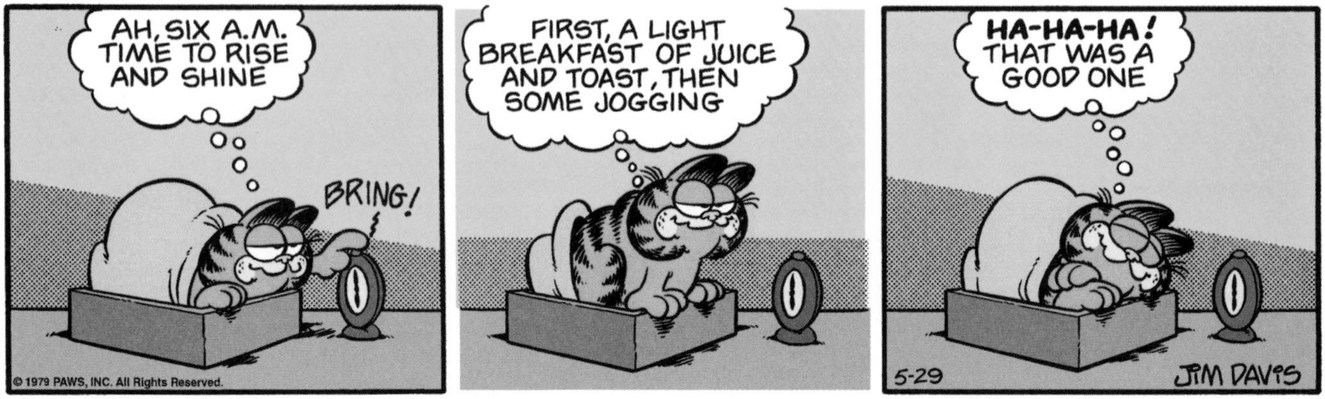
AH, SIX A.M. TIME TO RISE AND SHINE
BRING!
© 1979 PAWS, INC. All Rights Reserved.
FIRST, A LIGHT BREAKFAST OF JUICE AND TOAST, THEN SOME JOGGING
HA-HA-HA! THAT WAS A GOOD ONE
5-29
JIM DAVIS

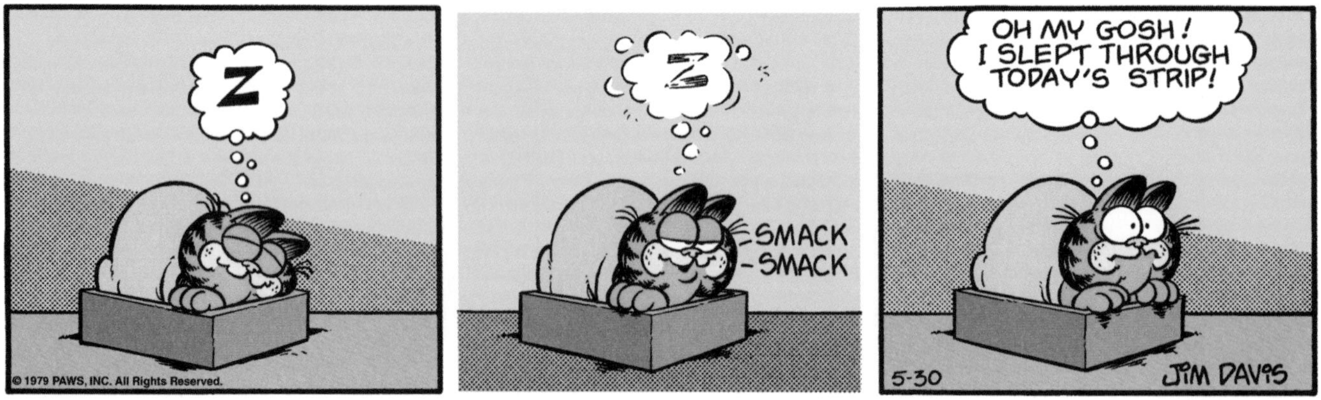
Z
© 1979 PAWS, INC. All Rights Reserved.
Z
SMACK -SMACK
OH MY GOSH! I SLEPT THROUGH TODAY'S STRIP!
5-30
JIM DAVIS

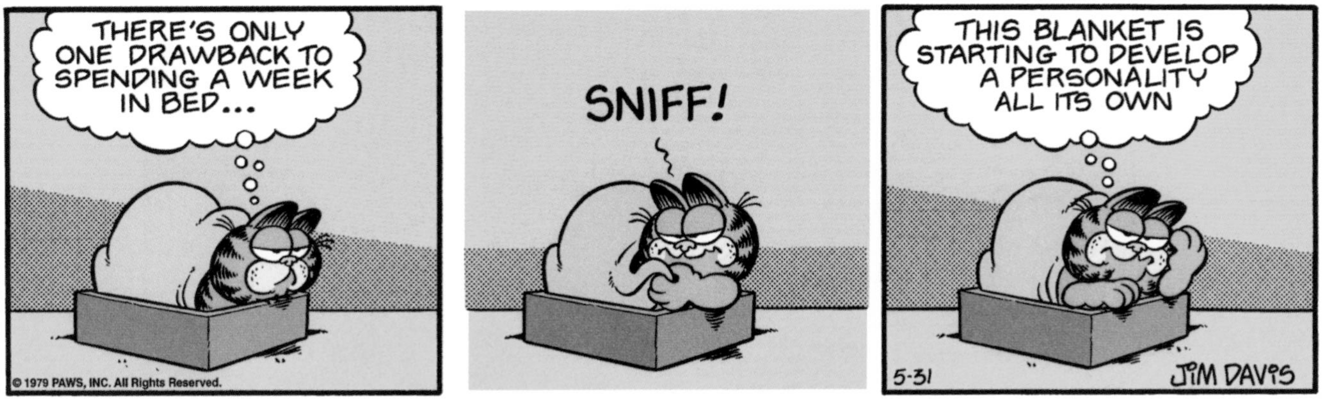
THERE'S ONLY ONE DRAWBACK TO SPENDING A WEEK IN BED...
SNIFF!
THIS BLANKET IS STARTING TO DEVELOP A PERSONALITY ALL ITS OWN
© 1979 PAWS, INC. All Rights Reserved.
5-31
JIM DAVIS

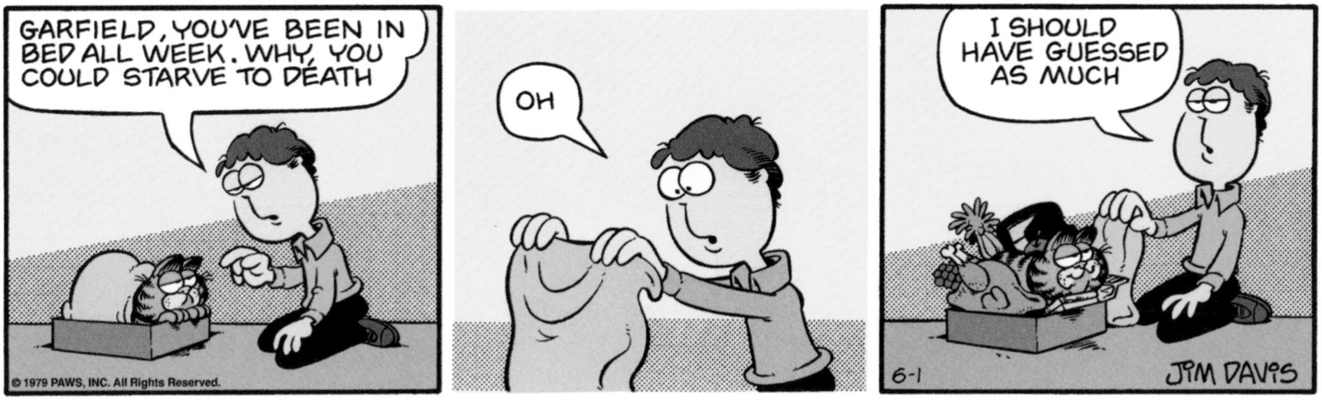
GARFIELD, YOU'VE BEEN IN BED ALL WEEK. WHY, YOU COULD STARVE TO DEATH
OH
I SHOULD HAVE GUESSED AS MUCH
© 1979 PAWS, INC. All Rights Reserved.
6-1
JIM DAVIS

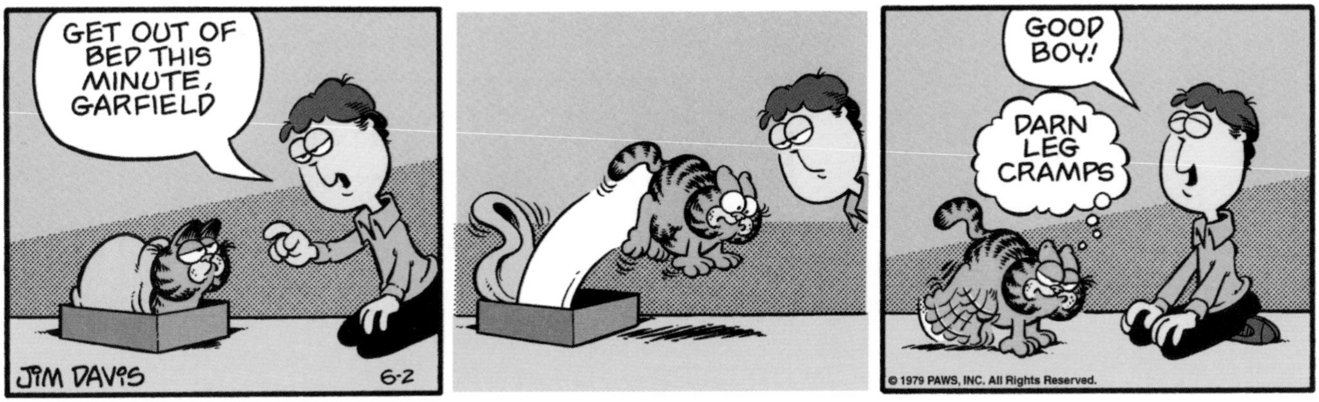
GET OUT OF BED THIS MINUTE, GARFIELD
GOOD BOY!
DARN LEG CRAMPS
JIM DAVIS
6-2
© 1979 PAWS, INC. All Rights Reserved.

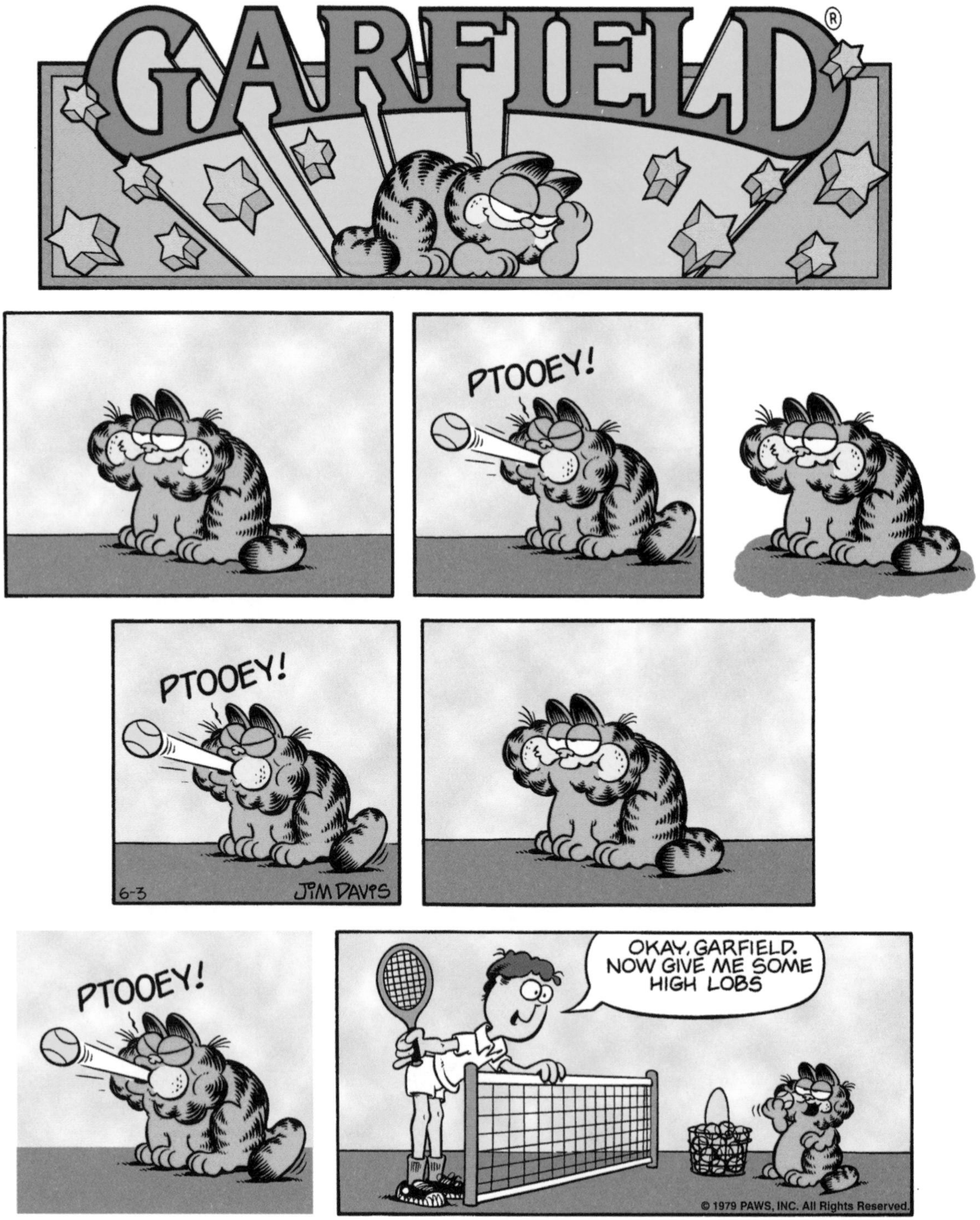
GARFIELD®
PTOOEY!
PTOOEY!
6-3
JIM DAVIS
PTOOEY!
OKAY, GARFIELD. NOW GIVE ME SOME HIGH LOBS
© 1979 PAWS, INC. All Rights Reserved.

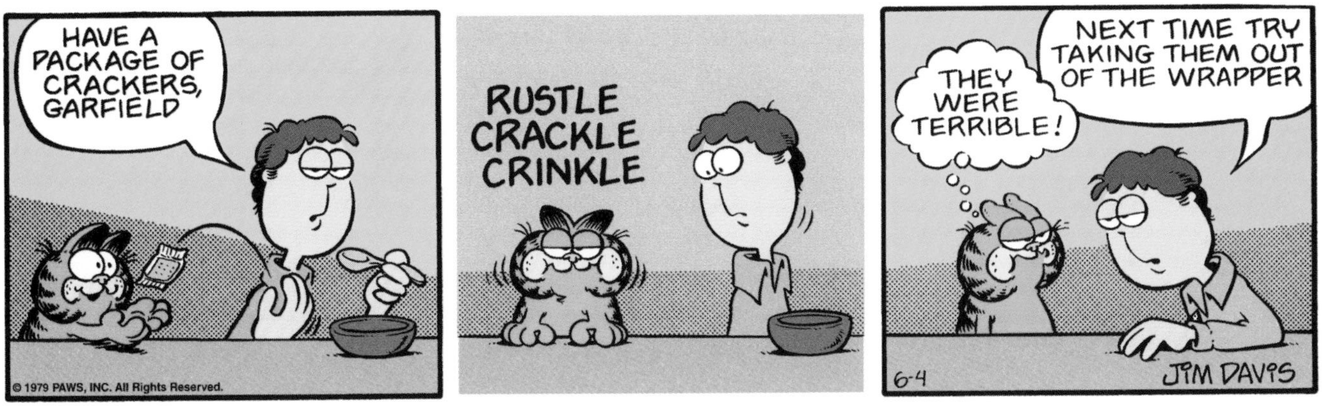
HAVE A PACKAGE OF CRACKERS, GARFIELD
© 1979 PAWS, INC. All Rights Reserved.
RUSTLE CRACKLE CRINKLE
THEY WERE TERRIBLE!
NEXT TIME TRY TAKING THEM OUT OF THE WRAPPER
6-4
JIM DAVIS

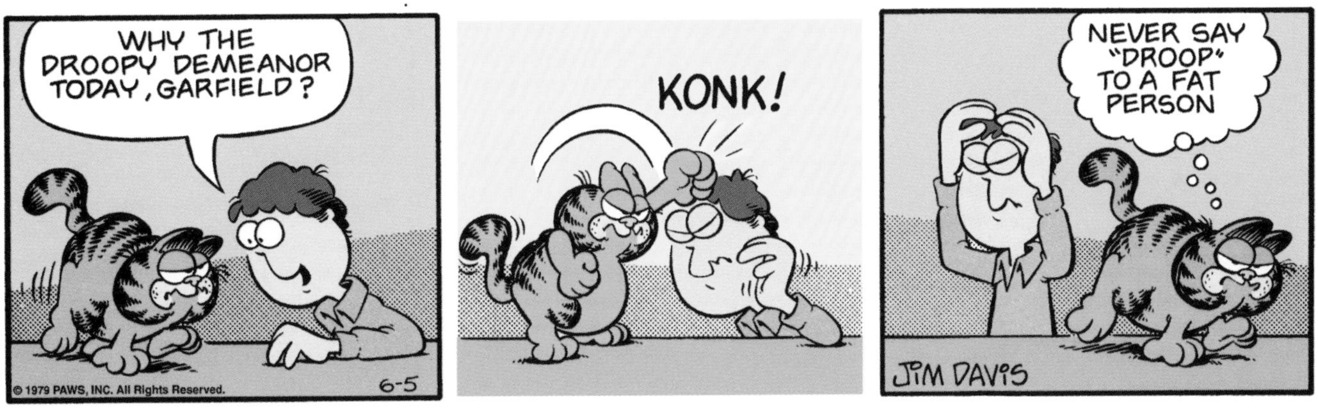
WHY THE DROOPY DEMEANOR TODAY, GARFIELD?
© 1979 PAWS, INC. All Rights Reserved.
6-5
KONK!
NEVER SAY "DROOP" TO A FAT PERSON
JIM DAVIS

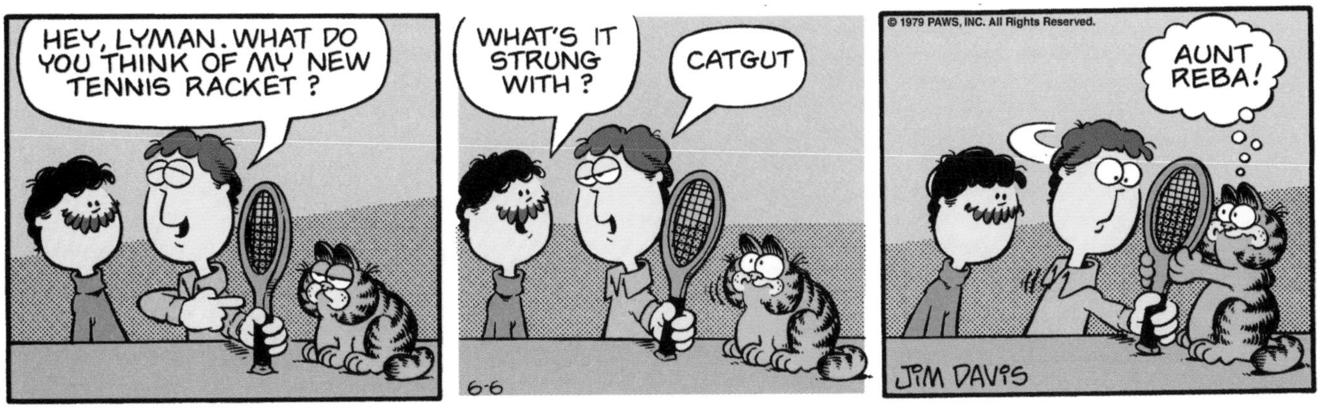
HEY, LYMAN. WHAT DO YOU THINK OF MY NEW TENNIS RACKET?
WHAT'S IT STRUNG WITH?
CATGUT
6-6
© 1979 PAWS, INC. All Rights Reserved.
AUNT REBA!
JIM DAVIS

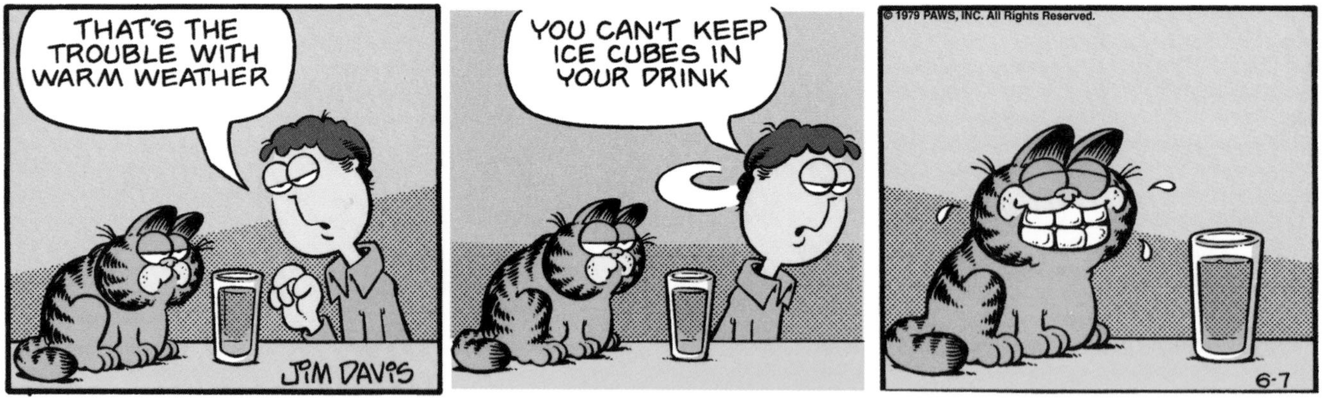
THAT'S THE TROUBLE WITH WARM WEATHER
JIM DAVIS
YOU CAN'T KEEP ICE CUBES IN YOUR DRINK
© 1979 PAWS, INC. All Rights Reserved.
6-7

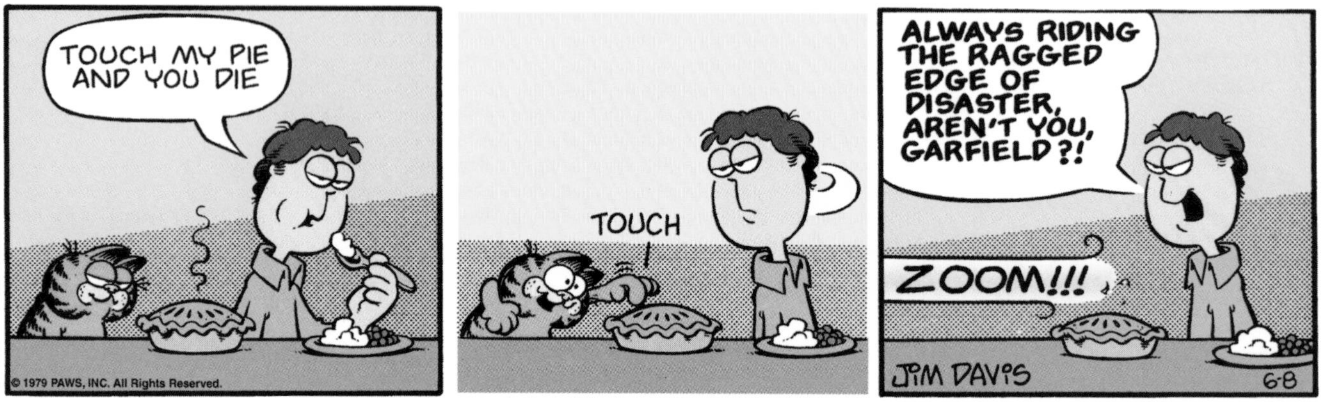
TOUCH MY PIE AND YOU DIE
© 1979 PAWS, INC. All Rights Reserved.
TOUCH
ALWAYS RIDING THE RAGGED EDGE OF DISASTER, AREN'T YOU, GARFIELD?!
ZOOM!!!
JIM DAVIS
6-8

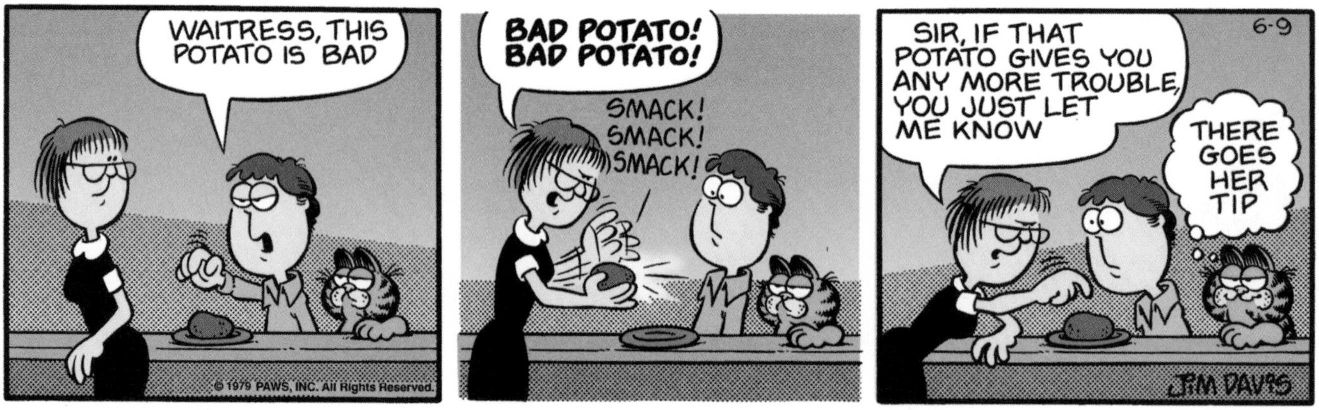
WAITRESS, THIS POTATO IS BAD
© 1979 PAWS, INC. All Rights Reserved.
BAD POTATO! BAD POTATO!
SMACK! SMACK! SMACK!
6-9
SIR, IF THAT POTATO GIVES YOU ANY MORE TROUBLE, YOU JUST LET ME KNOW
THERE GOES HER TIP
JIM DAVIS

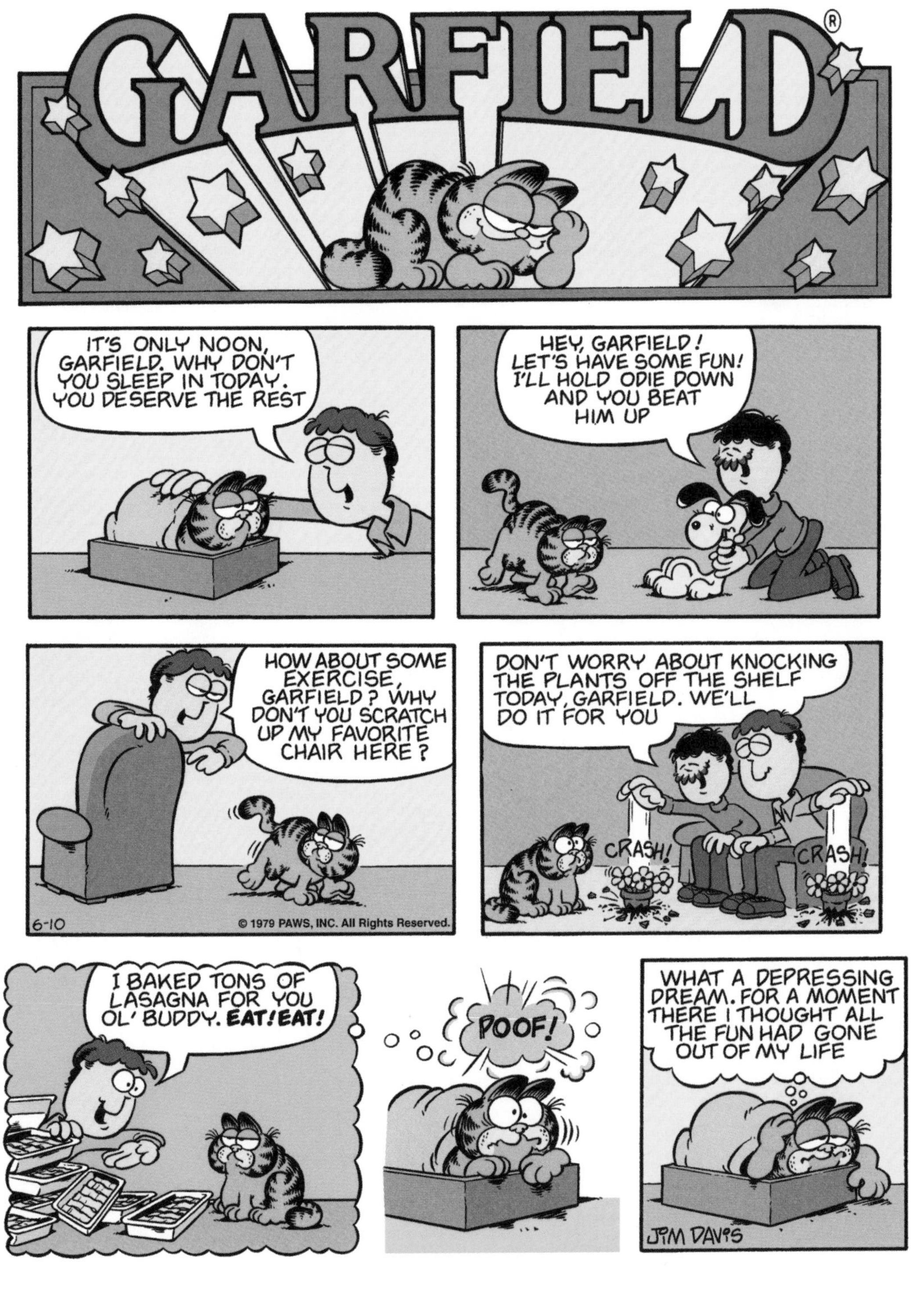
GARFIELD®
IT'S ONLY NOON, GARFIELD. WHY DON'T YOU SLEEP IN TODAY. YOU DESERVE THE REST
HEY, GARFIELD! LET'S HAVE SOME FUN! I'LL HOLD ODIE DOWN AND YOU BEAT HIM UP
HOW ABOUT SOME EXERCISE, GARFIELD? WHY DON'T YOU SCRATCH UP MY FAVORITE CHAIR HERE?
6-10
© 1979 PAWS, INC. All Rights Reserved.
DON'T WORRY ABOUT KNOCKING THE PLANTS OFF THE SHELF TODAY, GARFIELD. WE'LL DO IT FOR YOU
CRASH!
CRASH!
I BAKED TONS OF LASAGNA FOR YOU OL' BUDDY. EAT! EAT!
POOF!
WHAT A DEPRESSING DREAM. FOR A MOMENT THERE I THOUGHT ALL THE FUN HAD GONE OUT OF MY LIFE
JIM DAVIS

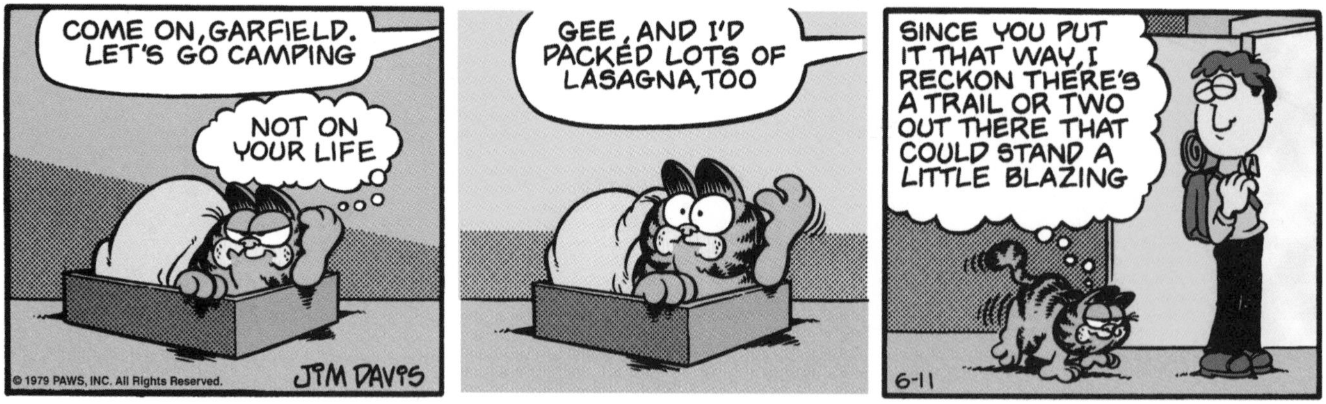
COME ON, GARFIELD. LET'S GO CAMPING
NOT ON YOUR LIFE
© 1979 PAWS, INC. All Rights Reserved.
JIM DAVIS
GEE, AND I'D PACKED LOTS OF LASAGNA, TOO
SINCE YOU PUT IT THAT WAY, I RECKON THERE'S A TRAIL OR TWO OUT THERE THAT COULD STAND A LITTLE BLAZING
6-11

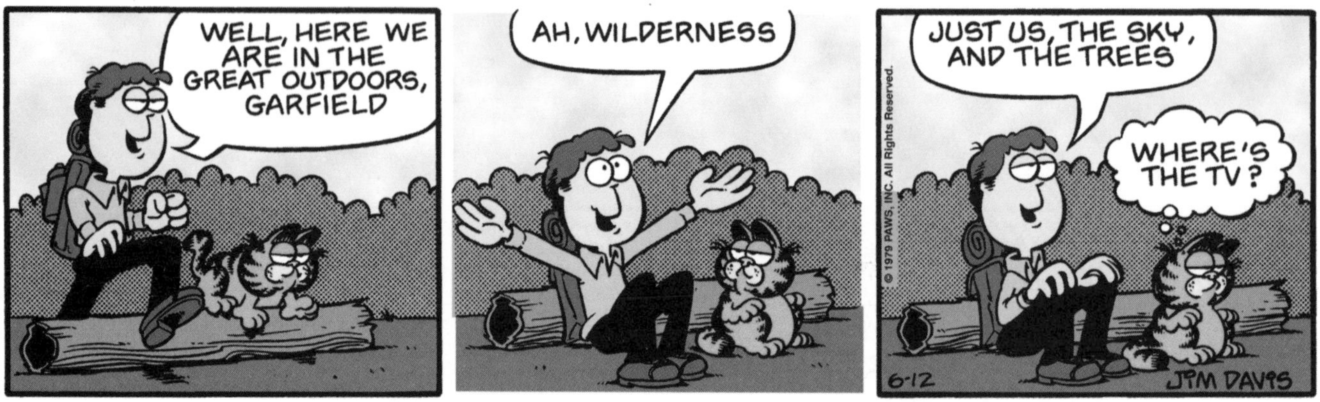
WELL, HERE WE ARE IN THE GREAT OUTDOORS, GARFIELD
AH, WILDERNESS
© 1979 PAWS, INC. All Rights Reserved.
JUST US, THE SKY, AND THE TREES
WHERE'S THE TV ?
6-12
JIM DAVIS

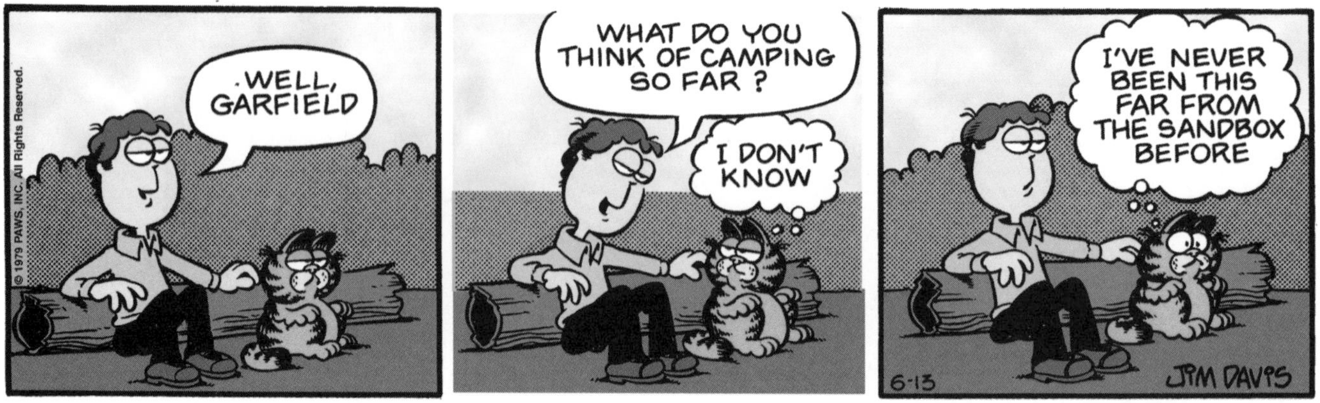
© 1979 PAWS, INC. All Rights Reserved.
WELL, GARFIELD
WHAT DO YOU THINK OF CAMPING SO FAR ?
I DON'T KNOW
I'VE NEVER BEEN THIS FAR FROM THE SANDBOX BEFORE
6-13
JIM DAVIS

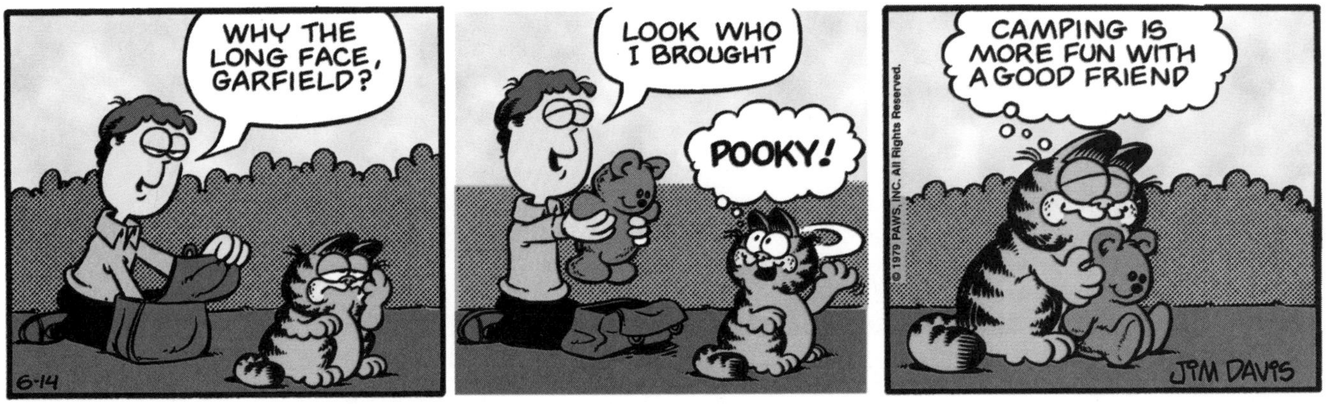
WHY THE LONG FACE, GARFIELD?
6-14
LOOK WHO I BROUGHT
POOKY!
CAMPING IS MORE FUN WITH A GOOD FRIEND
© 1979 PAWS, INC. All Rights Reserved.
JIM DAVIS

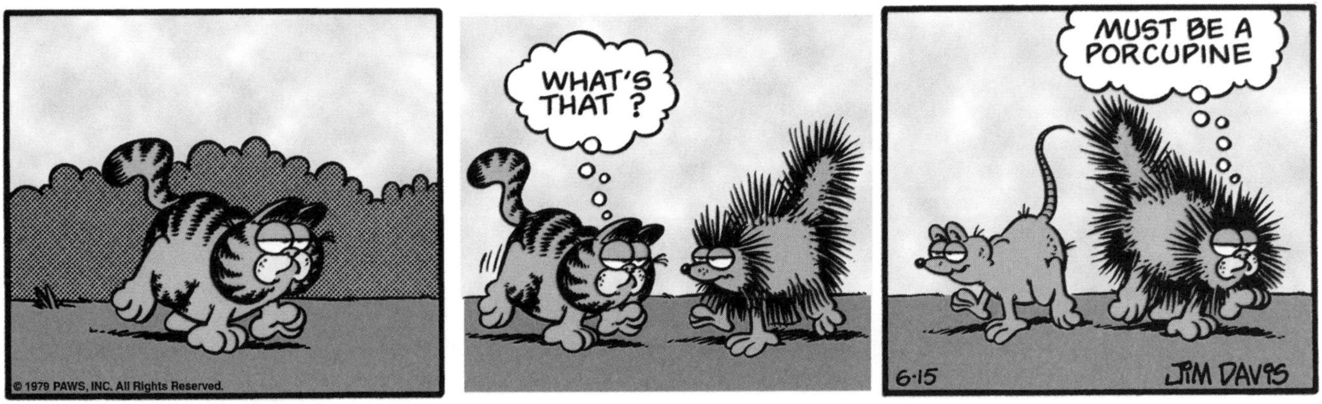
© 1979 PAWS, INC. All Rights Reserved.
WHAT'S THAT ?
MUST BE A PORCUPINE
6-15
JIM DAVIS

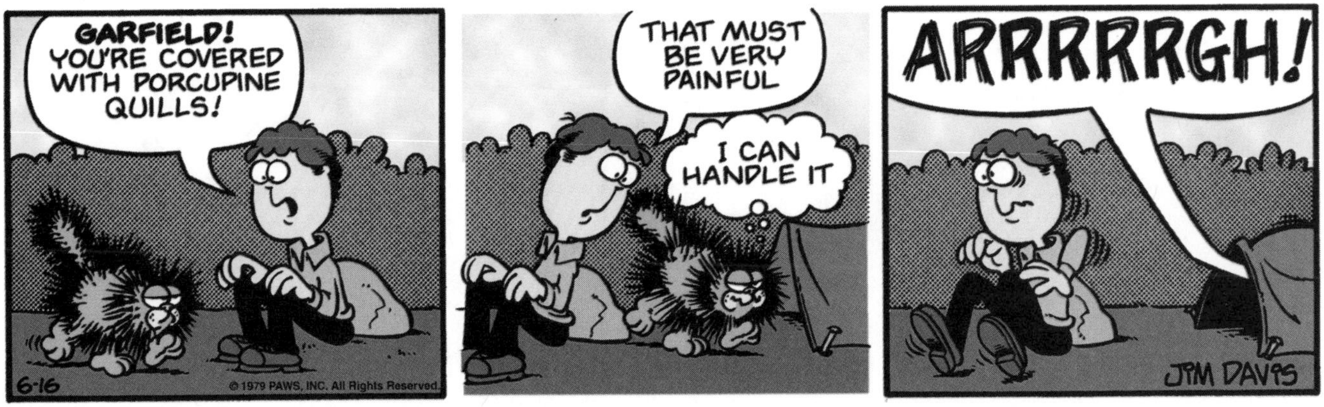
GARFIELD! YOU'RE COVERED WITH PORCUPINE QUILLS!
6-16
© 1979 PAWS, INC. All Rights Reserved.
THAT MUST BE VERY PAINFUL
I CAN HANDLE IT
ARRRRRGH!
JIM DAVIS

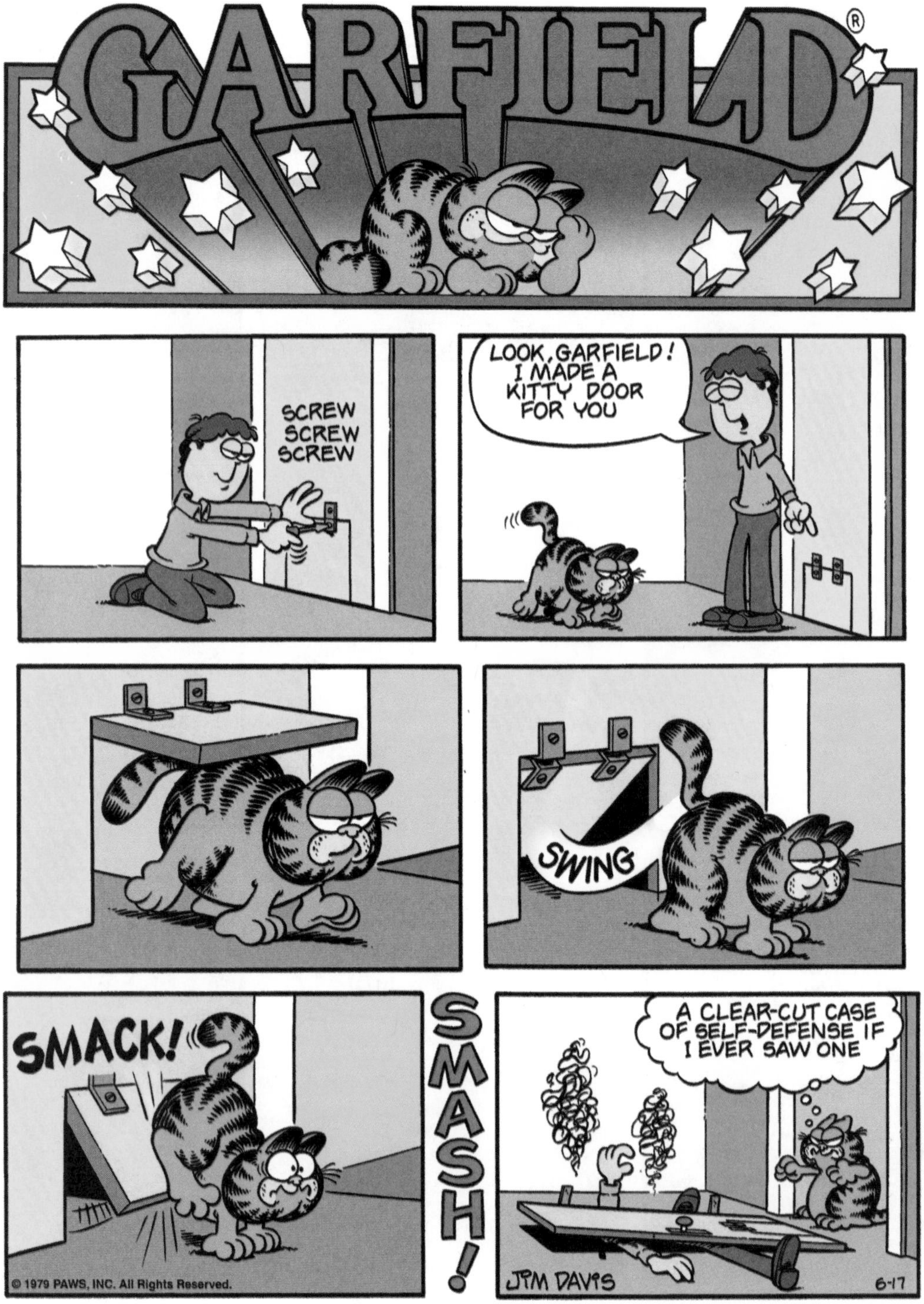
GARFIELD®
SCREW
SCREW
SCREW
LOOK, GARFIELD! I MADE A KITTY DOOR FOR YOU
SWING
SMACK!
SMASH!
A CLEAR-CUT CASE OF SELF-DEFENSE IF I EVER SAW ONE
© 1979 PAWS, INC. All Rights Reserved.
JIM DAVIS
6-17

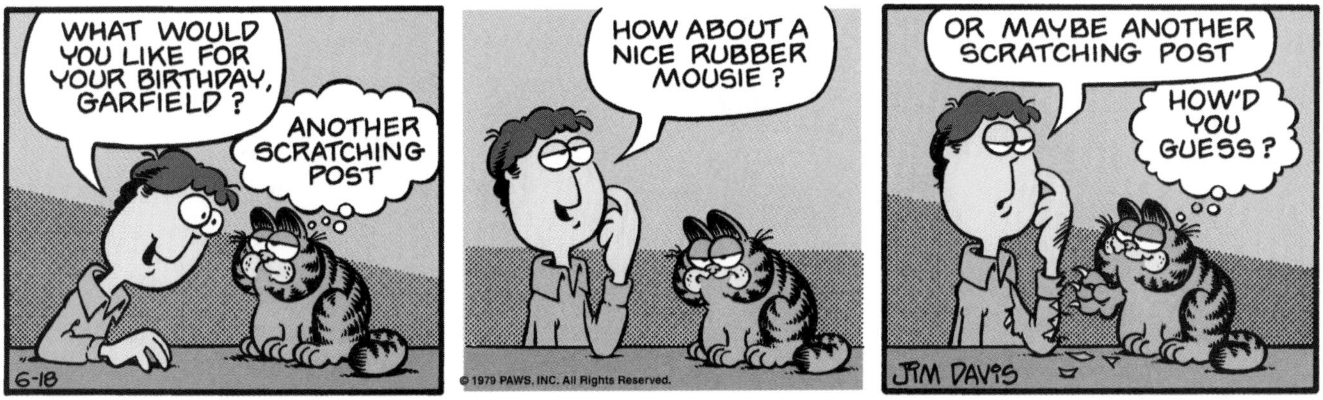
WHAT WOULD YOU LIKE FOR YOUR BIRTHDAY, GARFIELD ?
ANOTHER SCRATCHING POST
6-18
HOW ABOUT A NICE RUBBER MOUSIE ?
© 1979 PAWS, INC. All Rights Reserved.
OR MAYBE ANOTHER SCRATCHING POST
HOW'D YOU GUESS ?
JIM DAVIS

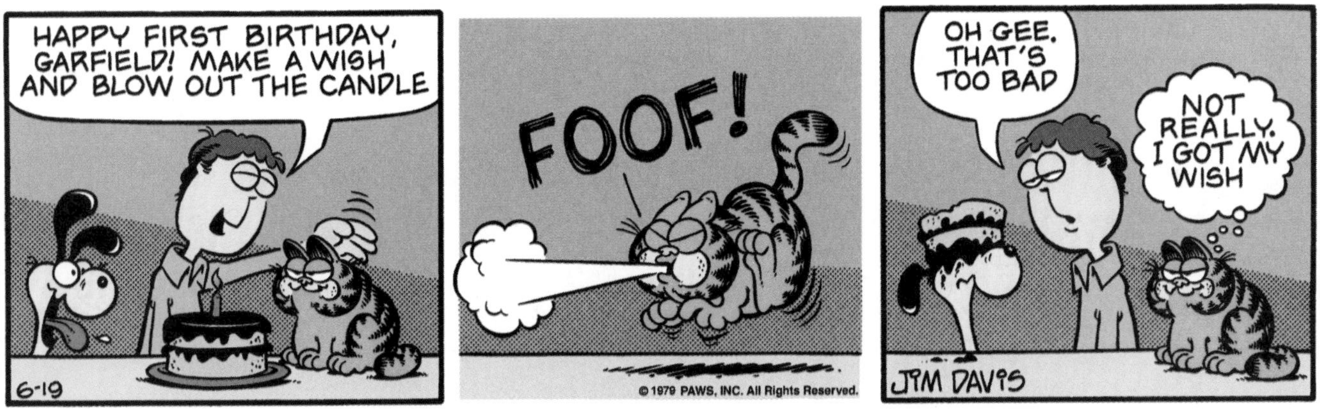
HAPPY FIRST BIRTHDAY, GARFIELD! MAKE A WISH AND BLOW OUT THE CANDLE
6-19
FOOF!
© 1979 PAWS, INC. All Rights Reserved.
OH GEE. THAT'S TOO BAD
NOT REALLY. I GOT MY WISH
JIM DAVIS

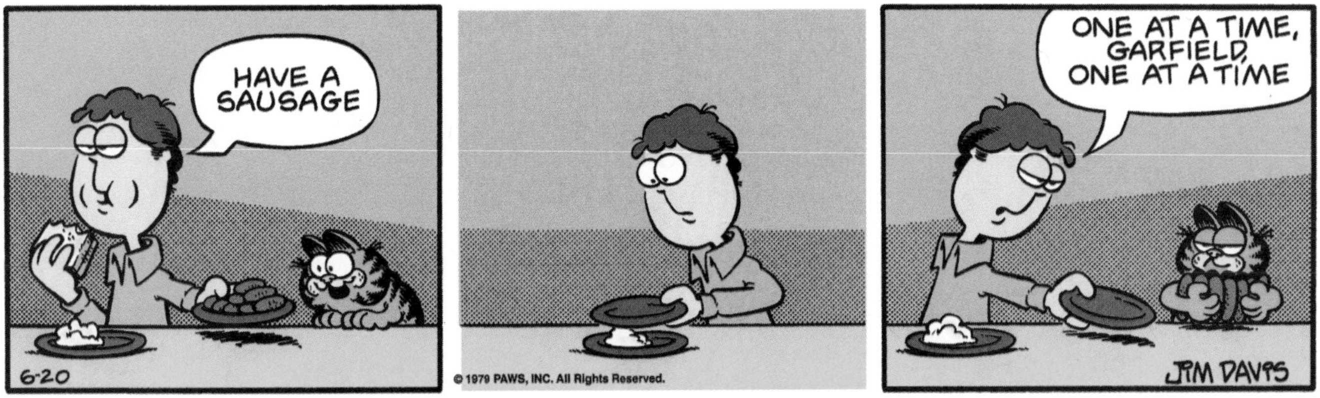
HAVE A SAUSAGE
6-20
© 1979 PAWS, INC. All Rights Reserved.
ONE AT A TIME, GARFIELD, ONE AT A TIME
JIM DAVIS

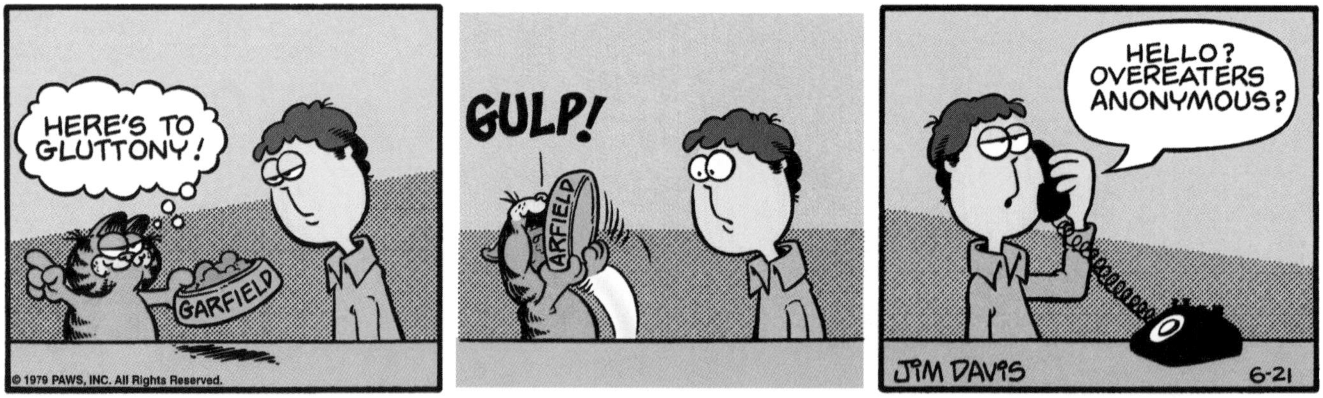
HERE'S TO GLUTTONY!
GARFIELD
© 1979 PAWS, INC. All Rights Reserved.
GULP!
ARFIELD
HELLO? OVEREATERS ANONYMOUS?
JIM DAVIS
6-21

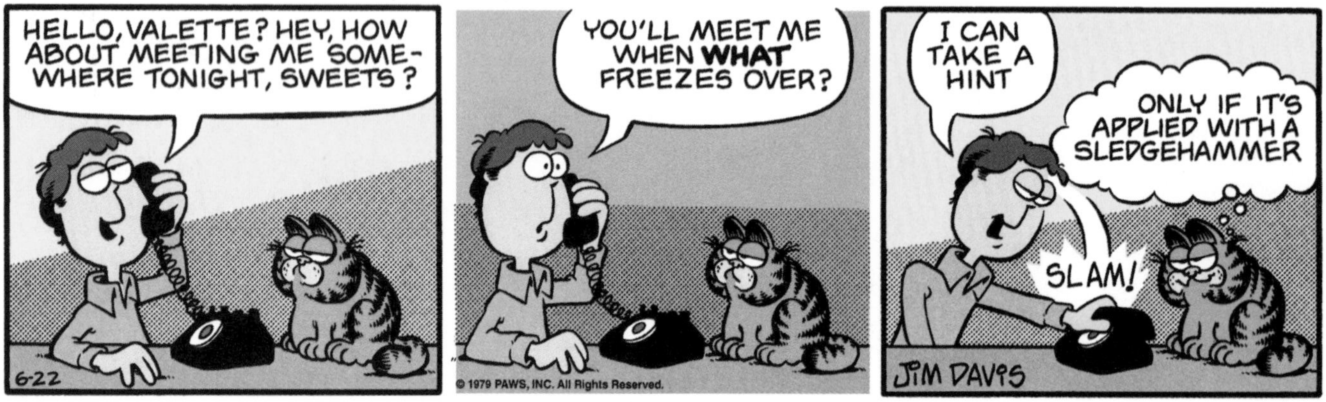
HELLO, VALETTE? HEY, HOW ABOUT MEETING ME SOME-WHERE TONIGHT, SWEETS?
6-22
YOU'LL MEET ME WHEN **WHAT** FREEZES OVER?
© 1979 PAWS, INC. All Rights Reserved.
I CAN TAKE A HINT
ONLY IF IT'S APPLIED WITH A SLEDGEHAMMER
SLAM!
JIM DAVIS

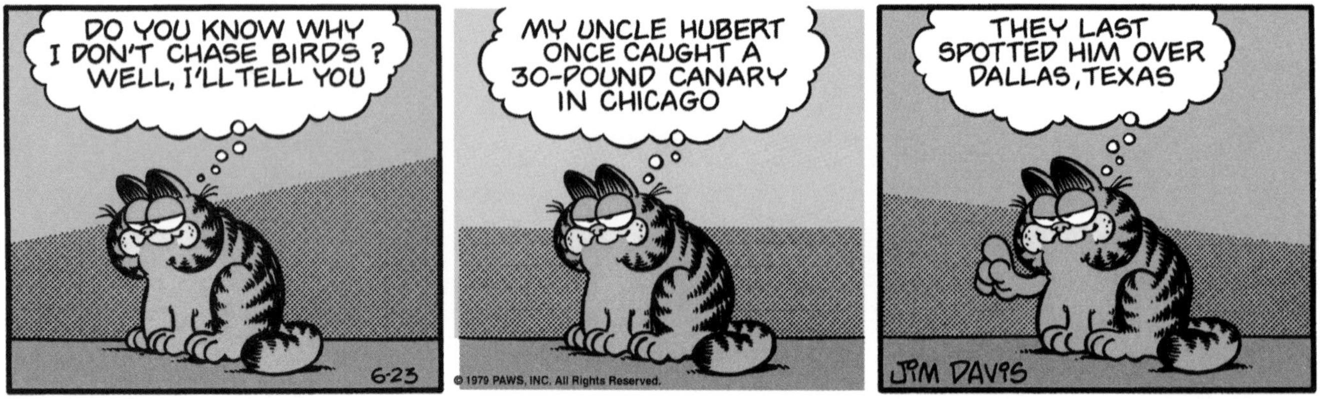
DO YOU KNOW WHY I DON'T CHASE BIRDS? WELL, I'LL TELL YOU
6-23
MY UNCLE HUBERT ONCE CAUGHT A 30-POUND CANARY IN CHICAGO
© 1979 PAWS, INC. All Rights Reserved.
THEY LAST SPOTTED HIM OVER DALLAS, TEXAS
JIM DAVIS

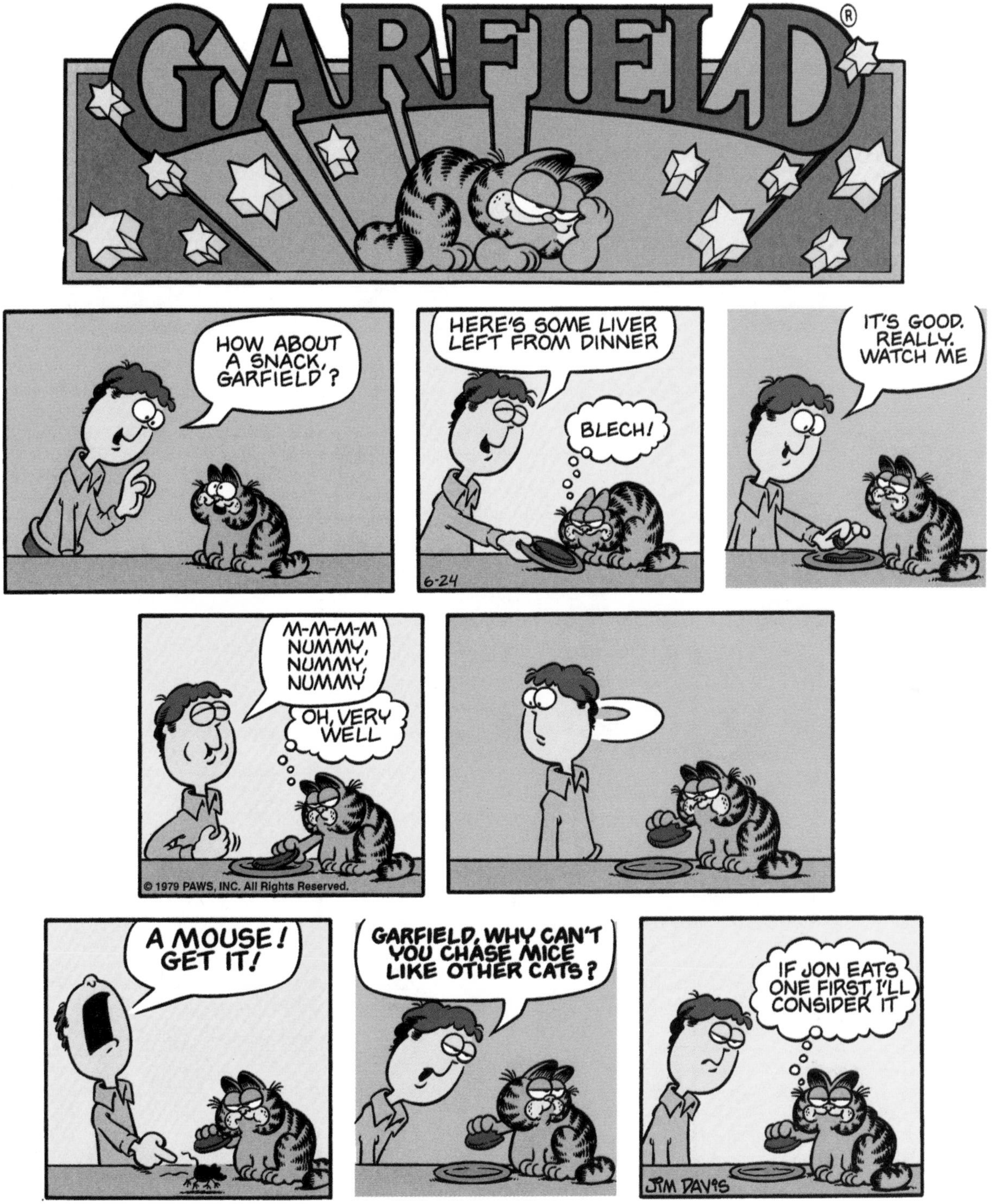
GARFIELD®
HOW ABOUT A SNACK, GARFIELD?
HERE'S SOME LIVER LEFT FROM DINNER
BLECH!
6-24
IT'S GOOD. REALLY. WATCH ME
M-M-M-M NUMMY, NUMMY, NUMMY
OH, VERY WELL
© 1979 PAWS, INC. All Rights Reserved.
A MOUSE! GET IT!
GARFIELD, WHY CAN'T YOU CHASE MICE LIKE OTHER CATS?
IF JON EATS ONE FIRST, I'LL CONSIDER IT
JIM DAVIS

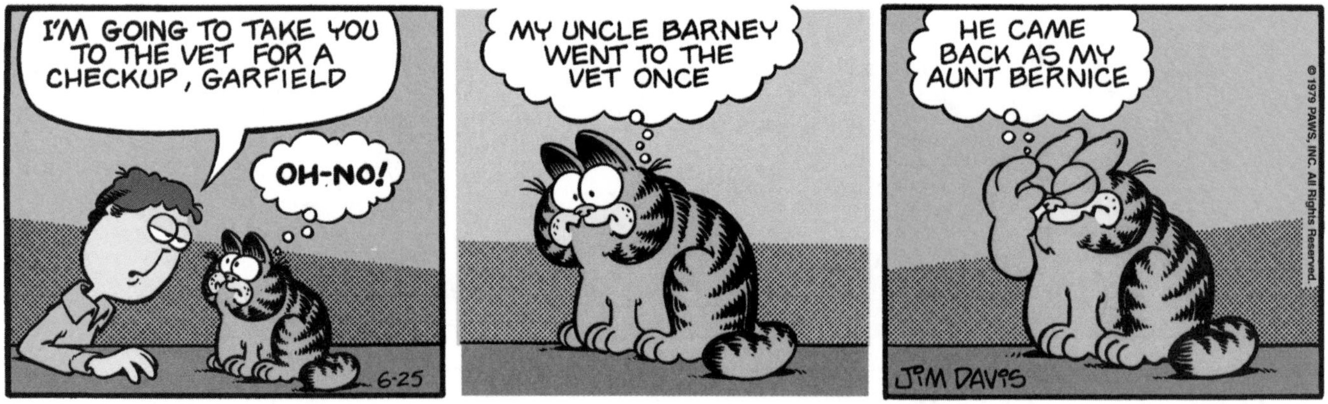
I'M GOING TO TAKE YOU TO THE VET FOR A CHECKUP, GARFIELD
OH-NO!
6-25
MY UNCLE BARNEY WENT TO THE VET ONCE
HE CAME BACK AS MY AUNT BERNICE
© 1979 PAWS, INC. All Rights Reserved.
JIM DAVIS

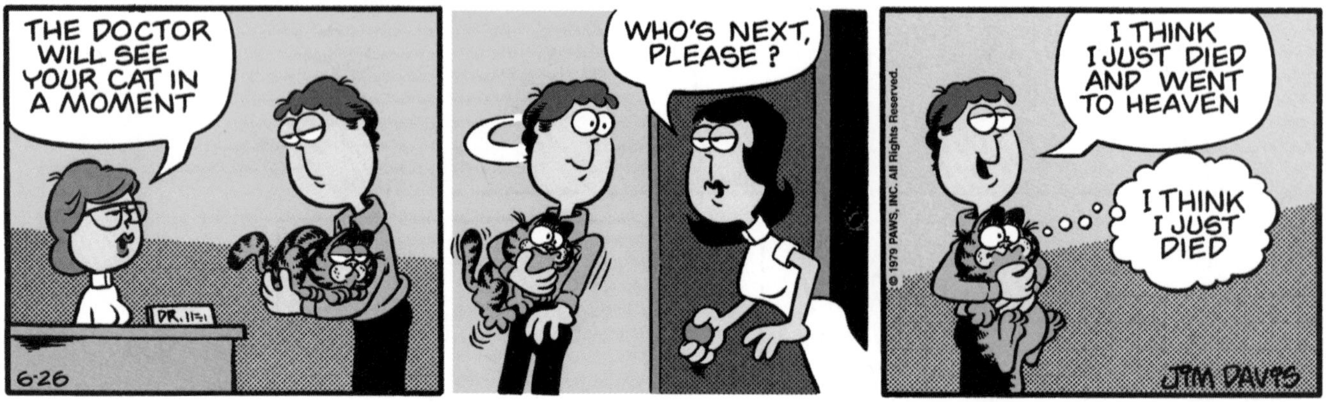
THE DOCTOR WILL SEE YOUR CAT IN A MOMENT
DR.
6-26
WHO'S NEXT, PLEASE?
© 1979 PAWS, INC. All Rights Reserved.
I THINK I JUST DIED AND WENT TO HEAVEN
I THINK I JUST DIED
JIM DAVIS

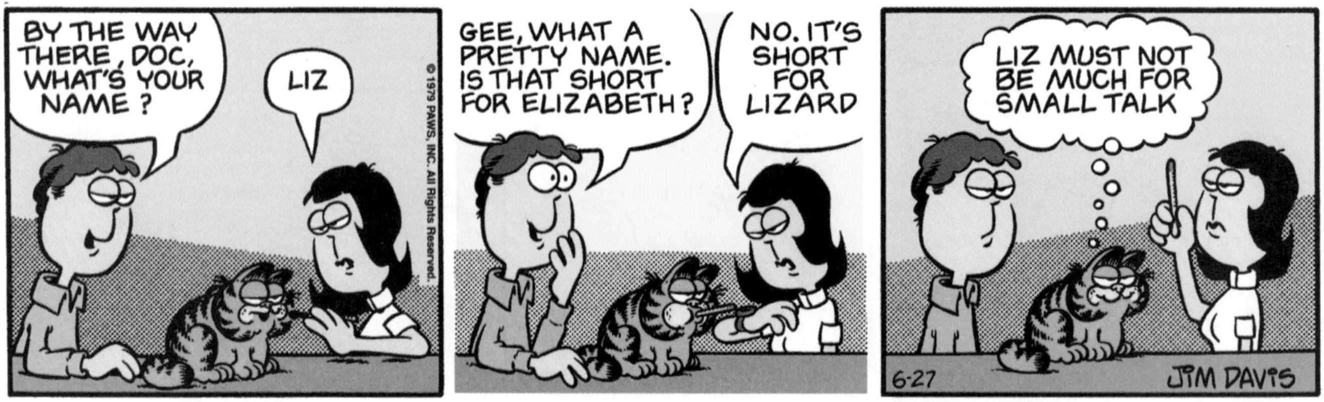
BY THE WAY THERE, DOC, WHAT'S YOUR NAME?
LIZ
© 1979 PAWS, INC. All Rights Reserved.
GEE, WHAT A PRETTY NAME. IS THAT SHORT FOR ELIZABETH?
NO. IT'S SHORT FOR LIZARD
LIZ MUST NOT BE MUCH FOR SMALL TALK
6-27
JIM DAVIS

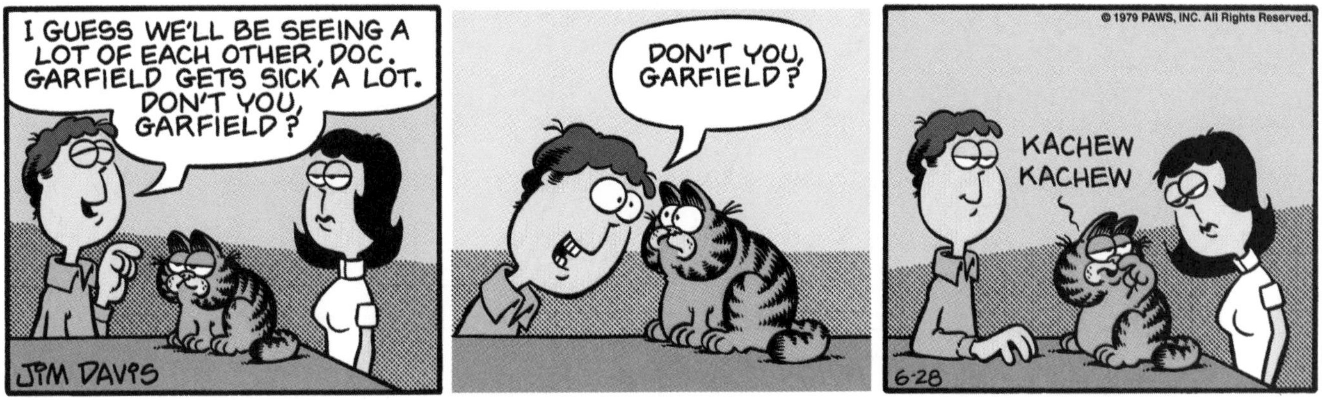
I GUESS WE'LL BE SEEING A LOT OF EACH OTHER, DOC. GARFIELD GETS SICK A LOT. DON'T YOU, GARFIELD?
JIM DAVIS
DON'T YOU, GARFIELD?
© 1979 PAWS, INC. All Rights Reserved.
KACHEW KACHEW
6-28

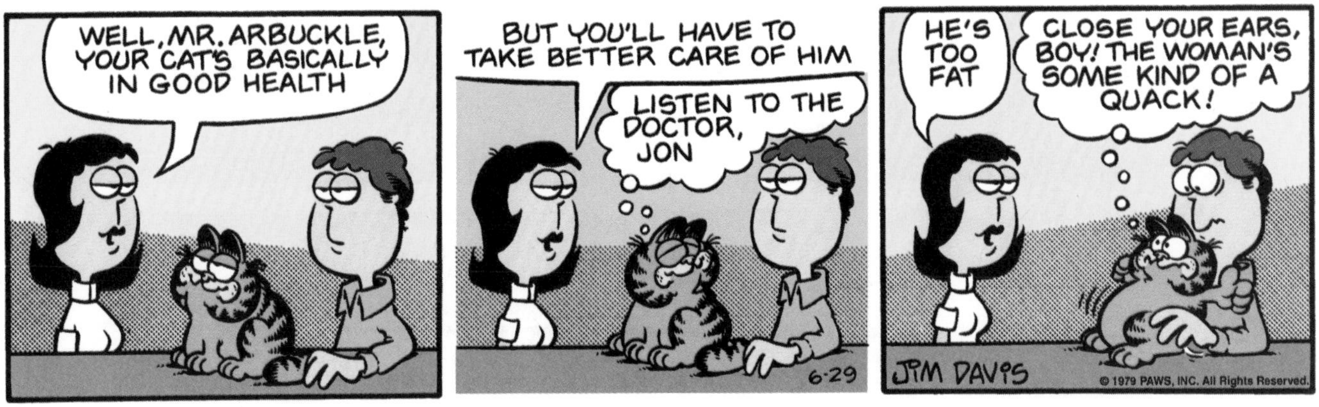
WELL, MR. ARBUCKLE, YOUR CAT'S BASICALLY IN GOOD HEALTH
BUT YOU'LL HAVE TO TAKE BETTER CARE OF HIM
LISTEN TO THE DOCTOR, JON
6-29
HE'S TOO FAT
CLOSE YOUR EARS, BOY! THE WOMAN'S SOME KIND OF A QUACK!
JIM DAVIS
© 1979 PAWS, INC. All Rights Reserved.

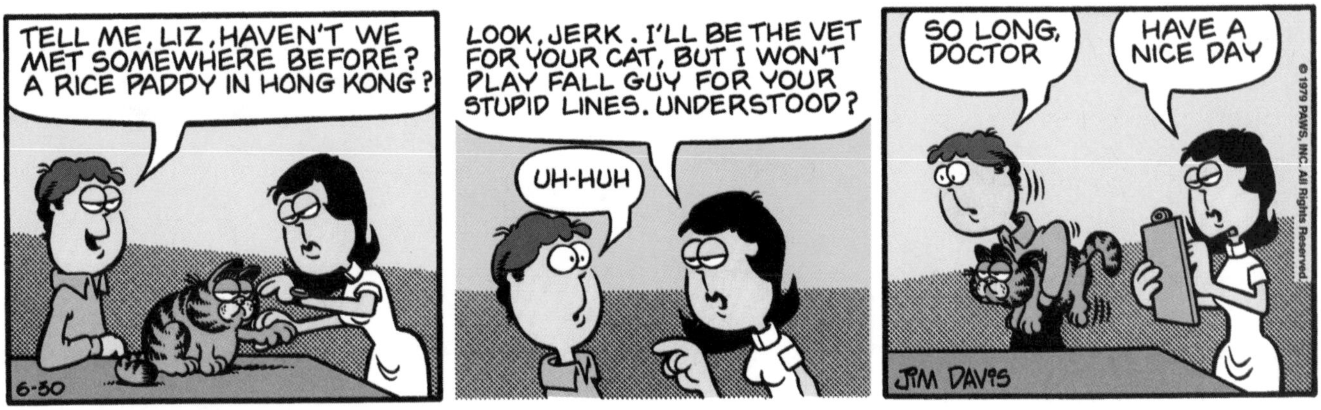
TELL ME, LIZ, HAVEN'T WE MET SOMEWHERE BEFORE? A RICE PADDY IN HONG KONG?
6-30
LOOK, JERK. I'LL BE THE VET FOR YOUR CAT, BUT I WON'T PLAY FALL GUY FOR YOUR STUPID LINES. UNDERSTOOD?
UH-HUH
SO LONG, DOCTOR
HAVE A NICE DAY
© 1979 PAWS, INC. All Rights Reserved.
JIM DAVIS

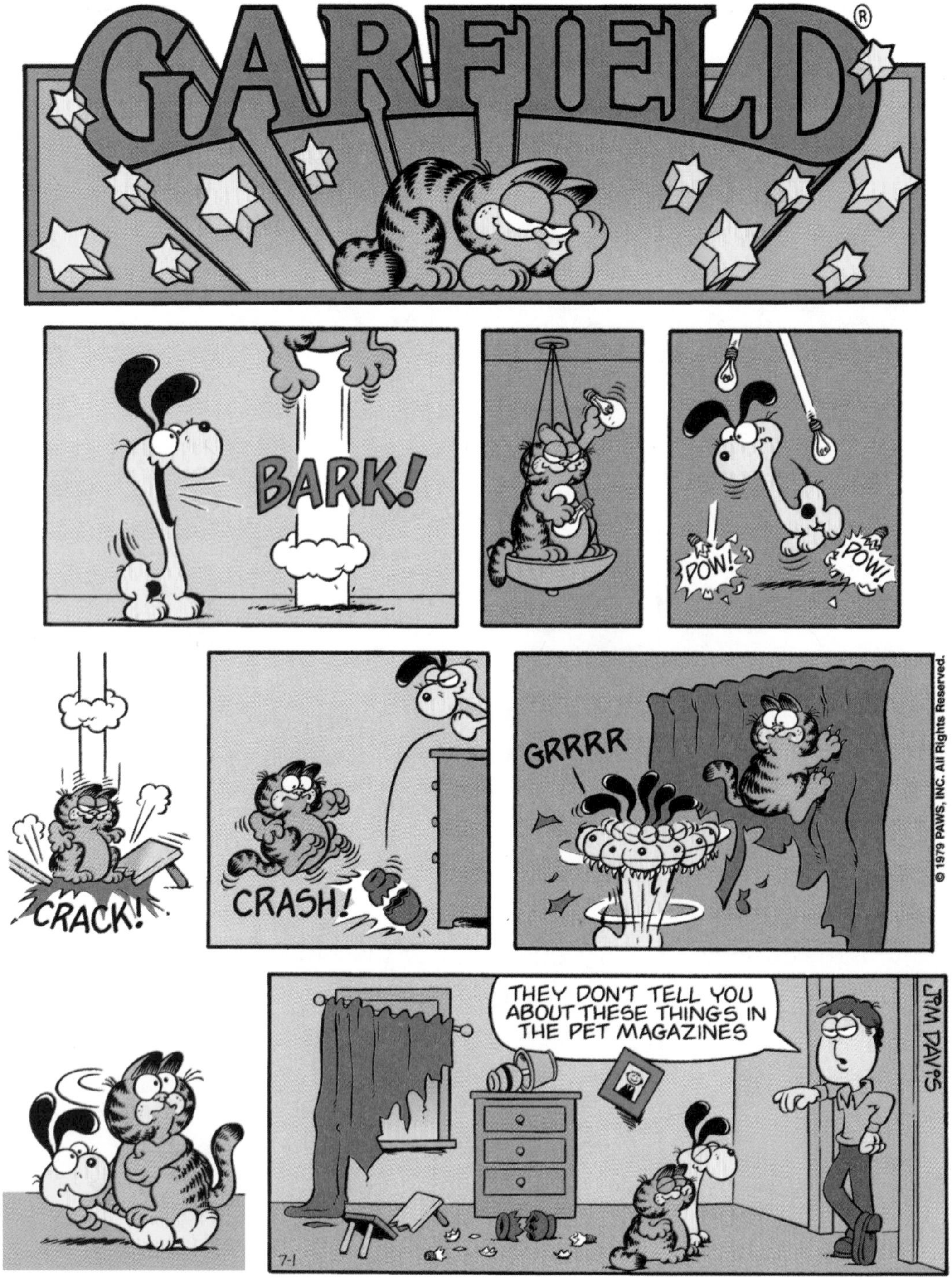
GARFIELD®
BARK!
POW!
POW!
CRACK!
CRASH!
GRRRR
© 1979 PAWS, INC. All Rights Reserved.
THEY DON'T TELL YOU ABOUT THESE THINGS IN THE PET MAGAZINES
JIM DAVIS
7-1

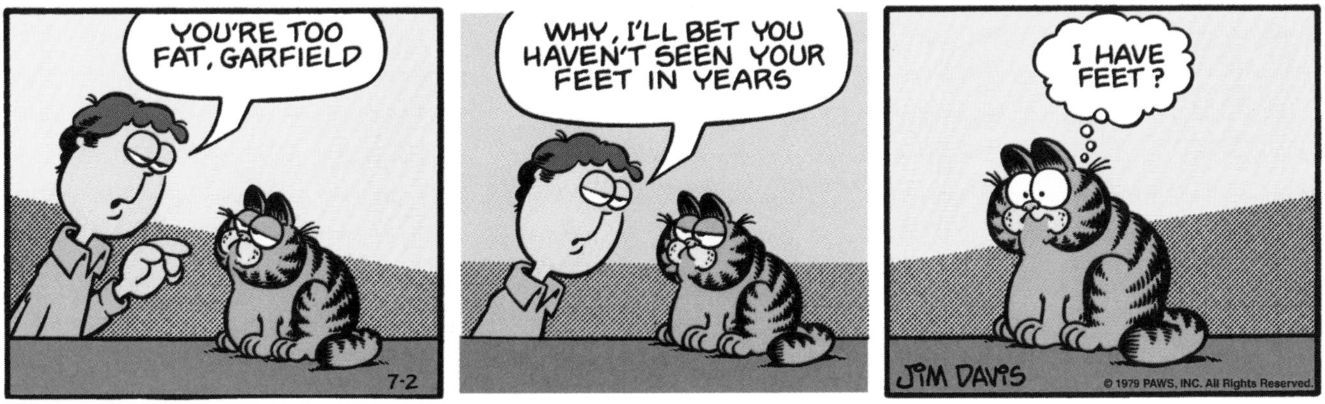
YOU'RE TOO FAT, GARFIELD
7-2
WHY, I'LL BET YOU HAVEN'T SEEN YOUR FEET IN YEARS
I HAVE FEET?
JIM DAVIS
© 1979 PAWS, INC. All Rights Reserved.

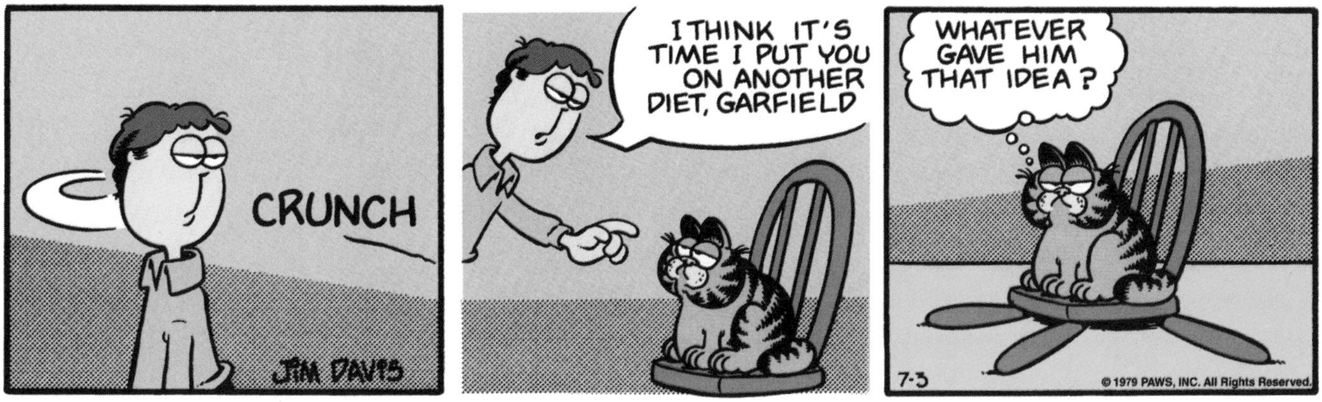
CRUNCH
JIM DAVIS
I THINK IT'S TIME I PUT YOU ON ANOTHER DIET, GARFIELD
WHATEVER GAVE HIM THAT IDEA?
7-3
© 1979 PAWS, INC. All Rights Reserved.

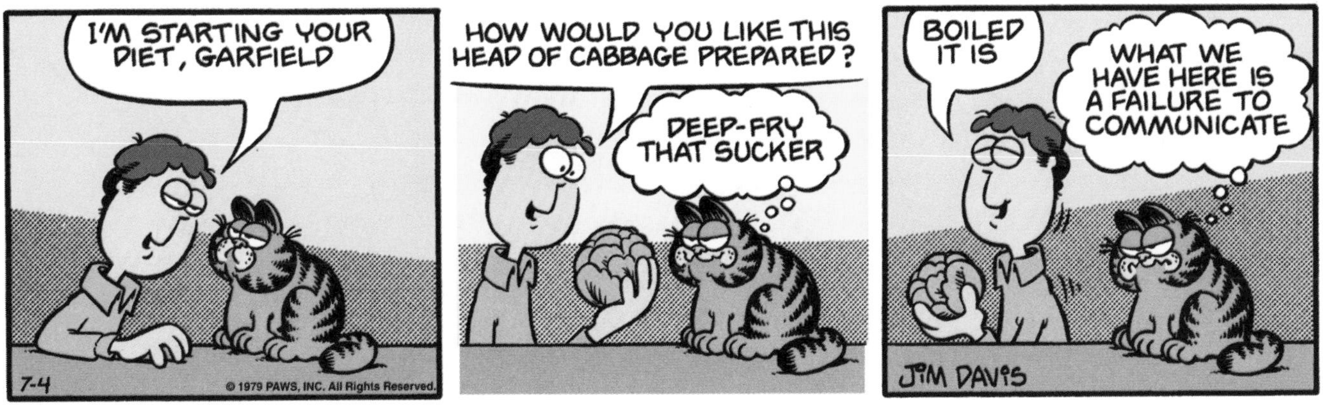
I'M STARTING YOUR DIET, GARFIELD
7-4
© 1979 PAWS, INC. All Rights Reserved.
HOW WOULD YOU LIKE THIS HEAD OF CABBAGE PREPARED?
DEEP-FRY THAT SUCKER
BOILED IT IS
WHAT WE HAVE HERE IS A FAILURE TO COMMUNICATE
JIM DAVIS

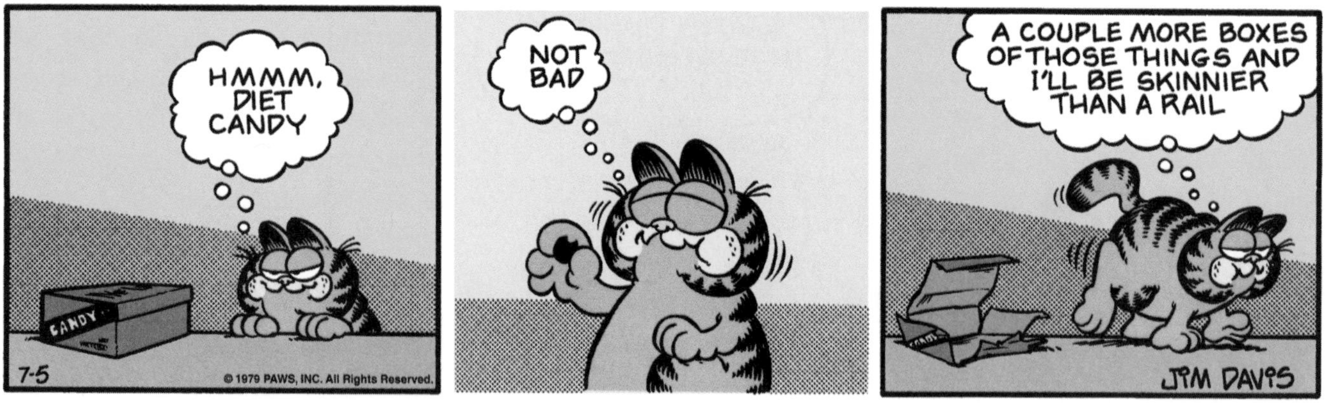

HMMM, DIET CANDY
CANDY
7-5
© 1979 PAWS, INC. All Rights Reserved.
NOT BAD
A COUPLE MORE BOXES OF THOSE THINGS AND I'LL BE SKINNIER THAN A RAIL
JIM DAVIS

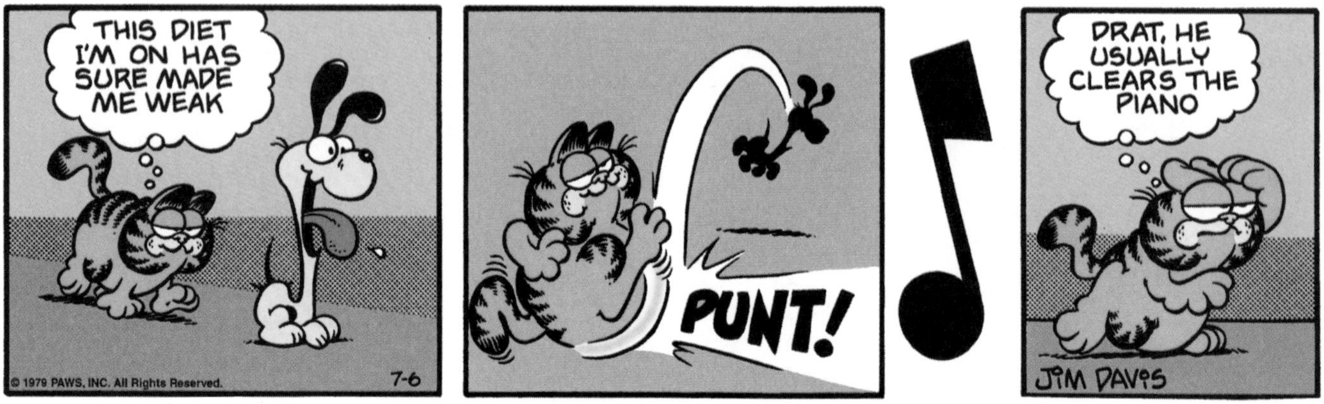

THIS DIET I'M ON HAS SURE MADE ME WEAK
© 1979 PAWS, INC. All Rights Reserved.
7-6
PUNT!
DRAT, HE USUALLY CLEARS THE PIANO
JIM DAVIS

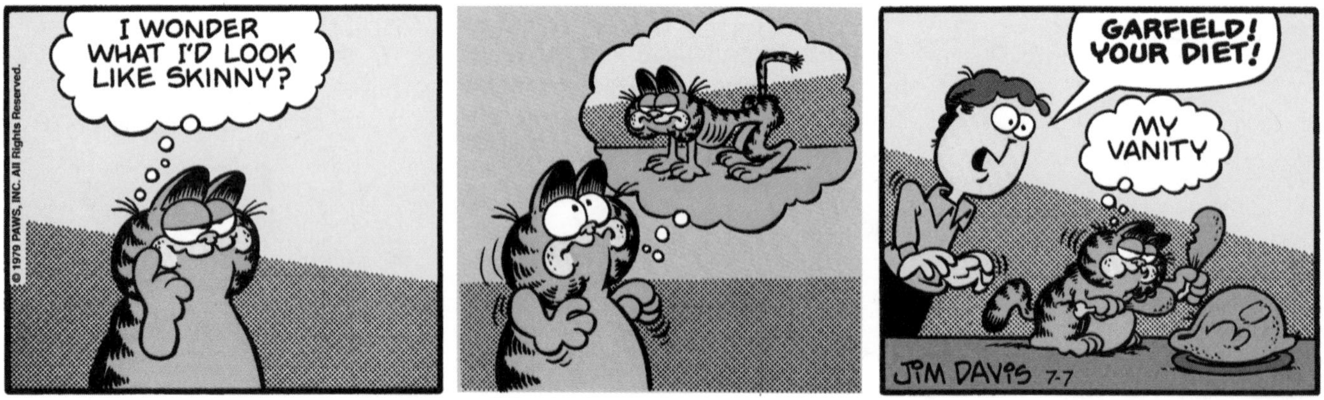

I WONDER WHAT I'D LOOK LIKE SKINNY?
© 1979 PAWS, INC. All Rights Reserved.
GARFIELD! YOUR DIET!
MY VANITY
JIM DAVIS 7-7

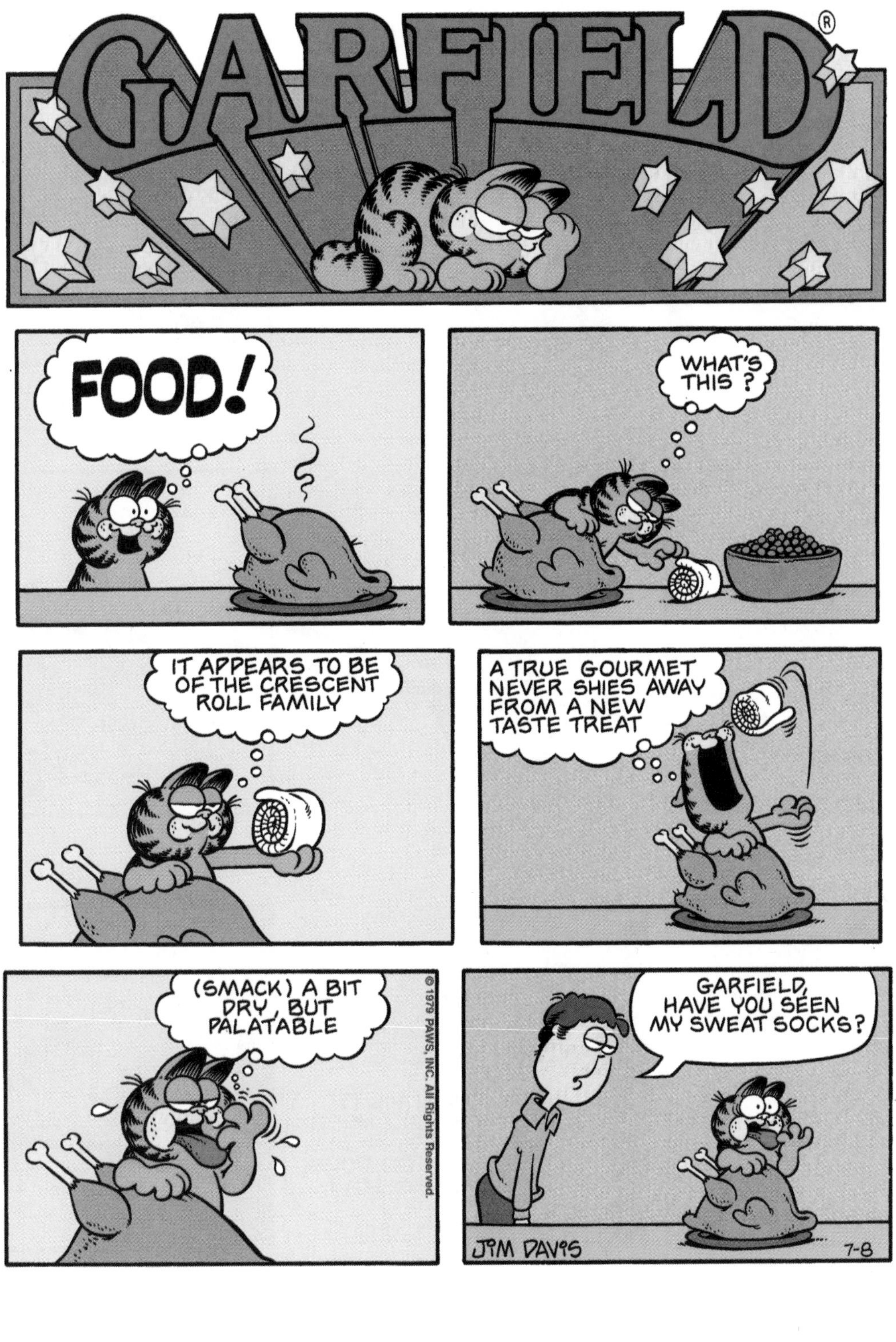
GARFIELD®
FOOD!
WHAT'S THIS ?
IT APPEARS TO BE OF THE CRESCENT ROLL FAMILY
A TRUE GOURMET NEVER SHIES AWAY FROM A NEW TASTE TREAT
(SMACK) A BIT DRY, BUT PALATABLE
GARFIELD, HAVE YOU SEEN MY SWEAT SOCKS?
JIM DAVIS
7-8

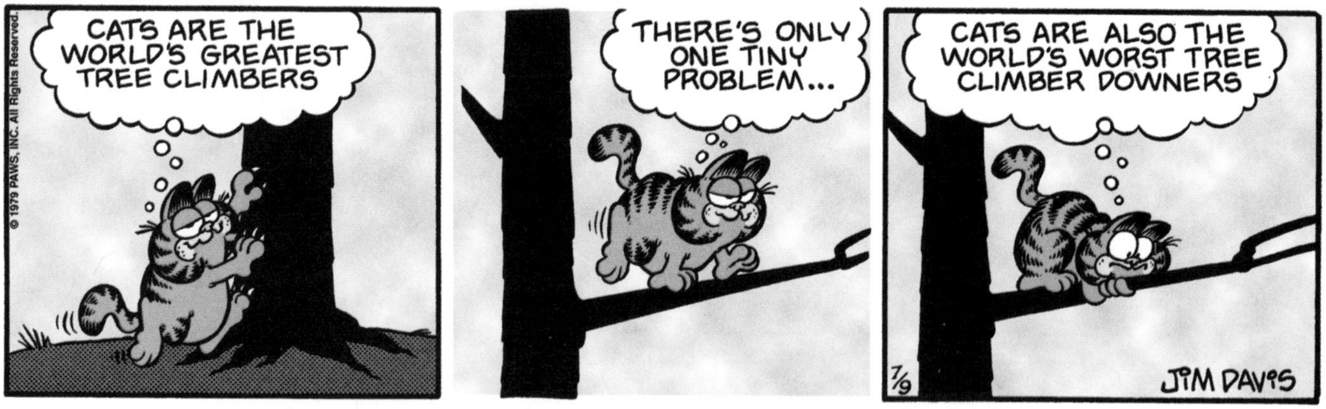
© 1979 PAWS, INC. All Rights Reserved.
CATS ARE THE WORLD'S GREATEST TREE CLIMBERS
THERE'S ONLY ONE TINY PROBLEM...
CATS ARE ALSO THE WORLD'S WORST TREE CLIMBER DOWNERS
7/9
JIM DAVIS

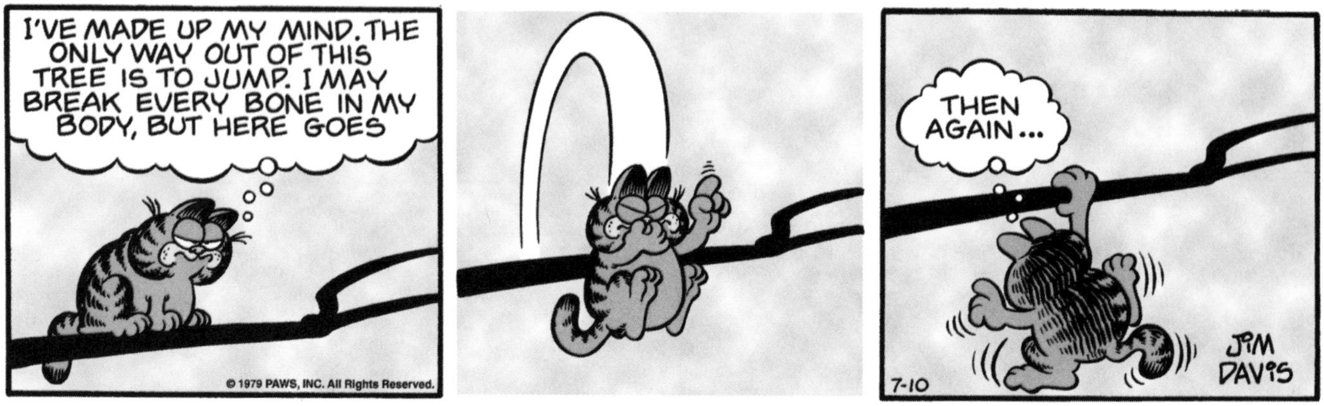
I'VE MADE UP MY MIND. THE ONLY WAY OUT OF THIS TREE IS TO JUMP. I MAY BREAK EVERY BONE IN MY BODY, BUT HERE GOES
© 1979 PAWS, INC. All Rights Reserved.
THEN AGAIN...
7-10
JIM DAVIS

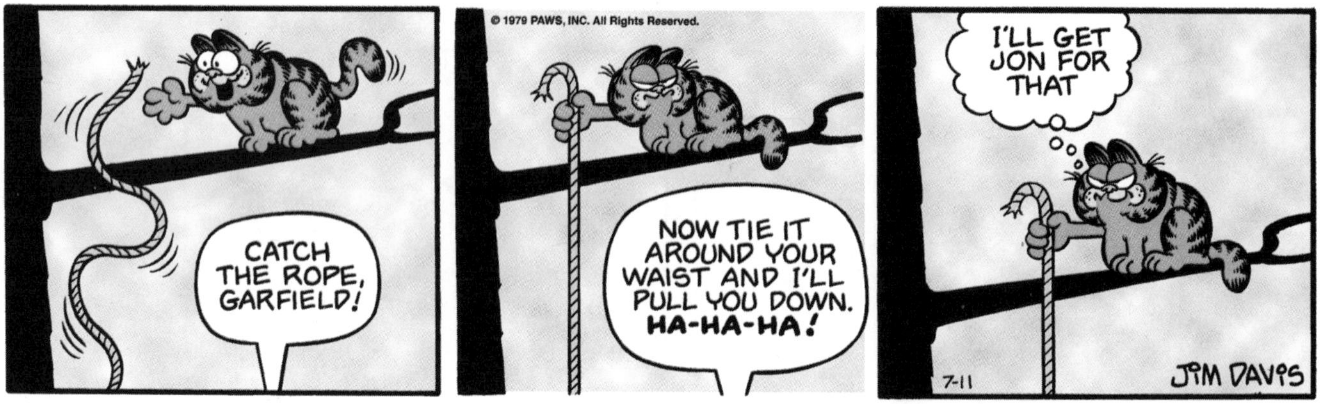
CATCH THE ROPE, GARFIELD!
© 1979 PAWS, INC. All Rights Reserved.
NOW TIE IT AROUND YOUR WAIST AND I'LL PULL YOU DOWN. HA-HA-HA!
I'LL GET JON FOR THAT
7-11
JIM DAVIS

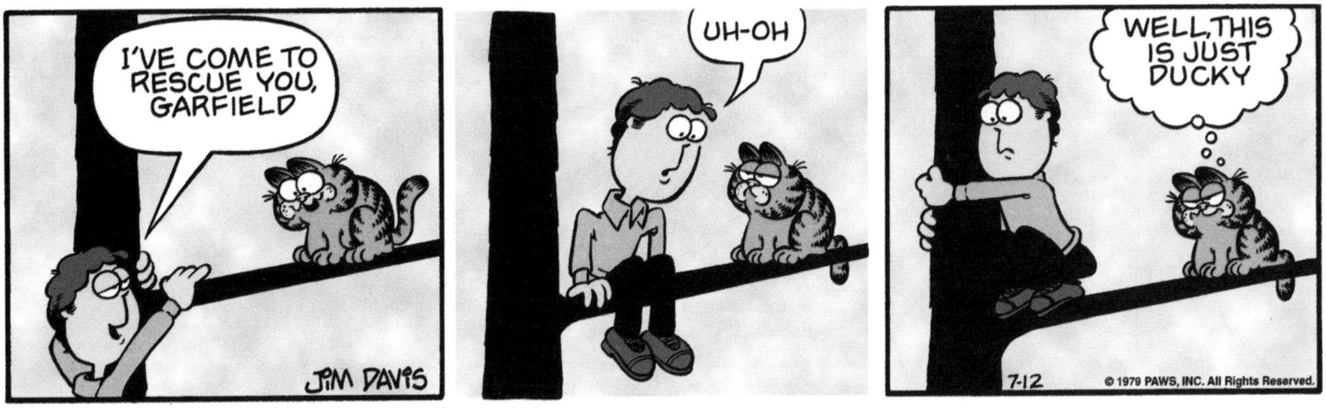
I'VE COME TO RESCUE YOU, GARFIELD
JIM DAVIS
UH-OH
WELL, THIS IS JUST DUCKY
7-12
© 1979 PAWS, INC. All Rights Reserved.

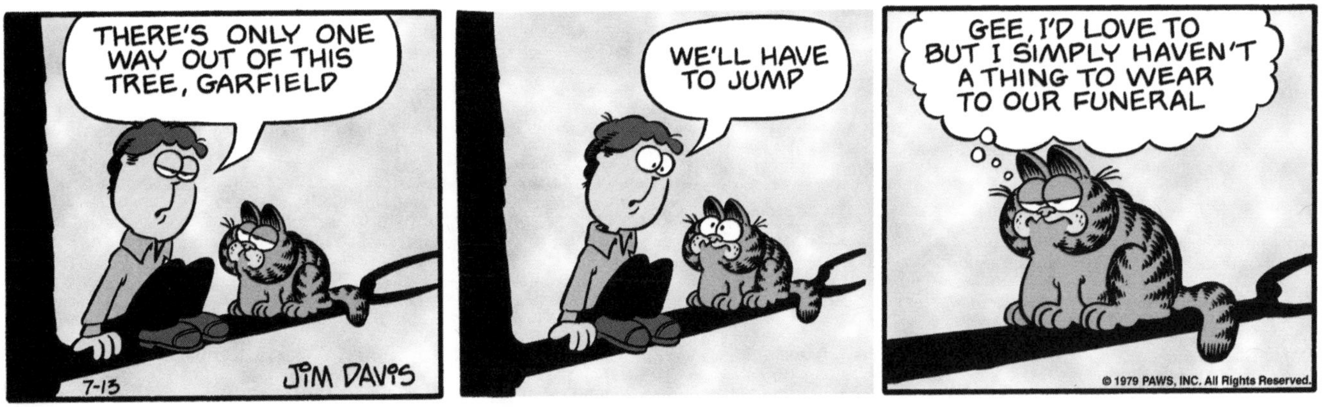
THERE'S ONLY ONE WAY OUT OF THIS TREE, GARFIELD
7-13
JIM DAVIS
WE'LL HAVE TO JUMP
GEE, I'D LOVE TO BUT I SIMPLY HAVEN'T A THING TO WEAR TO OUR FUNERAL
© 1979 PAWS, INC. All Rights Reserved.

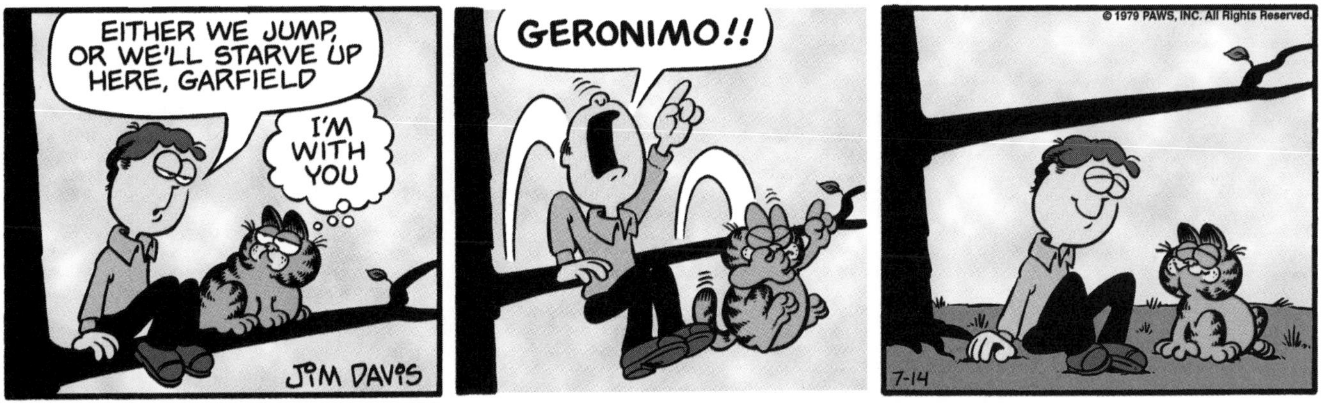
EITHER WE JUMP, OR WE'LL STARVE UP HERE, GARFIELD
I'M WITH YOU
JIM DAVIS
GERONIMO!!
© 1979 PAWS, INC. All Rights Reserved.
7-14

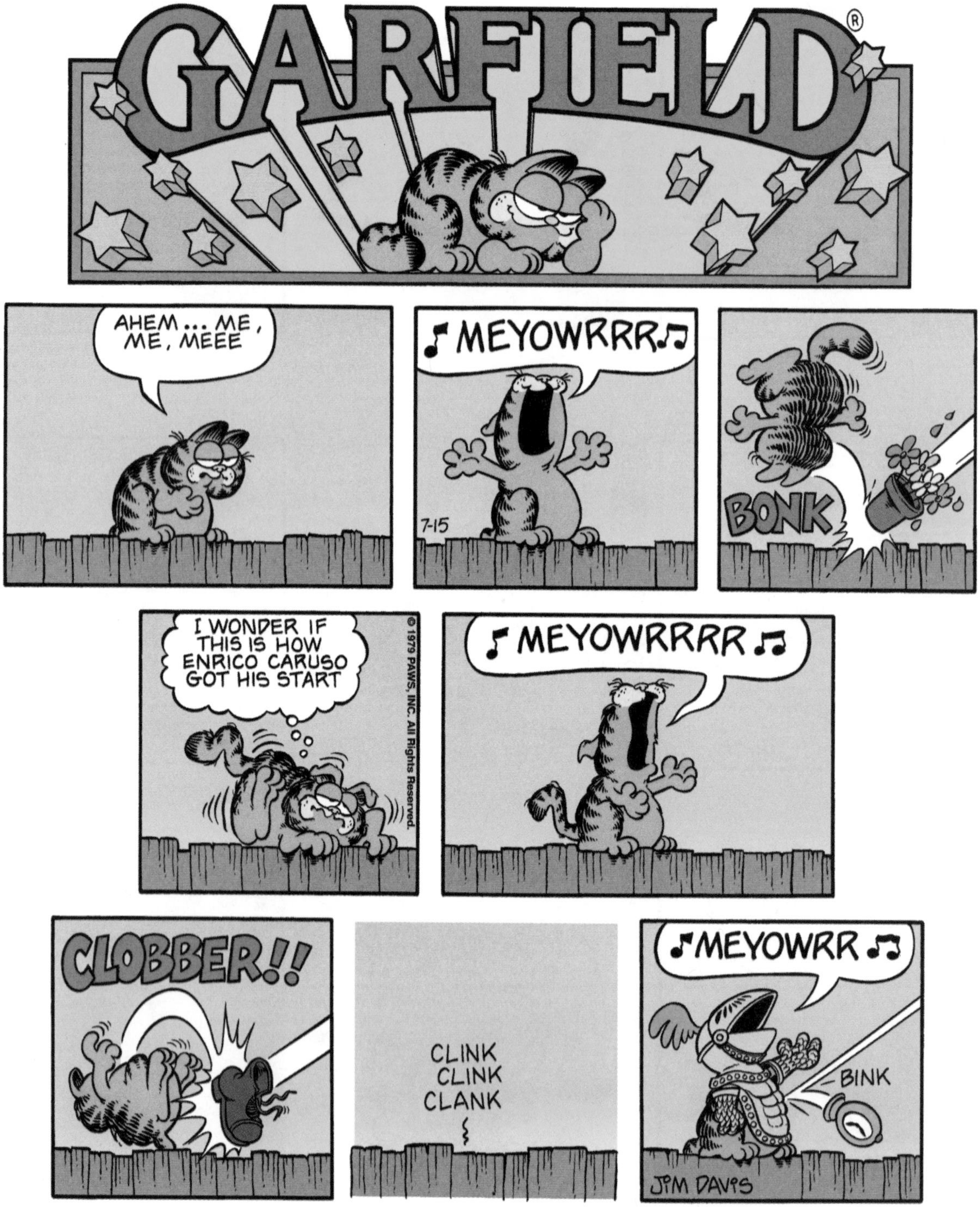
GARFIELD®
AHEM... ME, ME, MEEE
MEYOWRRR
7-15
BONK
I WONDER IF THIS IS HOW ENRICO CARUSO GOT HIS START
© 1979 PAWS, INC. All Rights Reserved.
MEYOWRRRR
CLOBBER!!
CLINK CLINK CLANK
MEYOWRR
BINK
JIM DAVIS

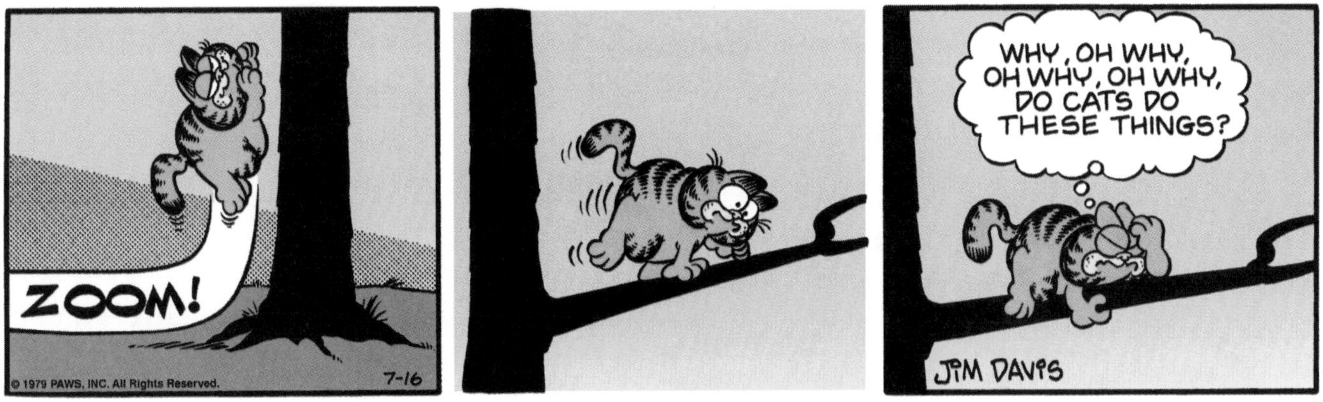
ZOOM!
© 1979 PAWS, INC. All Rights Reserved.
7-16
WHY, OH WHY, OH WHY, OH WHY, DO CATS DO THESE THINGS?
JIM DAVIS

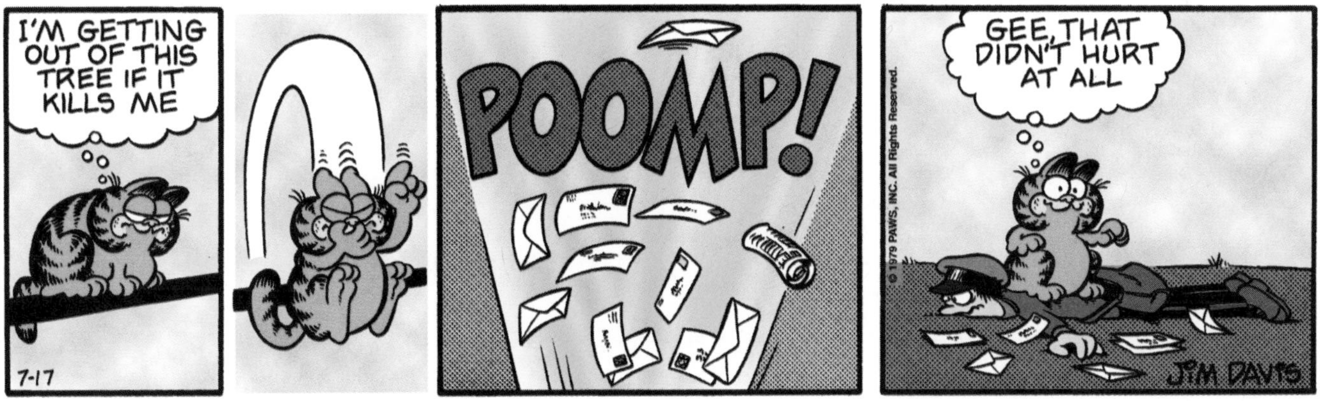
I'M GETTING OUT OF THIS TREE IF IT KILLS ME
7-17
POOMP!
© 1979 PAWS, INC. All Rights Reserved.
GEE, THAT DIDN'T HURT AT ALL
JIM DAVIS

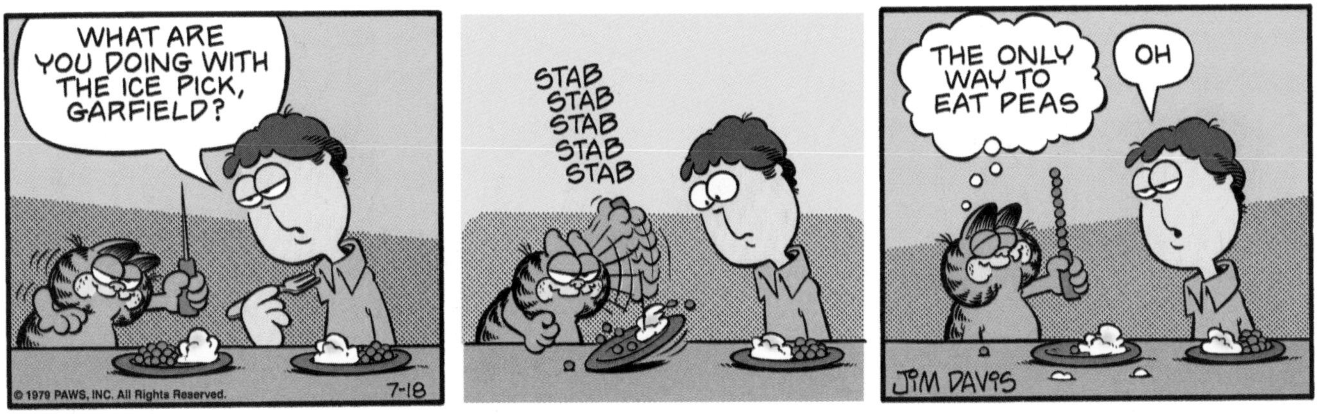
WHAT ARE YOU DOING WITH THE ICE PICK, GARFIELD?
© 1979 PAWS, INC. All Rights Reserved.
7-18
STAB STAB STAB STAB STAB
THE ONLY WAY TO EAT PEAS
OH
JIM DAVIS

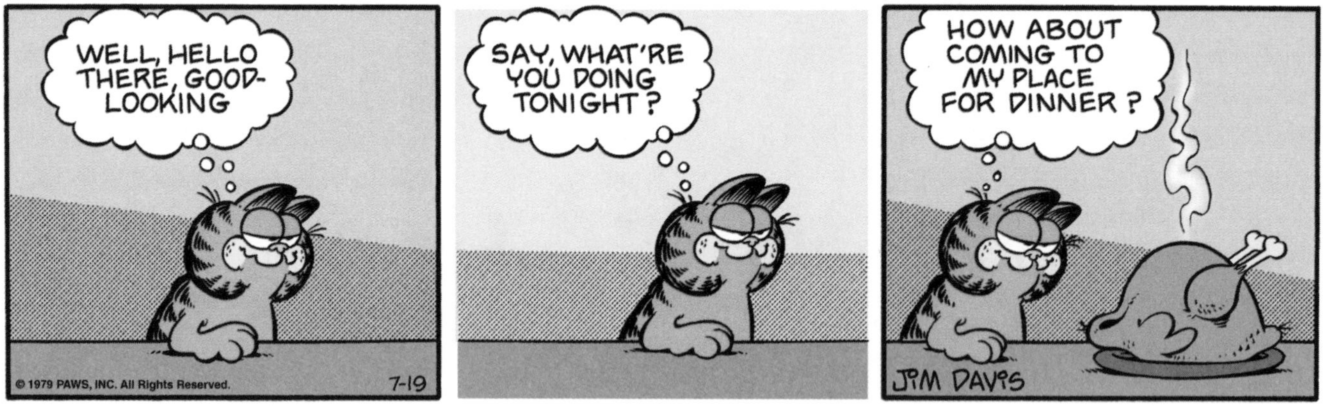
WELL, HELLO THERE, GOOD-LOOKING
SAY, WHAT'RE YOU DOING TONIGHT?
HOW ABOUT COMING TO MY PLACE FOR DINNER?
© 1979 PAWS, INC. All Rights Reserved.
7-19
JIM DAVIS

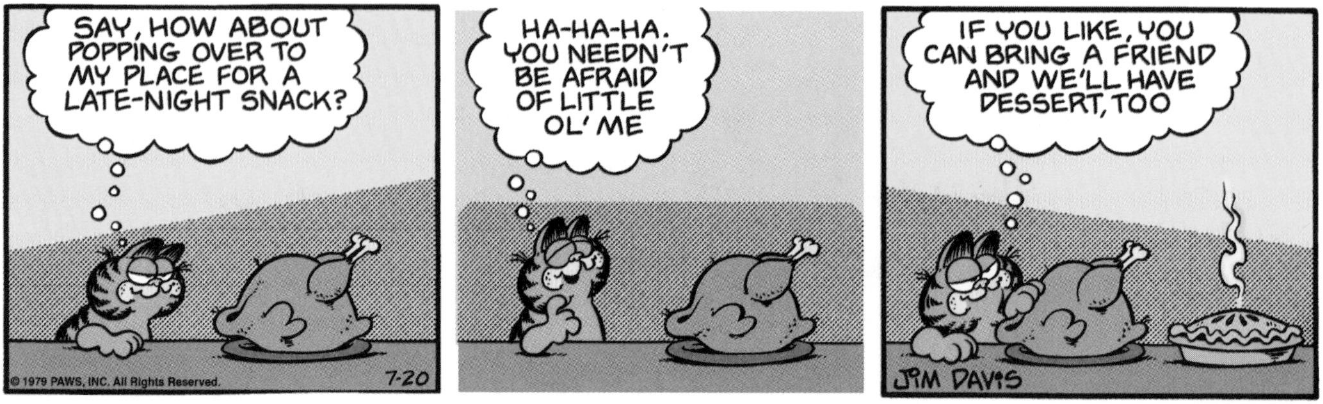
SAY, HOW ABOUT POPPING OVER TO MY PLACE FOR A LATE-NIGHT SNACK?
HA-HA-HA. YOU NEEDN'T BE AFRAID OF LITTLE OL' ME
IF YOU LIKE, YOU CAN BRING A FRIEND AND WE'LL HAVE DESSERT, TOO
© 1979 PAWS, INC. All Rights Reserved.
7-20
JIM DAVIS

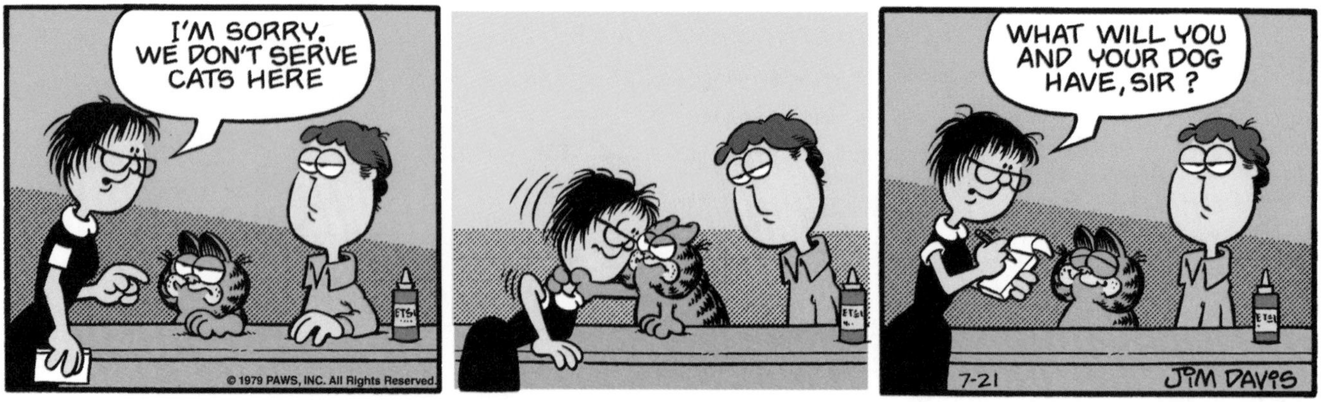
I'M SORRY. WE DON'T SERVE CATS HERE
WHAT WILL YOU AND YOUR DOG HAVE, SIR?
© 1979 PAWS, INC. All Rights Reserved.
7-21
JIM DAVIS

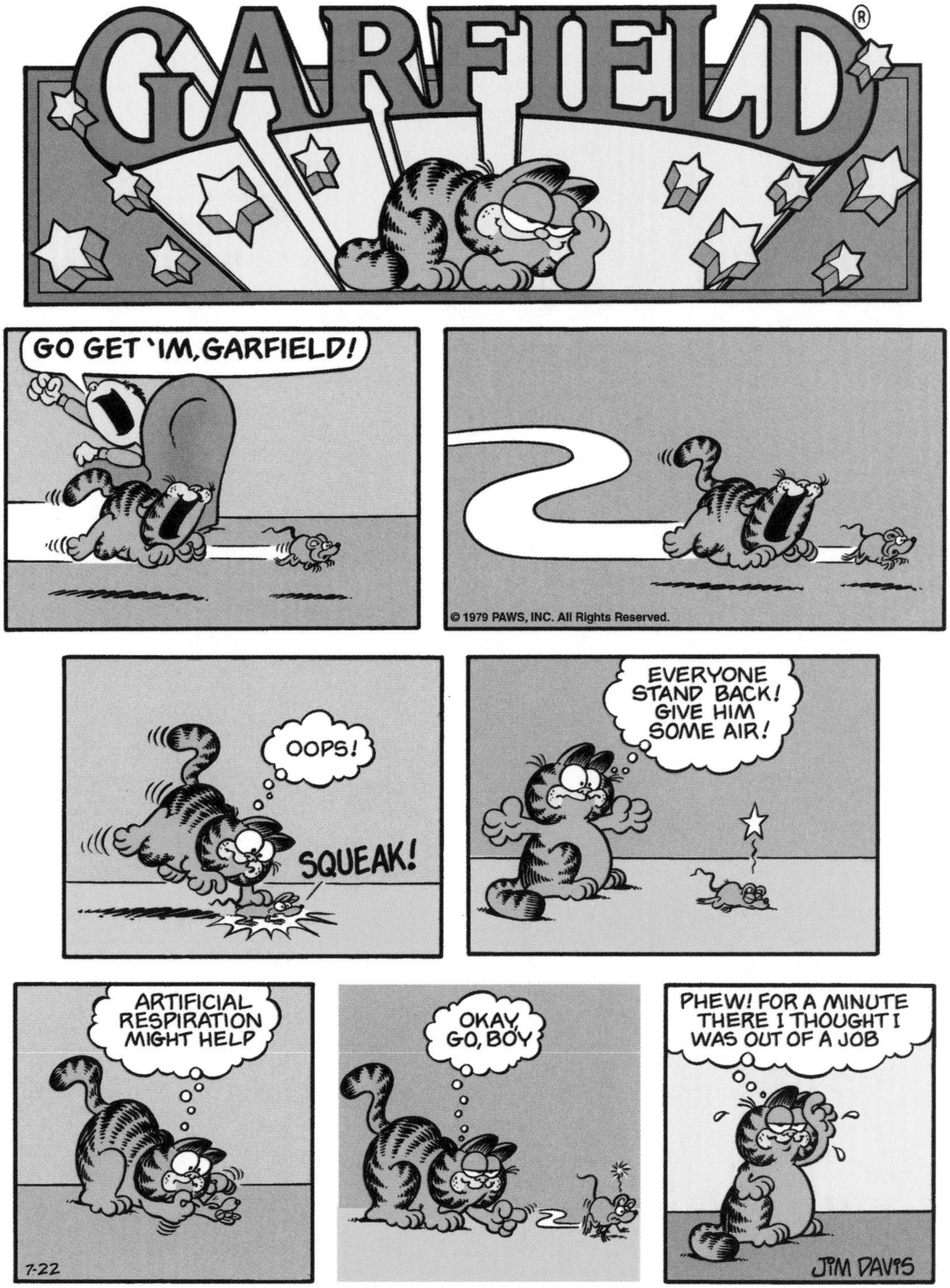
GARFIELD®
GO GET 'IM, GARFIELD!
© 1979 PAWS, INC. All Rights Reserved.
OOPS!
SQUEAK!
EVERYONE STAND BACK! GIVE HIM SOME AIR!
ARTIFICIAL RESPIRATION MIGHT HELP
OKAY, GO, BOY
PHEW! FOR A MINUTE THERE I THOUGHT I WAS OUT OF A JOB
7-22
JIM DAVIS

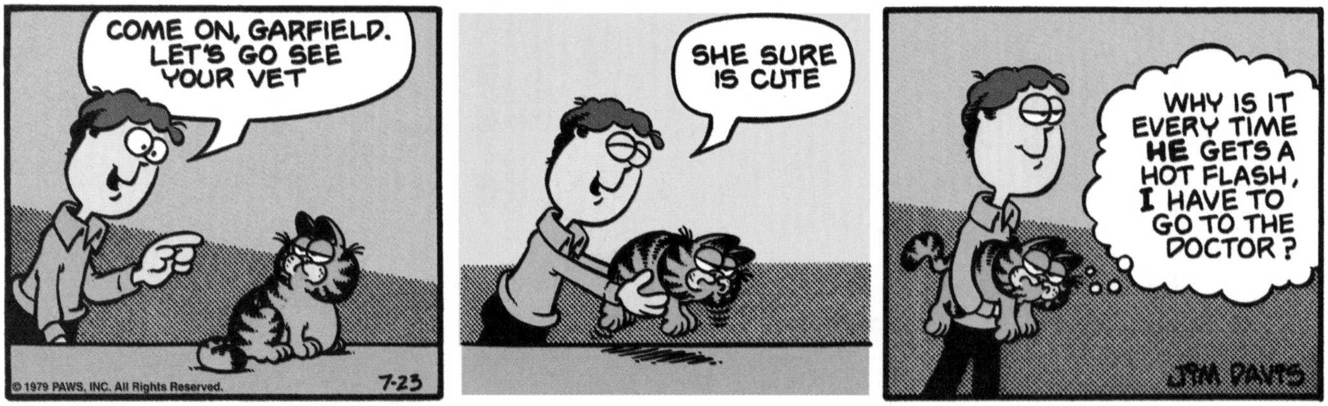
COME ON, GARFIELD. LET'S GO SEE YOUR VET
© 1979 PAWS, INC. All Rights Reserved.
7-23
SHE SURE IS CUTE
WHY IS IT EVERY TIME **HE** GETS A HOT FLASH, **I** HAVE TO GO TO THE DOCTOR?
JIM DAVIS

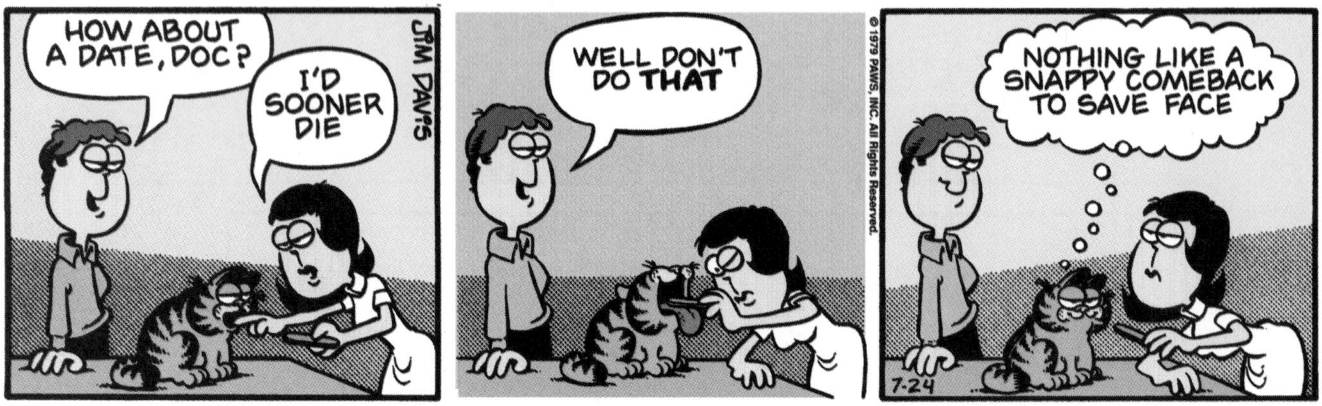
HOW ABOUT A DATE, DOC?
I'D SOONER DIE
JIM DAVIS
WELL DON'T DO **THAT**
© 1979 PAWS, INC. All Rights Reserved.
NOTHING LIKE A SNAPPY COMEBACK TO SAVE FACE
7-24

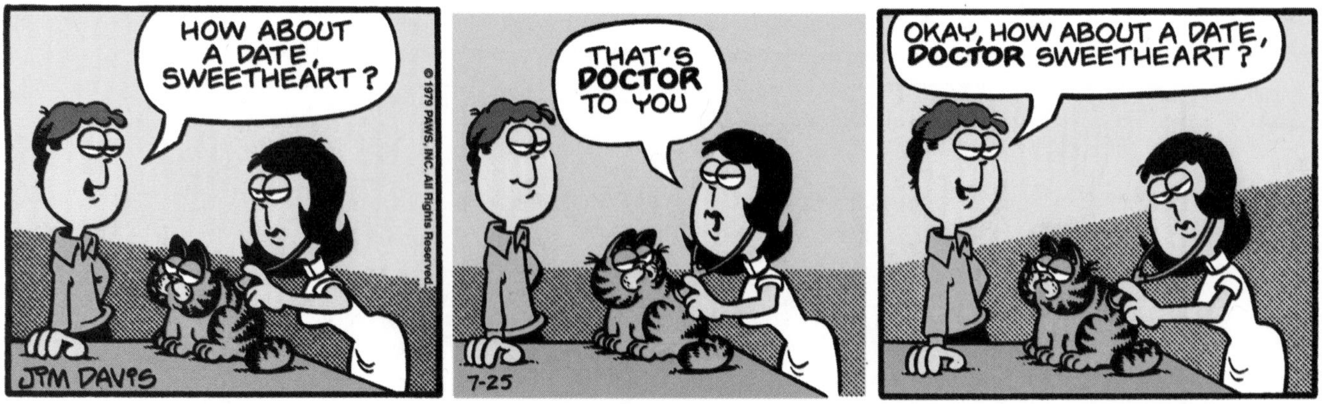
HOW ABOUT A DATE, SWEETHEART?
© 1979 PAWS, INC. All Rights Reserved.
JIM DAVIS
THAT'S **DOCTOR** TO YOU
7-25
OKAY, HOW ABOUT A DATE, **DOCTOR** SWEETHEART?

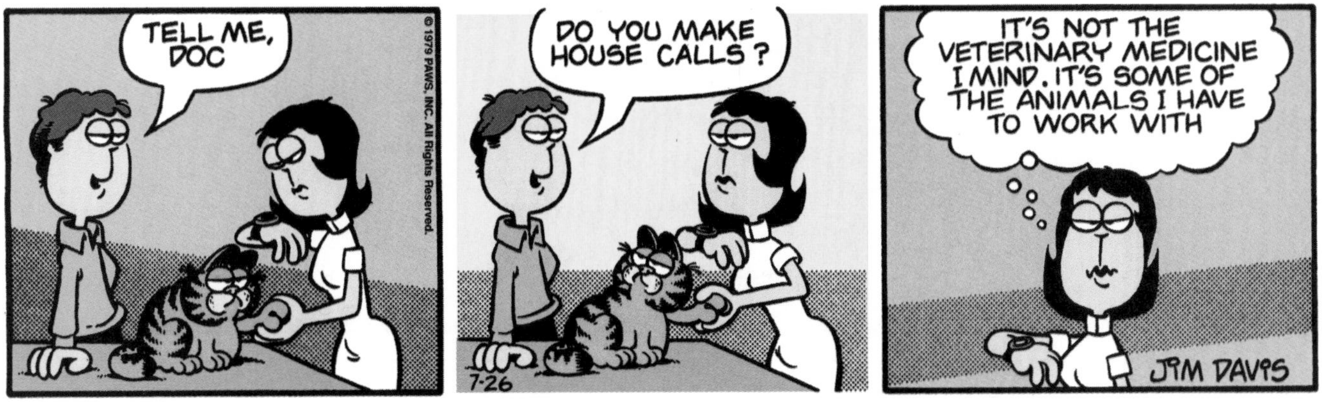
TELL ME, DOC
© 1979 PAWS, INC. All Rights Reserved.
DO YOU MAKE HOUSE CALLS?
7-26
IT'S NOT THE VETERINARY MEDICINE I MIND. IT'S SOME OF THE ANIMALS I HAVE TO WORK WITH
JIM DAVIS

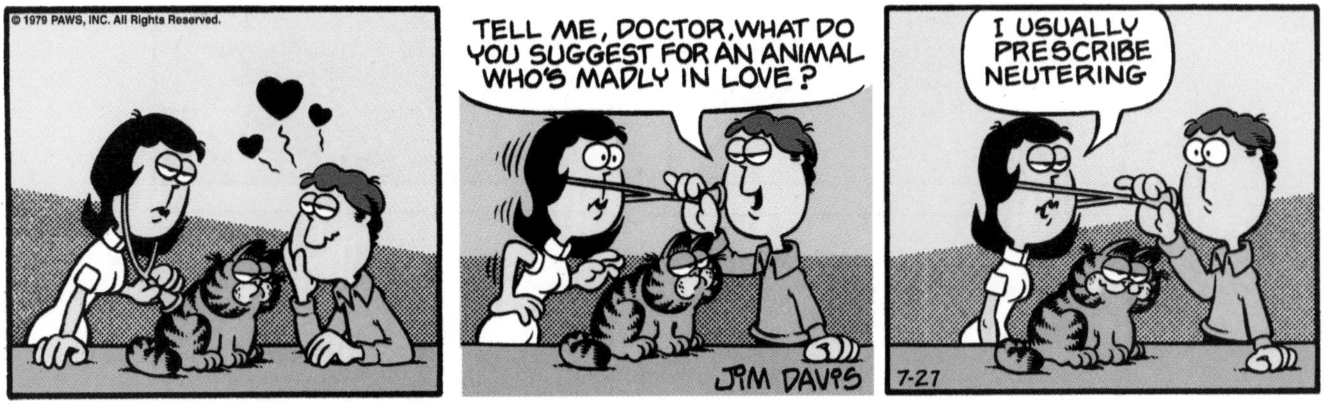
© 1979 PAWS, INC. All Rights Reserved.
TELL ME, DOCTOR, WHAT DO YOU SUGGEST FOR AN ANIMAL WHO'S MADLY IN LOVE?
JIM DAVIS
I USUALLY PRESCRIBE NEUTERING
7-27

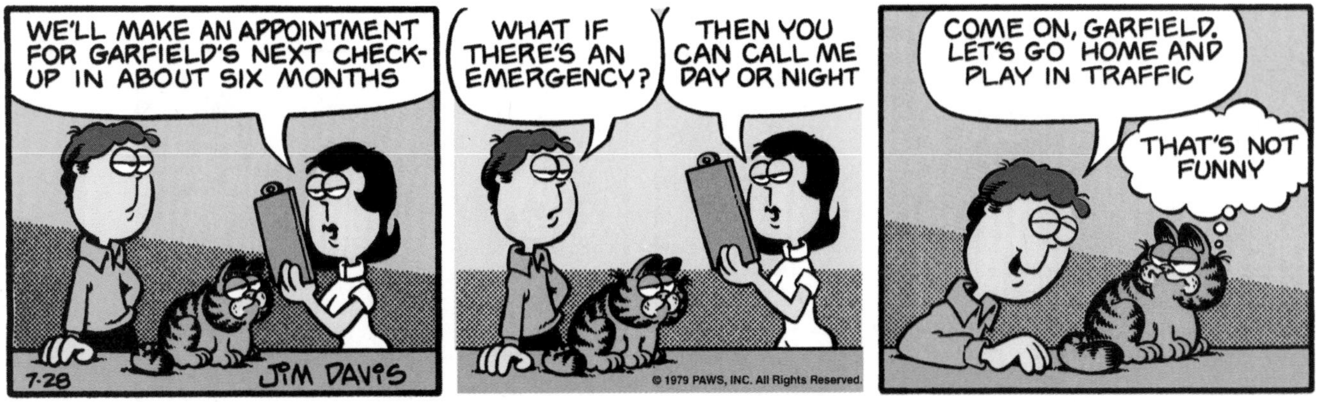
WE'LL MAKE AN APPOINTMENT FOR GARFIELD'S NEXT CHECK-UP IN ABOUT SIX MONTHS
7-28
JIM DAVIS
WHAT IF THERE'S AN EMERGENCY?
THEN YOU CAN CALL ME DAY OR NIGHT
© 1979 PAWS, INC. All Rights Reserved.
COME ON, GARFIELD. LET'S GO HOME AND PLAY IN TRAFFIC
THAT'S NOT FUNNY

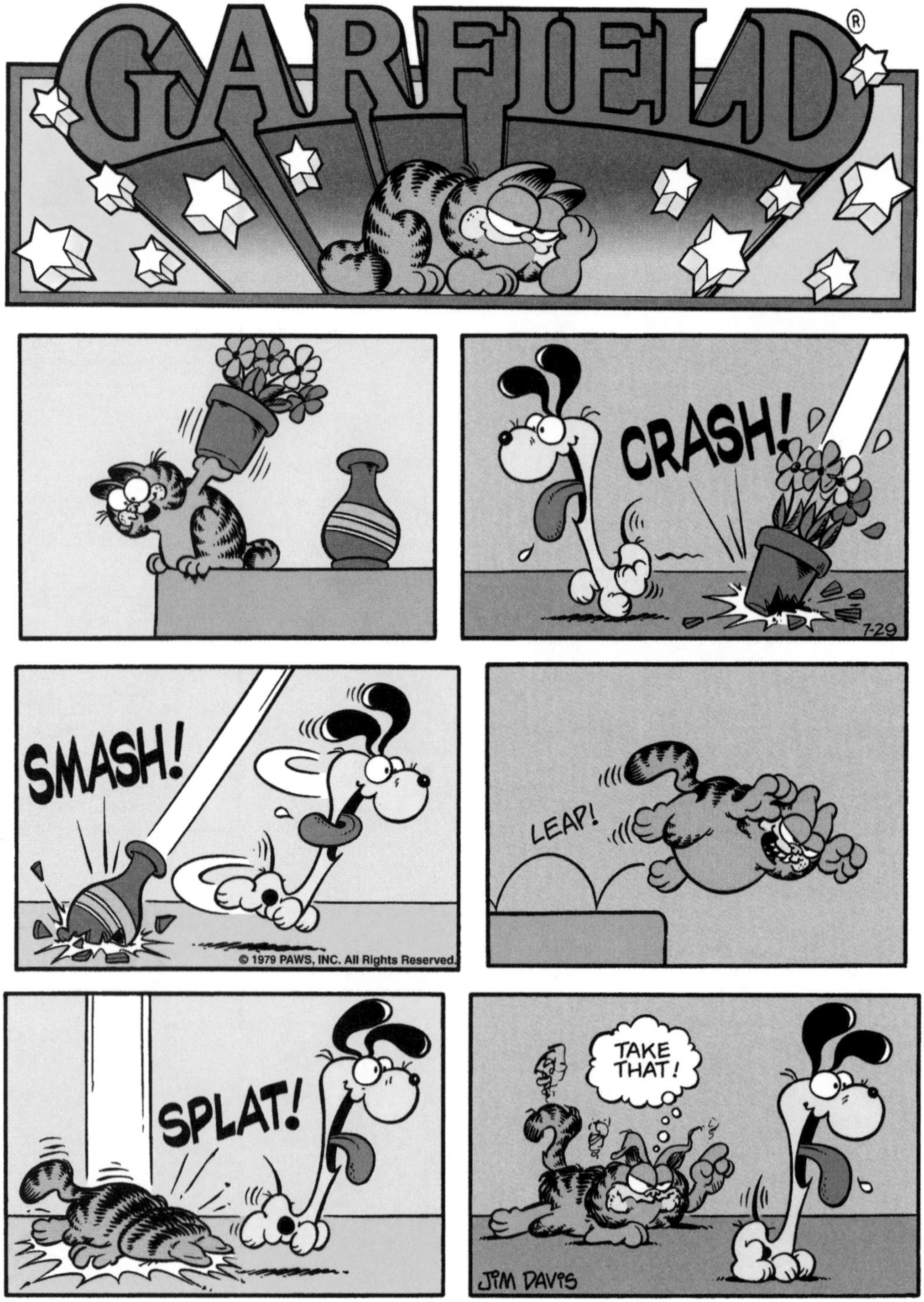
GARFIELD®
CRASH!
7-29
SMASH!
© 1979 PAWS, INC. All Rights Reserved.
LEAP!
SPLAT!
TAKE THAT!
JIM DAVIS

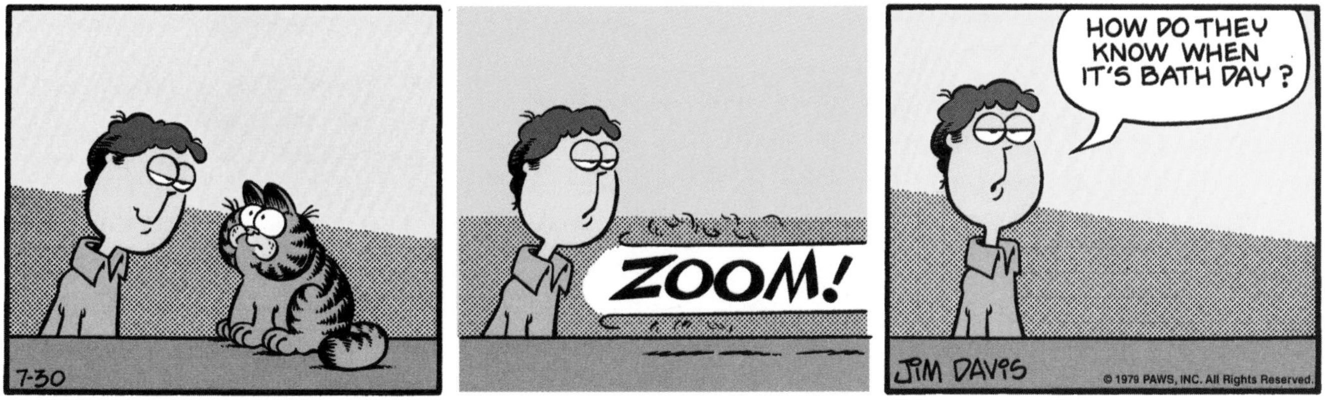
7-30
ZOOM!
HOW DO THEY KNOW WHEN IT'S BATH DAY?
JIM DAVIS
© 1979 PAWS, INC. All Rights Reserved.

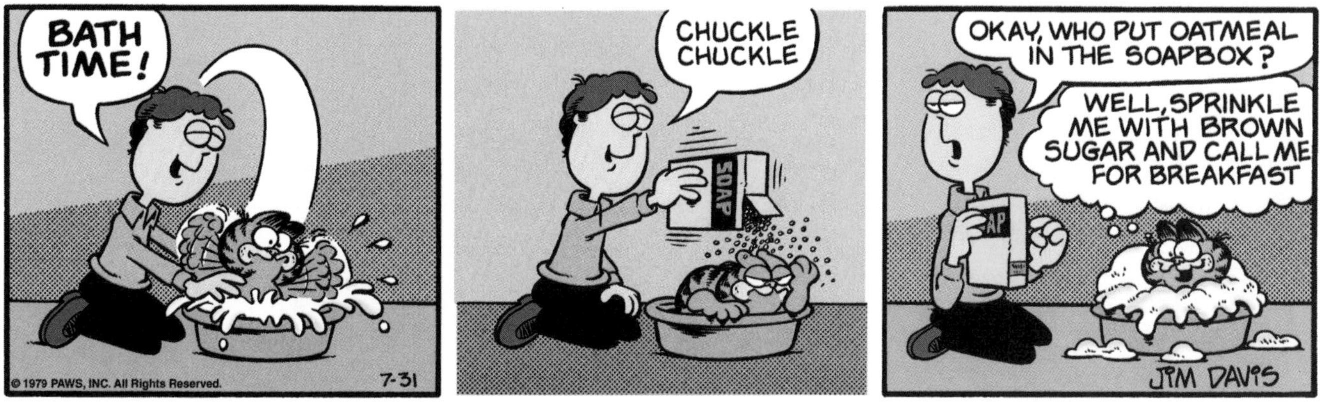
BATH TIME!
© 1979 PAWS, INC. All Rights Reserved.
7-31
CHUCKLE CHUCKLE
SOAP
OKAY, WHO PUT OATMEAL IN THE SOAPBOX?
WELL, SPRINKLE ME WITH BROWN SUGAR AND CALL ME FOR BREAKFAST
JIM DAVIS

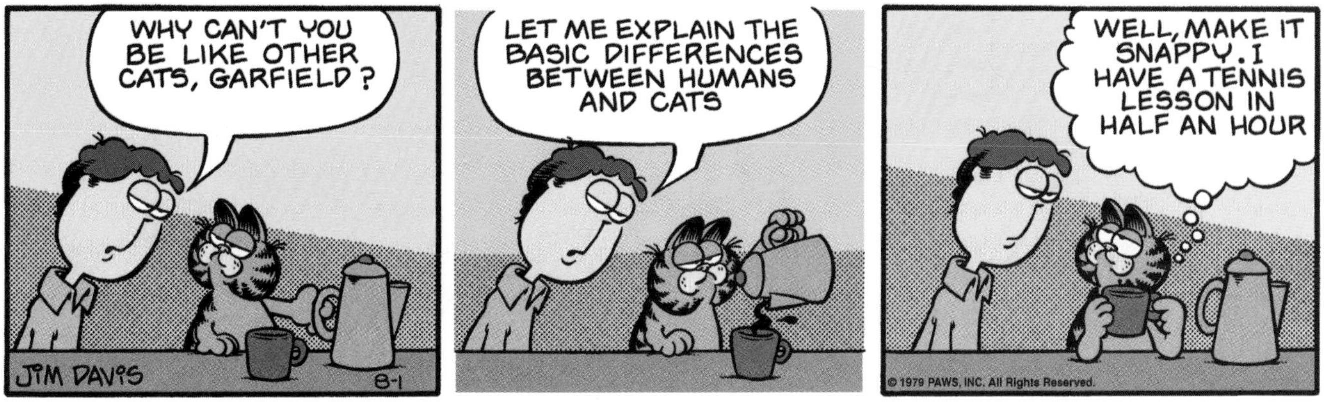
WHY CAN'T YOU BE LIKE OTHER CATS, GARFIELD?
JIM DAVIS
8-1
LET ME EXPLAIN THE BASIC DIFFERENCES BETWEEN HUMANS AND CATS
WELL, MAKE IT SNAPPY. I HAVE A TENNIS LESSON IN HALF AN HOUR
© 1979 PAWS, INC. All Rights Reserved.

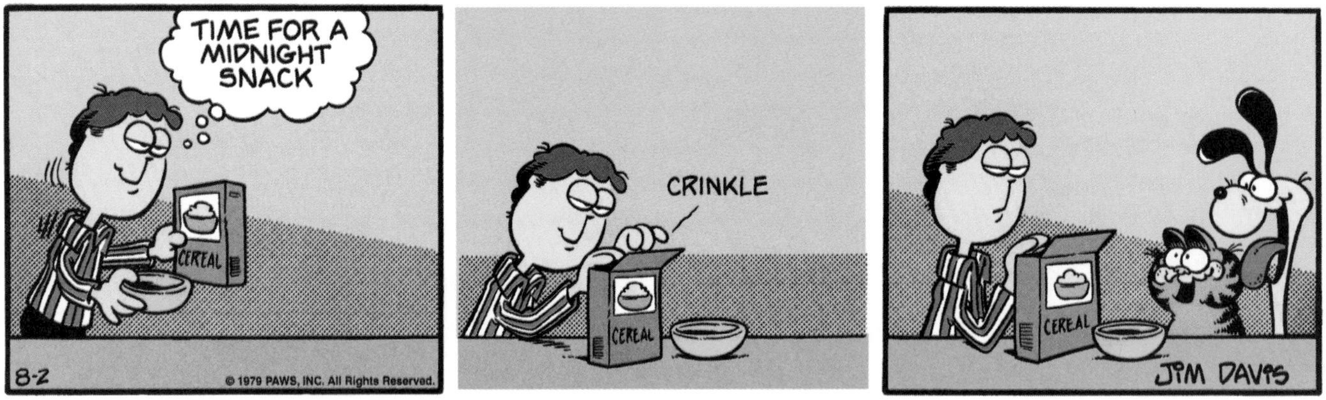
TIME FOR A MIDNIGHT SNACK
CEREAL
CRINKLE
CEREAL
CEREAL
8-2
© 1979 PAWS, INC. All Rights Reserved.
JIM DAVIS

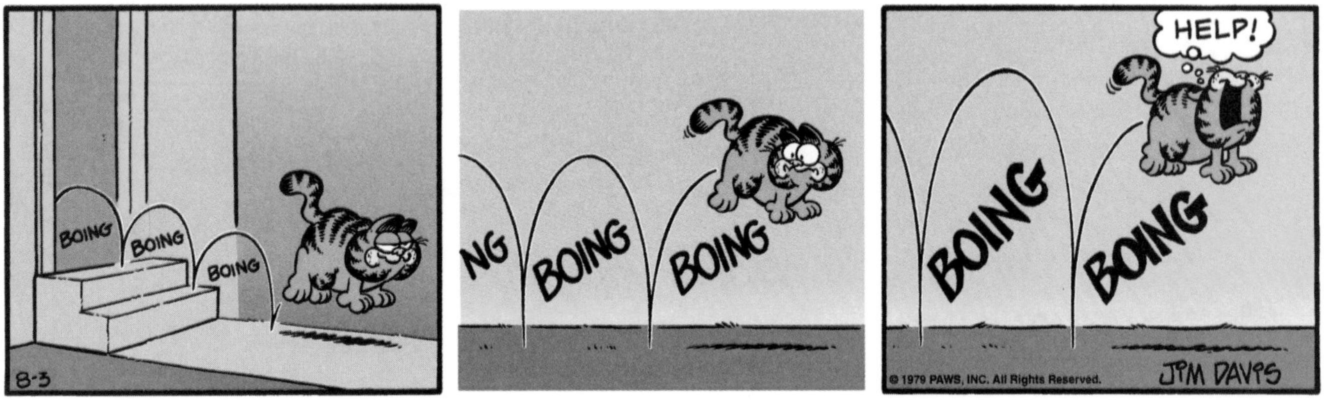
BOING
BOING
BOING
NG
BOING
BOING
HELP!
BOING
BOING
8-3
© 1979 PAWS, INC. All Rights Reserved.
JIM DAVIS

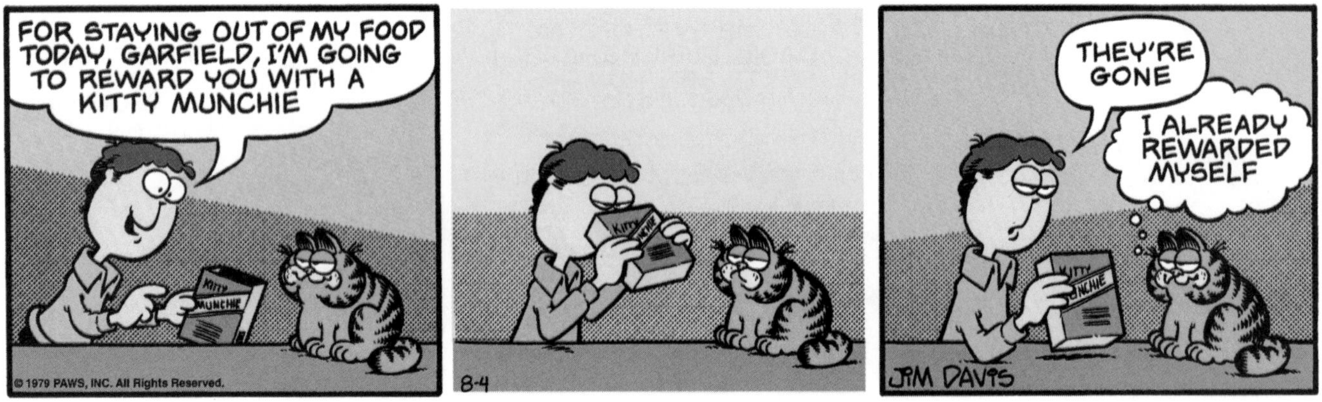
FOR STAYING OUT OF MY FOOD TODAY, GARFIELD, I'M GOING TO REWARD YOU WITH A KITTY MUNCHIE
KITTY MUNCHIE
THEY'RE GONE
I ALREADY REWARDED MYSELF
© 1979 PAWS, INC. All Rights Reserved.
8-4
JIM DAVIS

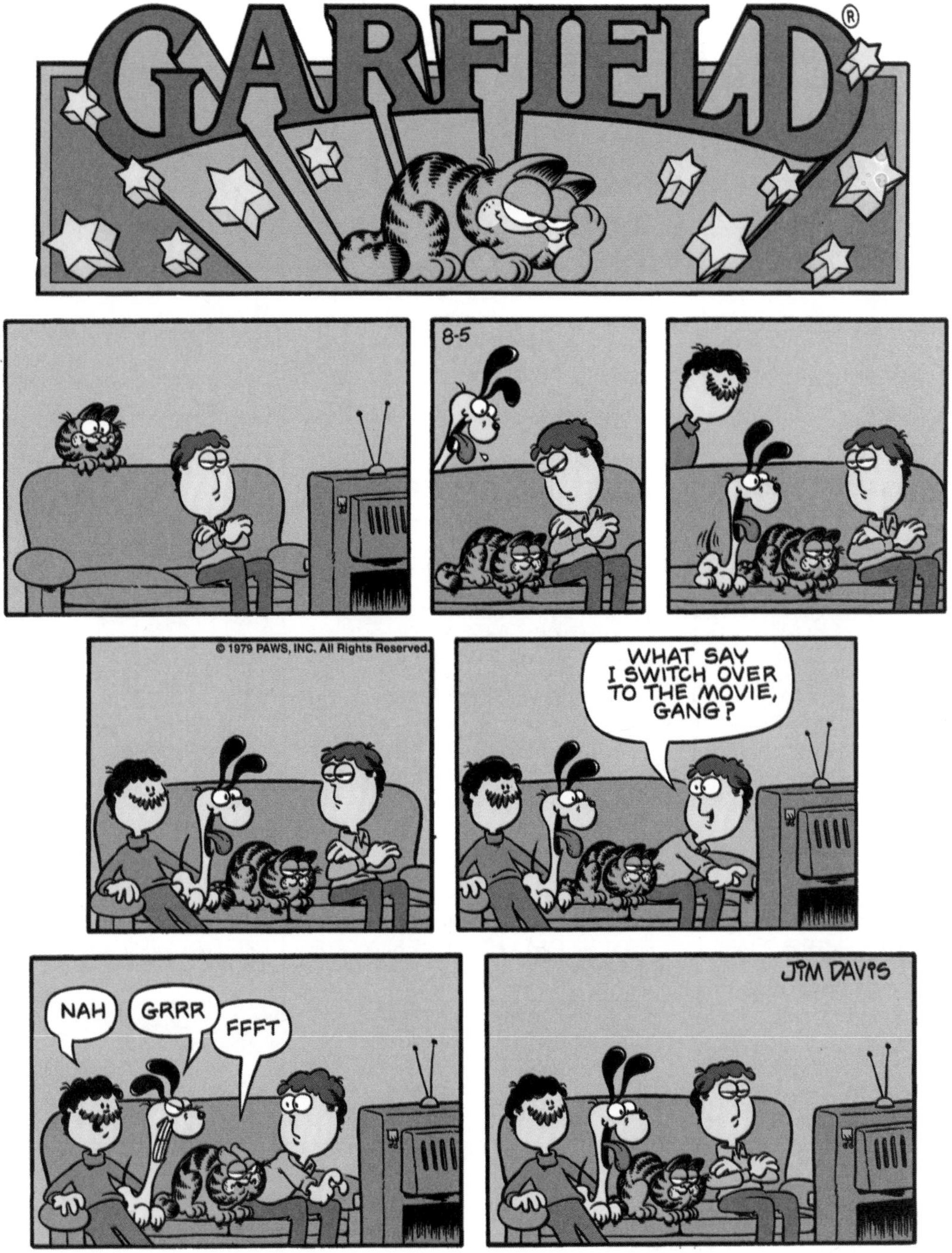
GARFIELD®
8-5
© 1979 PAWS, INC. All Rights Reserved.
WHAT SAY I SWITCH OVER TO THE MOVIE, GANG?
NAH
GRRR
FFFT
JIM DAVIS

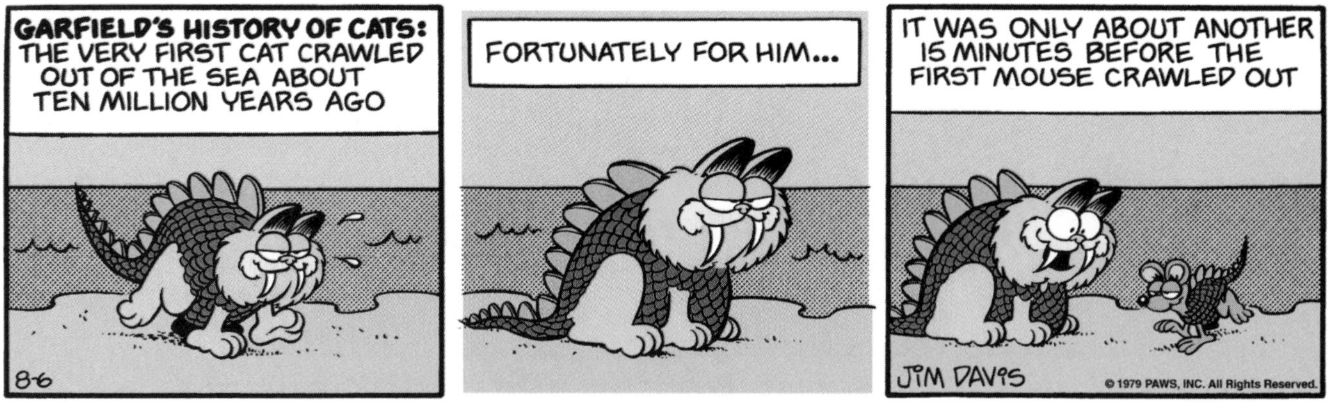
GARFIELD'S HISTORY OF CATS: THE VERY FIRST CAT CRAWLED OUT OF THE SEA ABOUT TEN MILLION YEARS AGO
8-6
FORTUNATELY FOR HIM...
IT WAS ONLY ABOUT ANOTHER 15 MINUTES BEFORE THE FIRST MOUSE CRAWLED OUT
JIM DAVIS
© 1979 PAWS, INC. All Rights Reserved.

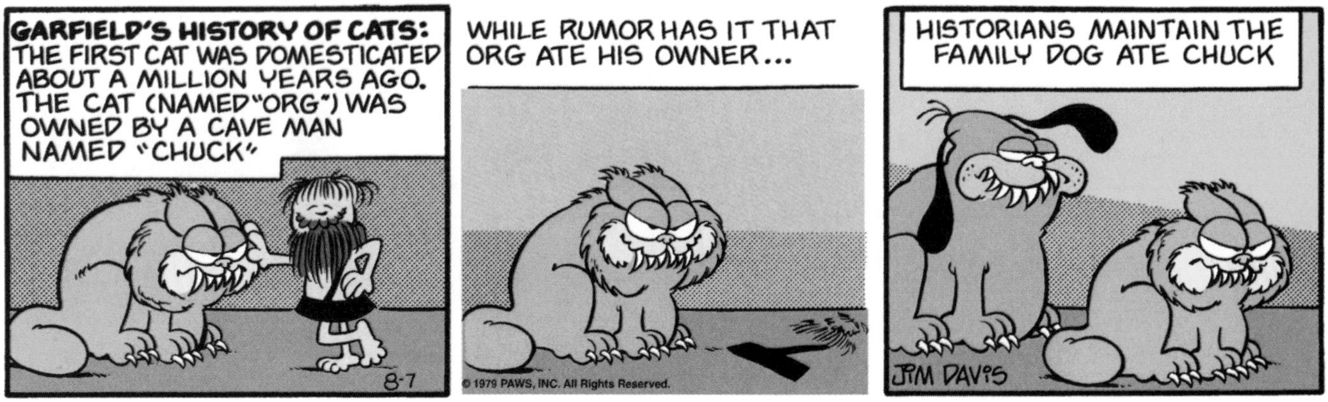
GARFIELD'S HISTORY OF CATS: THE FIRST CAT WAS DOMESTICATED ABOUT A MILLION YEARS AGO. THE CAT (NAMED "ORG") WAS OWNED BY A CAVE MAN NAMED "CHUCK"
8-7
WHILE RUMOR HAS IT THAT ORG ATE HIS OWNER...
© 1979 PAWS, INC. All Rights Reserved.
HISTORIANS MAINTAIN THE FAMILY DOG ATE CHUCK
JIM DAVIS

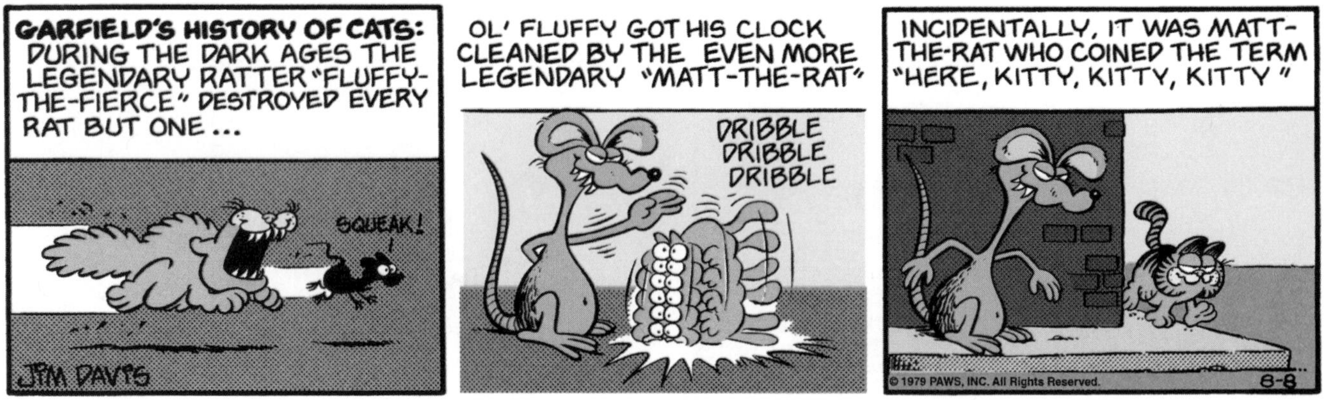
GARFIELD'S HISTORY OF CATS: DURING THE DARK AGES THE LEGENDARY RATTER "FLUFFY-THE-FIERCE" DESTROYED EVERY RAT BUT ONE...
SQUEAK!
JIM DAVIS
OL' FLUFFY GOT HIS CLOCK CLEANED BY THE EVEN MORE LEGENDARY "MATT-THE-RAT"
DRIBBLE
DRIBBLE
DRIBBLE
INCIDENTALLY, IT WAS MATT-THE-RAT WHO COINED THE TERM "HERE, KITTY, KITTY, KITTY"
© 1979 PAWS, INC. All Rights Reserved.
8-8

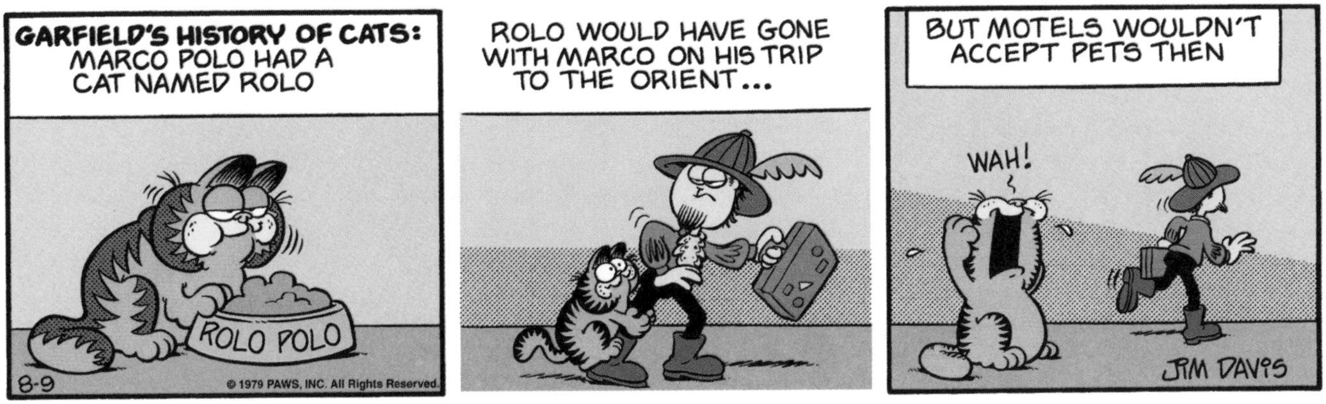
GARFIELD'S HISTORY OF CATS: MARCO POLO HAD A CAT NAMED ROLO
ROLO POLO
8-9
© 1979 PAWS, INC. All Rights Reserved.
ROLO WOULD HAVE GONE WITH MARCO ON HIS TRIP TO THE ORIENT...
BUT MOTELS WOULDN'T ACCEPT PETS THEN
WAH!
JIM DAVIS

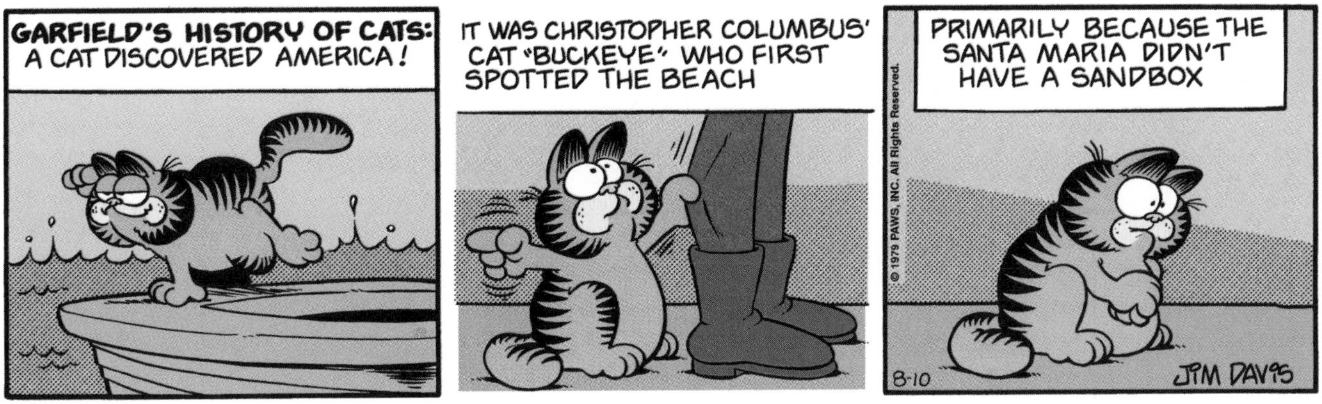
GARFIELD'S HISTORY OF CATS: A CAT DISCOVERED AMERICA!
IT WAS CHRISTOPHER COLUMBUS' CAT "BUCKEYE" WHO FIRST SPOTTED THE BEACH
© 1979 PAWS, INC. All Rights Reserved.
PRIMARILY BECAUSE THE SANTA MARIA DIDN'T HAVE A SANDBOX
8-10
JIM DAVIS

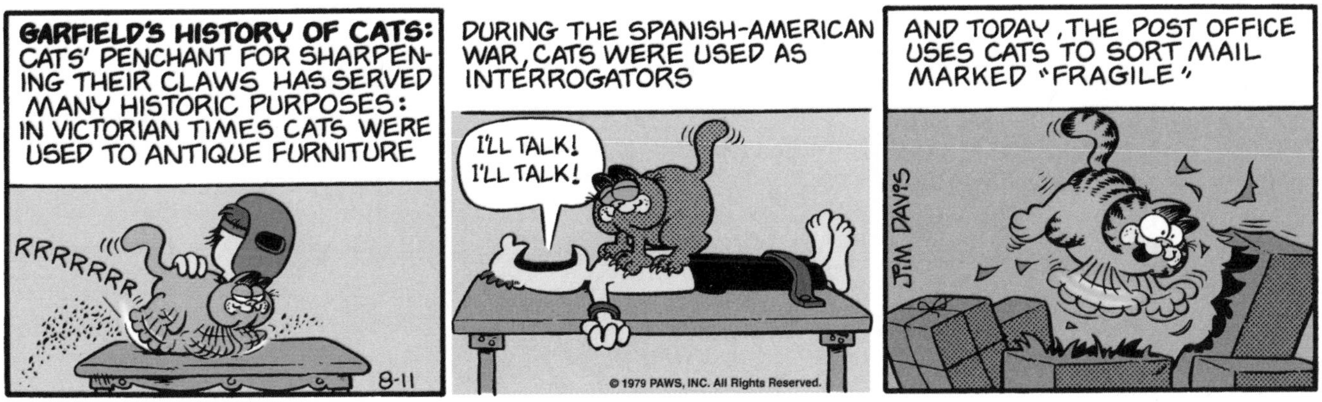
GARFIELD'S HISTORY OF CATS: CATS' PENCHANT FOR SHARPENING THEIR CLAWS HAS SERVED MANY HISTORIC PURPOSES: IN VICTORIAN TIMES CATS WERE USED TO ANTIQUE FURNITURE
RRRRRRRR
8-11
DURING THE SPANISH-AMERICAN WAR, CATS WERE USED AS INTERROGATORS
I'LL TALK! I'LL TALK!
© 1979 PAWS, INC. All Rights Reserved.
AND TODAY, THE POST OFFICE USES CATS TO SORT MAIL MARKED "FRAGILE"
JIM DAVIS

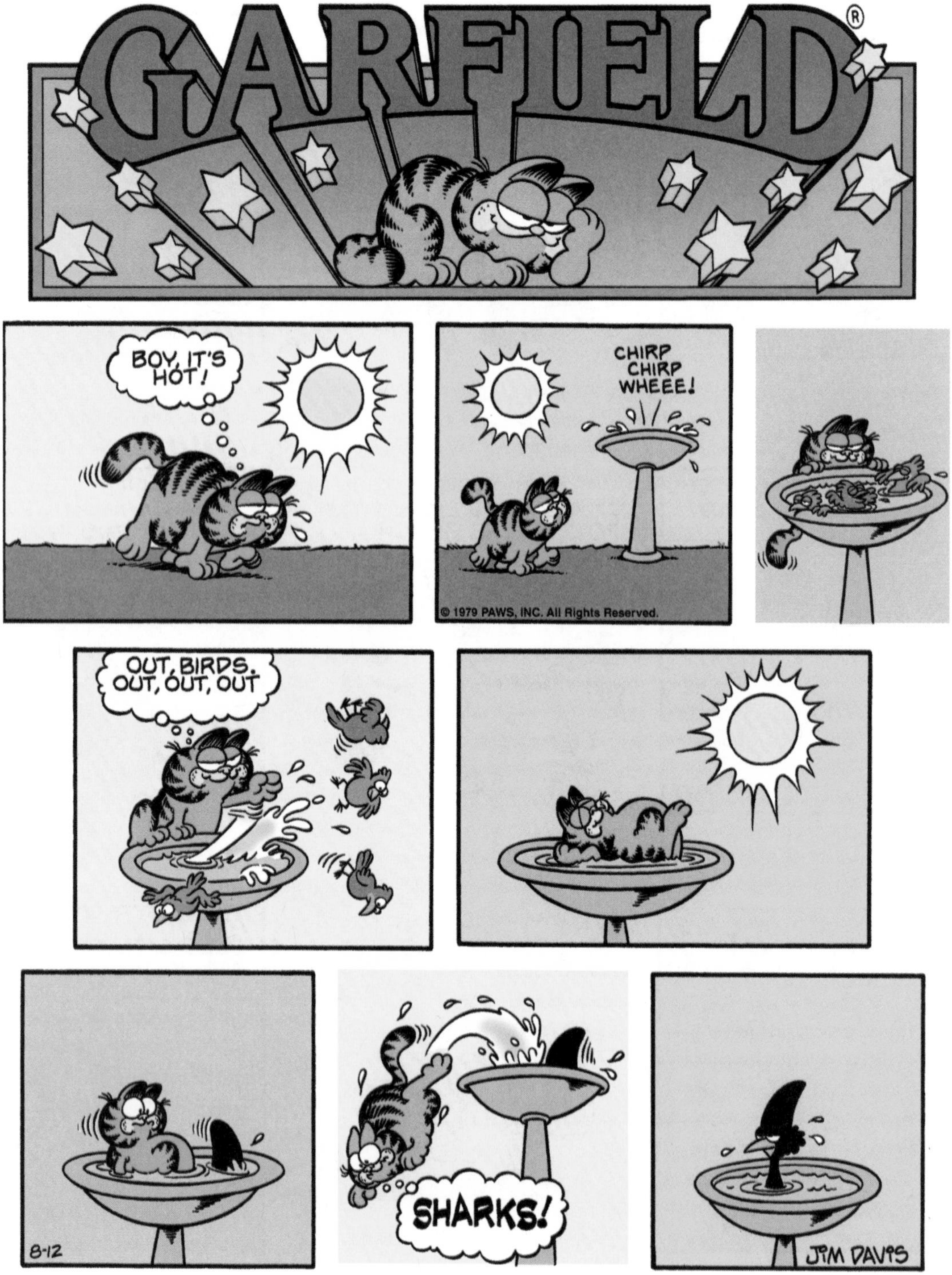
GARFIELD®
BOY, IT'S HOT!
CHIRP CHIRP WHEEE!
© 1979 PAWS, INC. All Rights Reserved.
OUT, BIRDS. OUT, OUT, OUT
8-12
SHARKS!
JIM DAVIS

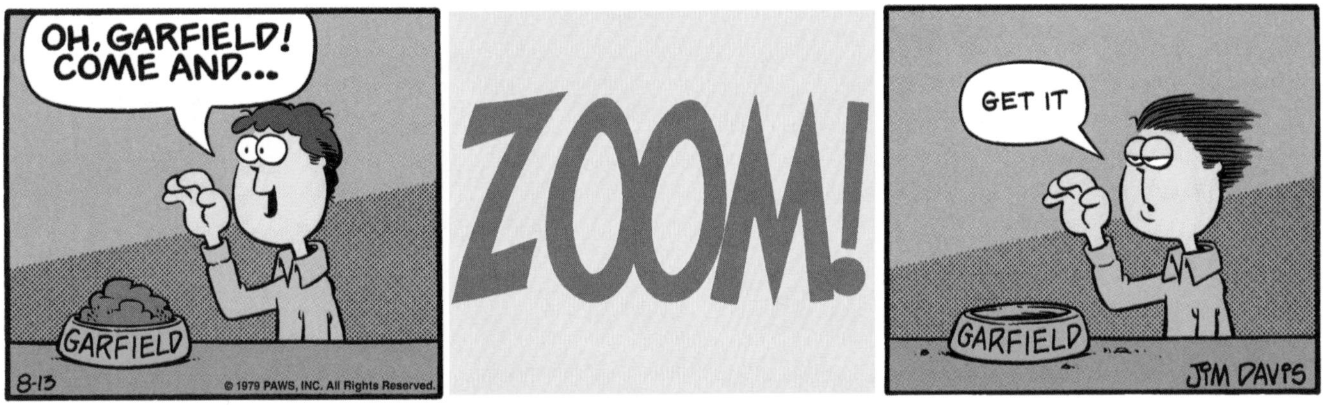
OH, GARFIELD! COME AND...
GARFIELD
8-13
© 1979 PAWS, INC. All Rights Reserved.
ZOOM!
GET IT
GARFIELD
JIM DAVIS

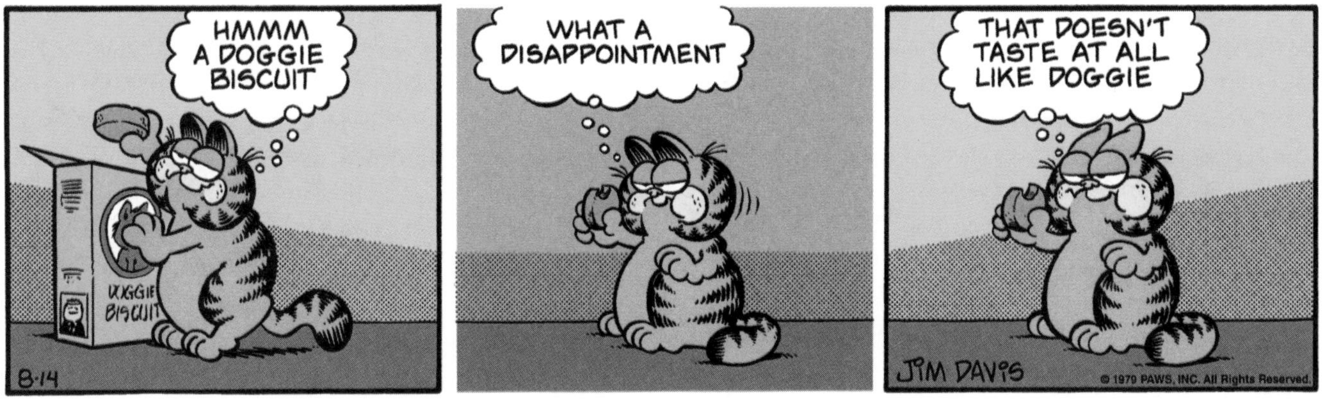
HMMM A DOGGIE BISCUIT
DOGGIE BISCUIT
8-14
WHAT A DISAPPOINTMENT
THAT DOESN'T TASTE AT ALL LIKE DOGGIE
JIM DAVIS
© 1979 PAWS, INC. All Rights Reserved.

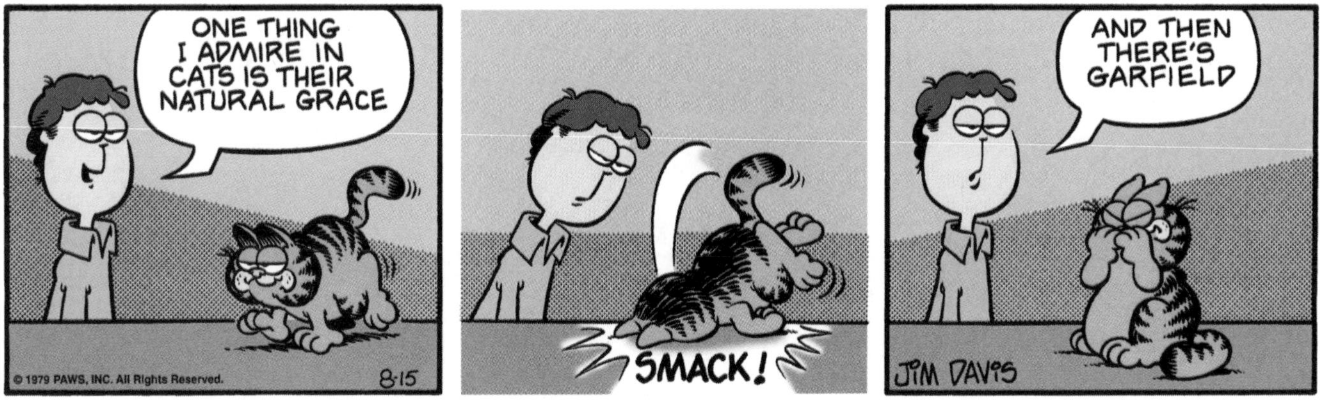
ONE THING I ADMIRE IN CATS IS THEIR NATURAL GRACE
© 1979 PAWS, INC. All Rights Reserved.
8-15
SMACK!
AND THEN THERE'S GARFIELD
JIM DAVIS

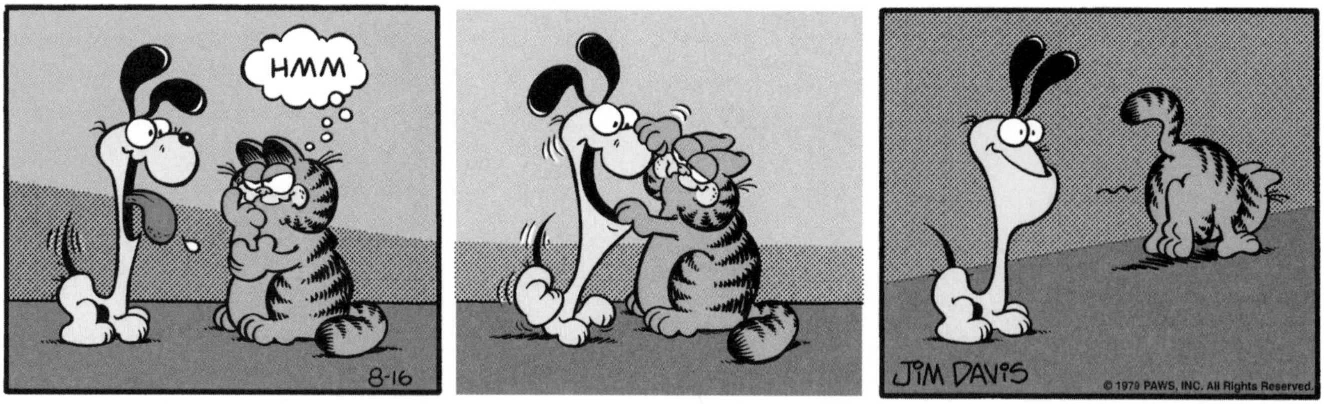
HMM
JIM DAVIS
8-16
© 1979 PAWS, INC. All Rights Reserved.

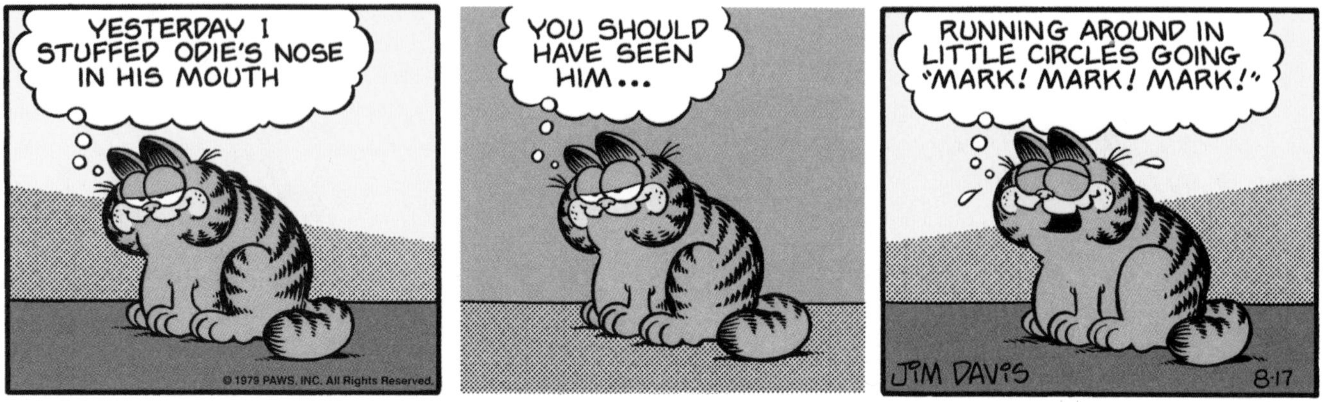
YESTERDAY I STUFFED ODIE'S NOSE IN HIS MOUTH
© 1979 PAWS, INC. All Rights Reserved.
YOU SHOULD HAVE SEEN HIM...
RUNNING AROUND IN LITTLE CIRCLES GOING "MARK! MARK! MARK!"
JIM DAVIS
8-17

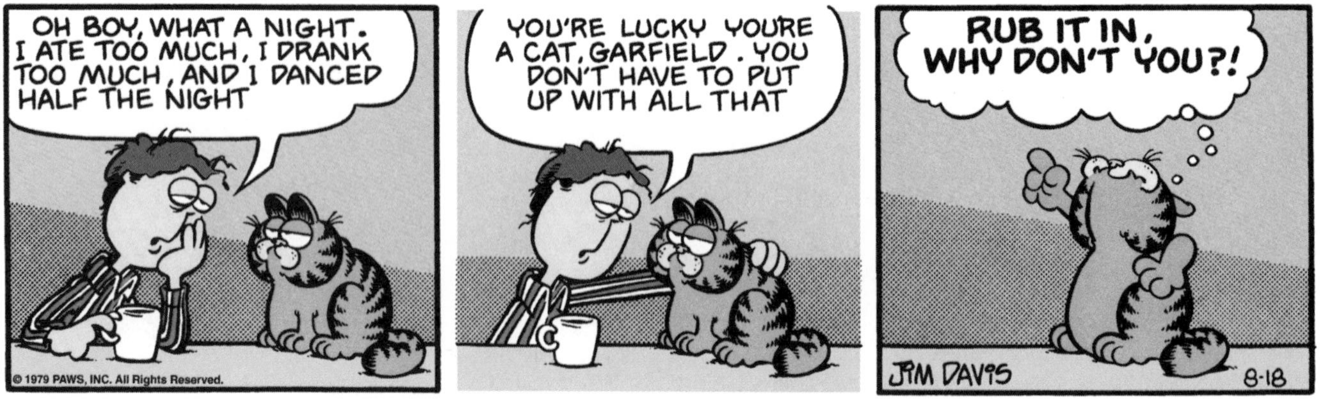
OH BOY, WHAT A NIGHT. I ATE TOO MUCH, I DRANK TOO MUCH, AND I DANCED HALF THE NIGHT
© 1979 PAWS, INC. All Rights Reserved.
YOU'RE LUCKY YOU'RE A CAT, GARFIELD. YOU DON'T HAVE TO PUT UP WITH ALL THAT
RUB IT IN, WHY DON'T YOU?!
JIM DAVIS
8-18

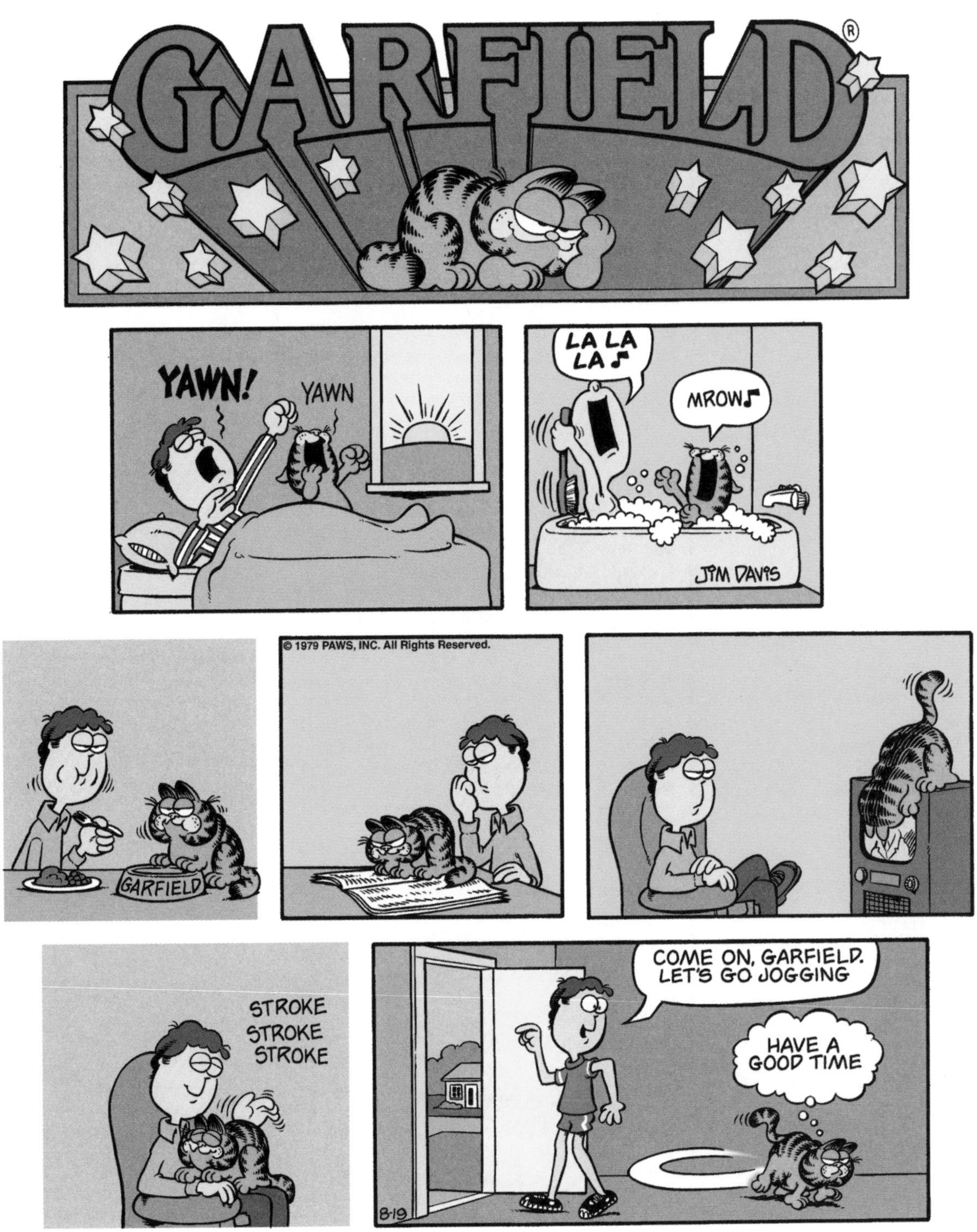
GARFIELD
YAWN!
YAWN
LA LA LA
MROW
JIM DAVIS
© 1979 PAWS, INC. All Rights Reserved.
GARFIELD
STROKE STROKE STROKE
COME ON, GARFIELD. LET'S GO JOGGING
HAVE A GOOD TIME
8-19

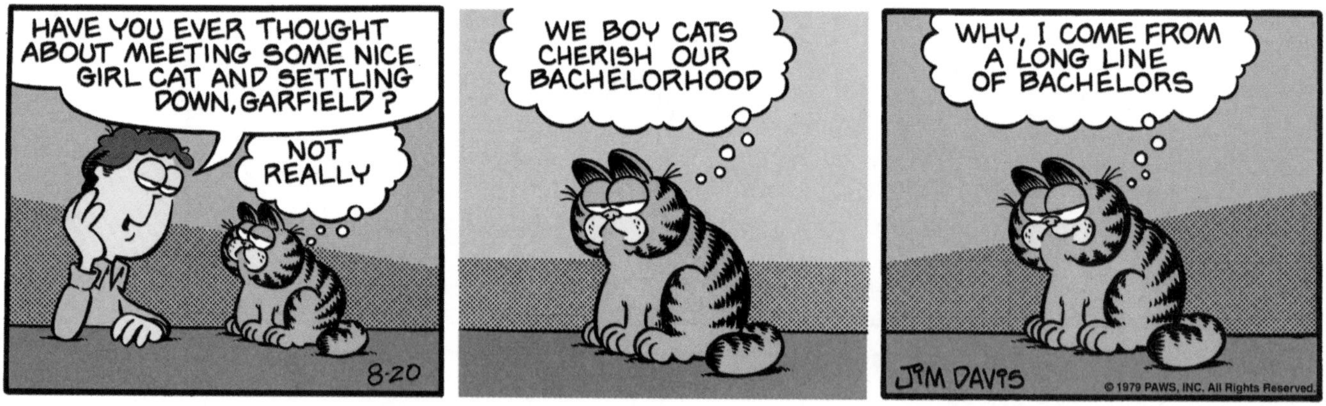
HAVE YOU EVER THOUGHT ABOUT MEETING SOME NICE GIRL CAT AND SETTLING DOWN, GARFIELD?
NOT REALLY
8-20
WE BOY CATS CHERISH OUR BACHELORHOOD
WHY, I COME FROM A LONG LINE OF BACHELORS
JIM DAVIS
© 1979 PAWS, INC. All Rights Reserved.

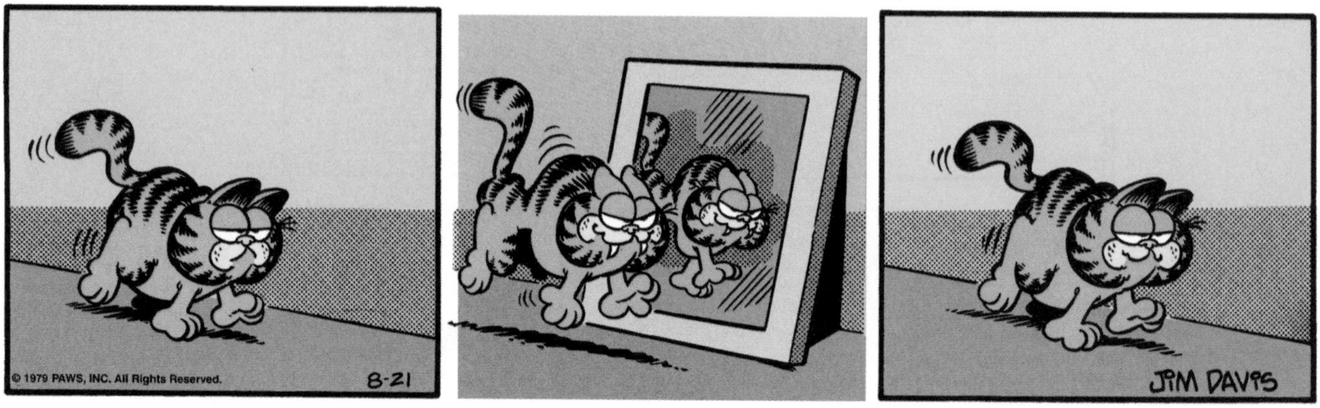
© 1979 PAWS, INC. All Rights Reserved.
8-21
JIM DAVIS

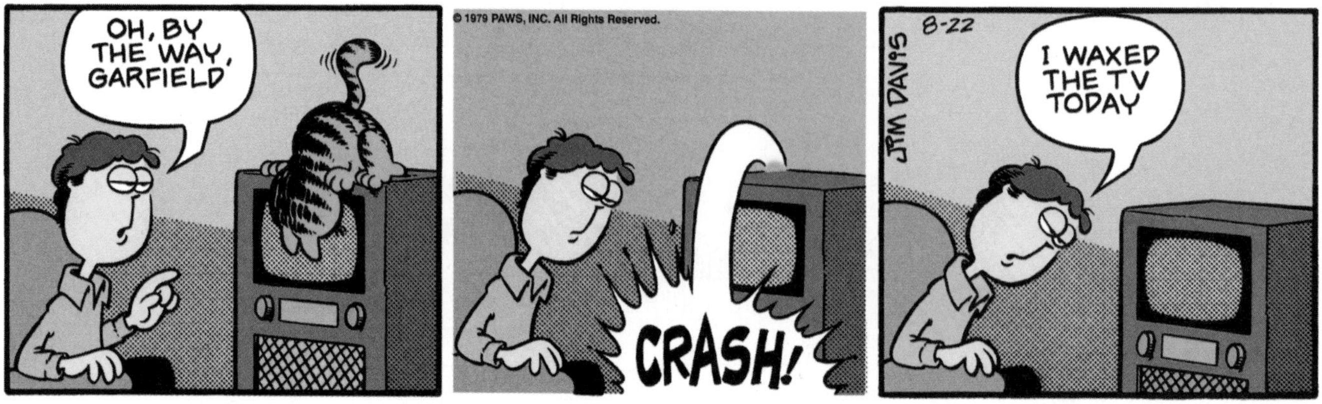
OH, BY THE WAY, GARFIELD
© 1979 PAWS, INC. All Rights Reserved.
CRASH!
JIM DAVIS
8-22
I WAXED THE TV TODAY

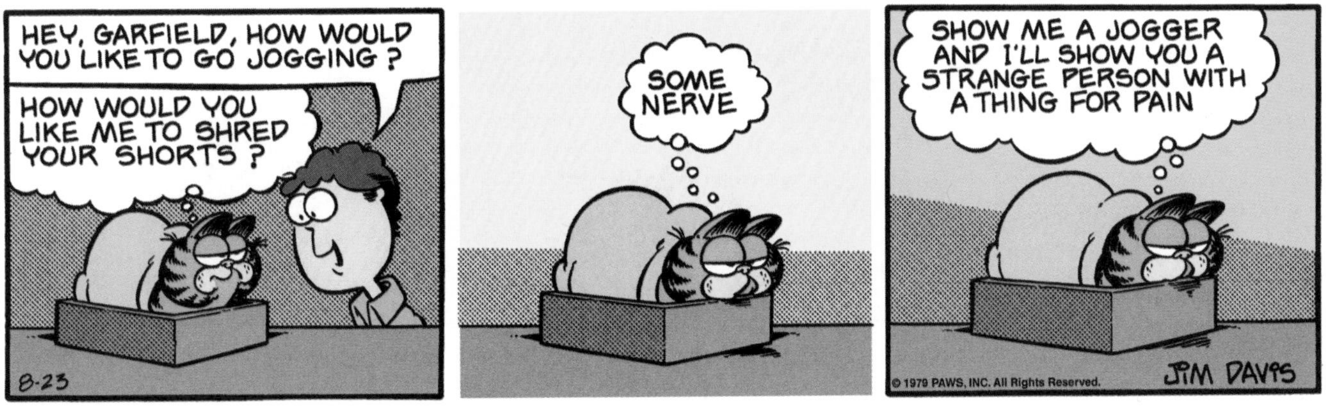
HEY, GARFIELD, HOW WOULD YOU LIKE TO GO JOGGING?
HOW WOULD YOU LIKE ME TO SHRED YOUR SHORTS?
8-23
SOME NERVE
SHOW ME A JOGGER AND I'LL SHOW YOU A STRANGE PERSON WITH A THING FOR PAIN
© 1979 PAWS, INC. All Rights Reserved.
JIM DAVIS

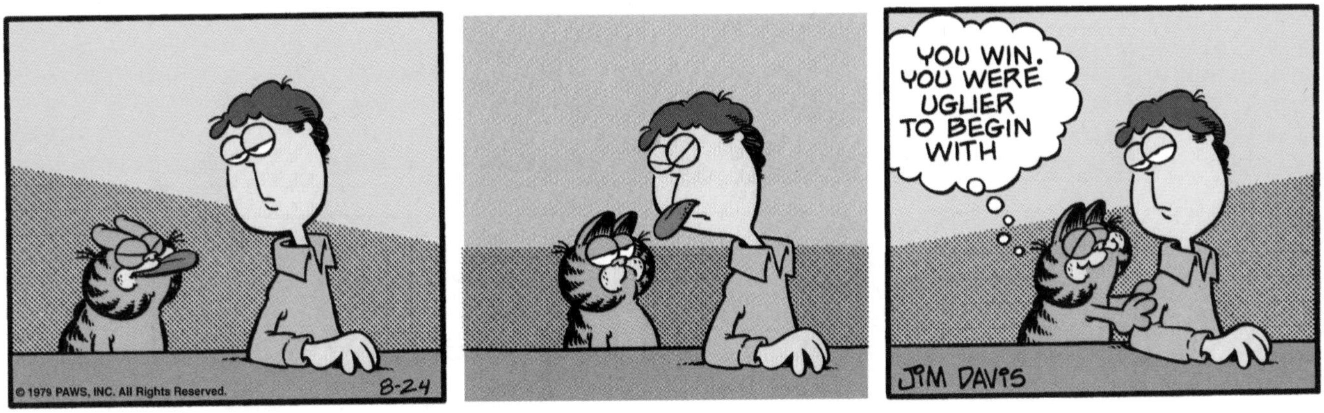
© 1979 PAWS, INC. All Rights Reserved.
8-24
YOU WIN. YOU WERE UGLIER TO BEGIN WITH
JIM DAVIS

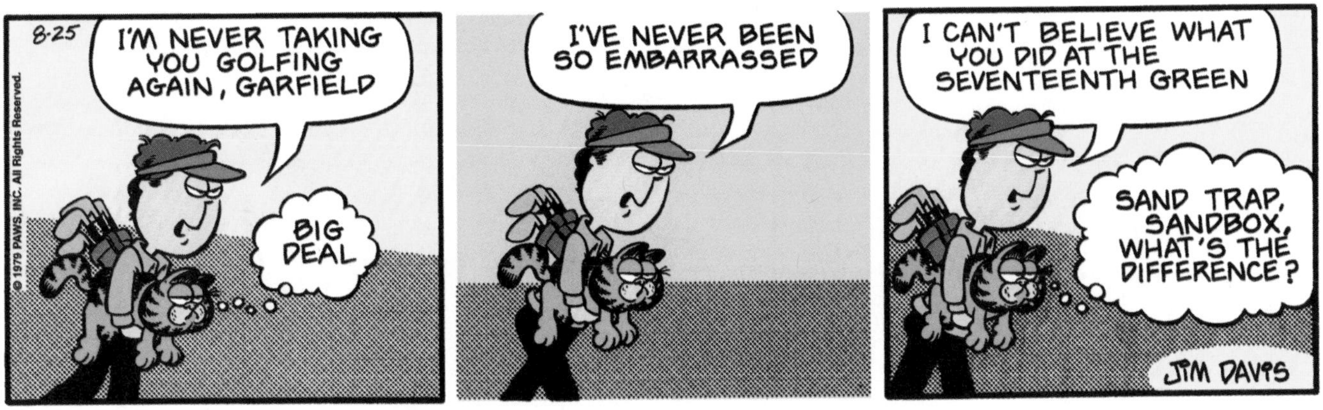
8-25
I'M NEVER TAKING YOU GOLFING AGAIN, GARFIELD
BIG DEAL
© 1979 PAWS, INC. All Rights Reserved.
I'VE NEVER BEEN SO EMBARRASSED
I CAN'T BELIEVE WHAT YOU DID AT THE SEVENTEENTH GREEN
SAND TRAP, SANDBOX, WHAT'S THE DIFFERENCE?
JIM DAVIS

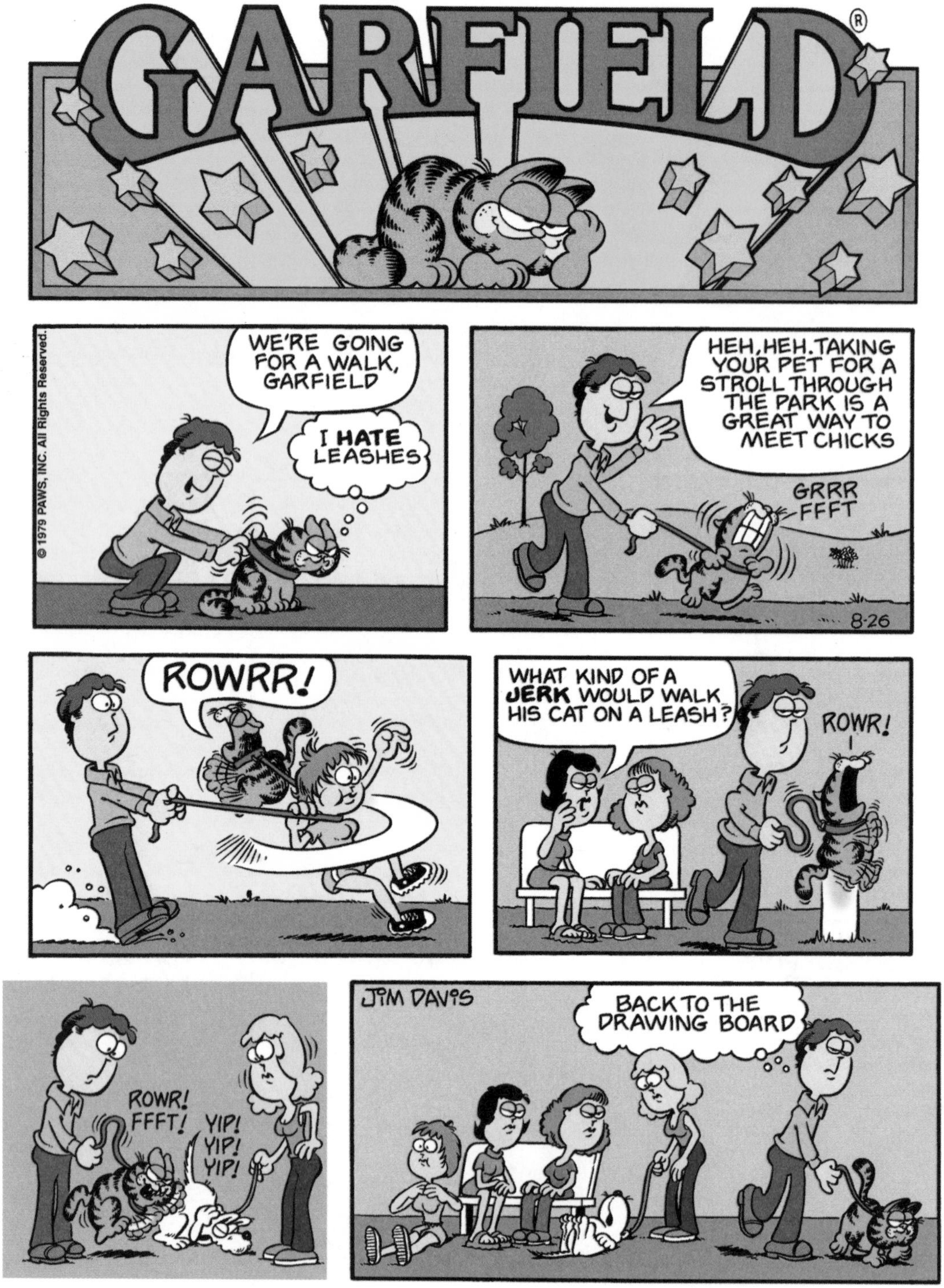
GARFIELD®
© 1979 PAWS, INC. All Rights Reserved.
WE'RE GOING FOR A WALK, GARFIELD
I **HATE** LEASHES
HEH, HEH. TAKING YOUR PET FOR A STROLL THROUGH THE PARK IS A GREAT WAY TO MEET CHICKS
GRRR FFFT
8-26
ROWRR!
WHAT KIND OF A **JERK** WOULD WALK HIS CAT ON A LEASH?
ROWR!
ROWR! FFFT!
YIP! YIP! YIP!
JIM DAVIS
BACK TO THE DRAWING BOARD